Down from the
Ivory Tower

Down from the Ivory Tower

Graduates and their Jobs

Peter Herriot

Birkbeck College
University of London

JOHN WILEY & SONS

Chichester . New York . Brisbane . Toronto . Singapore

Copyright © 1984 by John Wiley & Sons Ltd.

Library of Congress Cataloging in Publication Data:

Herriot, Peter.
  Down from the ivory tower

  Bibliography: p.
  Includes index.
  1. College graduates—Employment. 2. Recruiting of
employees—Psychological aspects. I. Title.
HD6277.H47 1984   653.3′111   83-16947

ISBN 0 471 90308 6

British Library Cataloguing in Publication Data:

Herriot, Peter.
  Down from the ivory tower: graduates and their jobs.
  1. College graduates—Employment—Great Britain
  I. Title
  331.11′42   HD6278.G7

ISBN 0 471 90308 6

Phototypeset by Input Typesetting Ltd, London SW19 8DR
and printed by The Pitman Press, Bath, Avon

Contents

Introduction

'The vision of a society devoted to, and capable of, conserving human talent seems within reach' (Dunnette and Borman, 1979). In its recruitment of its educational elite into organizations, Western industrialized society has some way to go before it can claim to have translated this optimistic vision into reality. It is the contention of this book that such an ideal cannot be approached until we have adopted a new theoretical framework for describing the process. My objective is not, therefore, primarily to recommend changes in recruitment or career guidance practices; this is not a practical book. It is, rather, an attempt to analyse the graduate recruitment process in more appropriate psychological terms. However, such a reanalysis does have practical implications, since it might affect the way practitioners conceptualize the recruitment process; and the models they carry about as part of their conceptual baggage are likely to carry over into what they do.

At present there are two different approaches to the recruitment of graduates, deriving from different historical traditions in psychology. The first tradition derives from *psychometrics*. Its assumptions are those embodied in our everyday use of language. We assume that we can describe persons in terms of various characteristics; and we also assume that we can describe jobs in terms of the tasks that they involve, and hence in terms of the characteristics they require in their occupants. The selection of graduates is therefore in principle a matter of fitting the person to the job; if the fit is not perfect, training will knock off the rough edges. The key features of this approach are first, its static nature. The individual is assumed to be an entity with relatively fixed characteristics, and so is the job. The second key assumption is that these two elements can be objectively observed and assessed, and that selection can and should be based on this assessment.

The second psychological tradition which has been brought to bear upon the graduate recruitment process has been the *developmental* approach. This assumes that individuals develop through unfolding stages of personal and occupational maturity. It is the credo of most careers advisers in US and UK universities, who regard students, not organizations, as their clients. Many careers advisers have recently taken on board two additional theoretical emphases. First, there is the adherence to the possibility of self-development and self-actualization, taken from the humanistic psychology of Rogers, Maslow and others. Second, there is the increasing realization derived from life-span psychology, that transitions from one developmental stage to another are very difficult to make. Many careers advisers see their task as helping the student to develop himself by making the transition from education to work effectively.

Thus the two institutional parties to the graduate recruitment process have very different models, implicit and explicit, according to which they operate. Organizations are concerned to assess the individual student in terms of his suitability for employment. They hope to predict the future development of their relationship with the employee on the basis of this assessment. They make the psychometric assumptions that personality characteristics do not change very much, and that they predict behaviours across different situations. Thus, their assessment is in effect a prediction.

Careers advisers, on the other hand, see the student as their client, whom they counsel in such a way as to assist his development. They may perceive organizations as serving their own interests by their recruitment practices, while they themselves serve the student's interests. These perceptions imply at best an uneasy relationship between careers advisers and organizations. The apparently contradictory psychological theories which each party holds, one static and the other developmental in nature, give an ideological framework for these differences.

It is the basic argument of this book that neither a psychometric nor a developmental model is the most appropriate to describe graduate recruitment. Both these approaches centre upon the person, either as a relatively stable and predictable individual possessing certain characteristics to differing degrees, or as a follower of a stage-by-stage developmental progression, which he may enhance or even transcend by self-actualization. Both approaches largely ignore the fact that psychology is social. It is an indictment of the insularity of different branches of psychology that the empirical and theoretical advances in one field have had little effect upon the development of others. The importance of recent developments in social psychology for the psychometric approach in particular is immense. It is only when we stop looking at recruitment as though the individual student were the object of study that we can understand what is going on. We are not primarily concerned either with the assessment of the student, or with his self-actualization. We are interested above all in a *relationship*—that between the student and the organization. Since this relationship is constantly changing and developing as each party communicates with the other, we are concerned with a dynamic *social process*.

The earlier chapters of the book look at the graduate recruitment process largely from the point of view of the organization. The assumptions of the psychometric tradition are spelt out in some detail in Chapter 1. The growing realization of the need to choose outcome criteria other than simply the job performance of the individual reflects the insistence of organizational psychologists that the recruitment and selection systems have wide-ranging consequences for the organization. However, the predictors used for selection purposes are still overwhelmingly assessments of various characteristics of the applicant. Such assessments assume that people's behaviour at work can be predicted by various personality traits and aptitudes; that these traits predict behaviour across a wide range of work situations; and that they remain constant over time. These assumptions are then questioned closely in the light of developments in social psychology. The historical departure from the trait approach to the prediction of behaviour, and the advent of interactionism is briefly touched upon, if only to show that one of the basic assumptions of the psychometric approach has long been abandoned elsewhere. In particular, the interaction between the individual and the organization as a social context is stressed.

The assumption that objective assessment of traits on the basis of the observation of behaviour is possible is questioned in Chapter 2, where the social psychological evidence from attribution theory is outlined. The inference of personal and/or situational causes of behaviour on the part of the assessor is anything but clear-cut, and observers are subject to sundry biases in this respect. Moreover, various theories about other people that we carry about with us as part of our conceptual baggage, our implicit personality theories, mean that any judgements we make about others tell people as much about ourselves as about those we are assessing.

However, social psychology does far more than indicate that 'objective' assessment is a chimera. It also explores the nature of the processes involved when assessments of different sorts are made. Once we know what these processes are, we can start to appreciate the strengths and weaknesses of each mode of assessment. We can begin to utilize our natural capacities for social intercourse rather than treat them as interfering subjectivity. The important questions are not so much the traditional psychometric ones regarding the reliability and validity of psychological measuring instruments. They are rather the cognitive and social questions regarding how judgements are made. Chapter 3 explores the nature of ratings of one individual by another, and also that of self-ratings. These are particularly important for two reasons. First, it is argued that the self-concept, for which self-ratings provide some indirect evidence, is a major determinant of our actions. Second, it is one of the elements involved in the social process of communication between individual and organization of which recruitment and selection is the first stage. Thus the interpersonal judgements which appeared initially to interfere with scientific objectivity can now actually be utilized in their natural setting—that of social communication.

Chapter 4 describes the various things that organizations communicate to their members—role expectations, norms, values, and image. It differentiates organizations in terms of the degree to which they seek to maintain their structures or to adapt them to a changing environment, and explores the implications of this difference for the messages which will be sent to their members. Next, the actual social process of communication and negotiation is explored. It is seen in terms of the individual applicant's reception of the messages sent by the organization, and her matching of her understanding of these with her self-concept, in its past, present, and future aspects. It is argued that it is the outcomes of different episodes of social negotiation which will determine whether the relationship between individual and organization ceases or continues. The graduate recruitment process is a short series of such episodes, and the implications for recruitment practices of analysing recruitment in these terms are explored. As usual, it appears that theoretical realignments imply a change in practice, by which old procedures are put to new purposes.

Chapters 5, 6, and 7 examine in detail the evidence available regarding the three usual stages of the graduate recruitment process: pre-selection, interview, and final assessment. In Chapter 5 the evidence regarding the application form and the decisions based upon it is reviewed, and it is concluded that subjective factors enter into decisions. An alternative use for the application form as evidence of the applicant's self-concept is suggested. The selection interview is treated at length in Chapter 6, and analysed in terms of a social episode in which parties follow rules and play roles. It is suggested that, at present, the parties to the interview have different objectives; consequently confusion results, making assessment by the interviewer of the applicant yet more hazardous. In Chapter 7 assessment centres are discussed, and their benefits are assumed, somewhat cynically, to be other than those originally intended. An overall summary of the three stages of the procedure indicates that the social psychological analyses are acceptable interpretations of much of the evidence.

Now we turn to the graduate applicant rather than concentrating upon the organization's recruitment procedures. It is argued in Chapter 8 that only the broadest definition of the term career can do justice to the graduate's development. She is under pressure to make the transition from the education system to the world of work, but at about the same time other cultural expectations are made of her too. For example, she may also be expected to undertake the role of wife. All such transitions have their difficulties, so that the decisions taken in their passage are unlikely to be cool, rational, and free of stress. On the contrary, far from being calculations of costs and benefits, decisions are often avoided or taken prematurely. Only when the graduate has built up a notion of the sort of person she intends to be, and of the world of work, can such decisions be taken meaningfully.

Chapter 9 moves on to describe the ways in which the student's self-concept predicts her occupational choice. It is evident that occupational as well as organizational choice is important to employers, since it is the student's performance as a professional, as well as her performance as a member of the organization, that is relevant. It is the student's self-esteem and her aspirations for herself in the future which seem the most important factors in her occupational choice. All features of the self-concept, however, can only be seen in the context of her previous history; the single most profound influence upon her occupational self-concept, and especially upon her aspirations, is the socioeconomic class of her parental home.

Another profound influence, both upon the graduate's occupational choice and upon recruiters' selection procedures, are sex-role stereotypes. In Chapter 10 we discuss how certain occupations and statuses are conceived as masculine or feminine, and indeed are numerically dominated by males or females. Women graduates may self-select for feminine occupations, seeing themselves as having feminine characteristics and therefore as suited to feminine jobs. On the other hand, there are many women with masculine or androgynous sex-stereotypes of themselves. It is only if organizations adjust their expectations to the self-concept of the woman graduate rather than to her sex that appropriate appointments will be made.

Discussion hitherto has been primarily of process; the process of the organization discovering the nature of the applicant's self-concept, and of the applicant discovering the nature of occupations and organizations. A major part of the research in occupational and vocational psychology has been into structure rather than process, however, This research is reviewed in Chapter 11, with particular reference to Holland's typology of persons and of environments. It was argued that, valuable and thorough though this research is, it has not offered a sufficiently full description of the person, nor has it explained the nature of the relationship between person and environment. Hence it is difficult, for example, to ascertain the extent to which college affects students' interests and values, a task already rendered next to impossible by methodological problems.

The part played by careers counsellors is explored in Chapter 12, where it is argued that the clinical model of an expert diagnosing problems and their causes, and helping to discover remedies, is inappropriate. Rather, it is suggested that the emphasis should be on careers education. While the student's understanding of the world of work and of herself are important objectives, it is proposed that the counsellor should also be educating for the social exchange process itself. Hence, the counsellor will be concerned to help the student to acquire the skills of communicating appropriately in the phases of the recruitment process.

In the final chapter some of the context of graduate recruitment is outlined, and a somewhat modified recruitment process is advocated. This book is concerned with theoretical change—a different paradigm for looking at graduate recruitment. This has to be matched by institutional and organizational change if we really are to achieve the objective of Dunnette and Borman quoted at the beginning of this introduction.

I would like to thank my wife and family for their support and forbearance during the writing of this book; my colleagues for their willingness to undertake administrative tasks which allowed me the time, and for the stimulating academic environment which they provided; Alice Gamlen, Linda Batten, and Gabrielle Ballantine for typing the manuscript; and Dianne Leader for her help with the Bibliography.

1

The Psychometric Tradition

1.1 BASIC ASSUMPTIONS

The recruitment and selection of graduates is typically seen in terms of an organization choosing between applicants on the basis of its assessment of them. Much less attention is paid to the other party in the transaction, the graduate, and to his choice of organization. Particularly is this true when, as at present, the selection ratio is very favourable, with many more applicants than positions. It is the purpose of this first chapter to explore the assumptions upon which organizations' assessments of graduates are made.

First, however, it is worth describing some of the circumstances of these assessments, in order to define the area of discussion. It is worth noting, for a start, that it is graduates who are being recruited. Many organizations have a policy of going to universities and polytechnics in order to recruit general management trainees. That is, they employ annually a cohort of graduates, whom they place in specific positions only after an initial period of varied training and familiarization with the organization. Others appoint graduates to specific vacant positions. Either way, organizations assume that the education system has done part of their task for them already. It has selected out a group of higher-than-average intelligence, and it has possibly given them a sound basic scientific education. Hence, they do not see much need to assess the general intellectual aptitude nor the technical competence of graduate applicants. They may not be too happy about the more practical skills that graduates leave university with (or in some cases without) (Glover and Herriot, 1982). However, they assume that graduates are intelligent enough to acquire these with training or on the job.

Thus, organizations tend not to assess the intellectual and technical abilities of graduates. Rather, they concentrate upon characteristics which they believe are important for anyone working for them. In particular, they lay especial stress upon personality traits, and assess the extent to which the

1

graduate possesses the ones judged appropriate on the basis of three types of evidence: first, the applicant's personal history, as indicated by his application form and any references they may have obtained; second, the interview, often held at the applicant's university; and third, the final assessment, which more and more frequently now is conducted using the assessment centre technique. At each of these stages some applicants are rejected and others passed on to the next stage. These stages are all described in detail in Chapters 5, 6, and 7. Suffice it to say here that at each stage it is personality characteristics which are being considered as well as aptitudes.

Underlying this idea of assessing the characteristics of individuals are certain general assumptions, which must be spelled out. These assumptions are embodied in the way we talk about people in our everyday speech. We refer, for example, to people being ambitious, or sociable, or whatever, implying that these descriptions are true of them in general, over a wide variety of situations. Further, we assume when using these descriptions that they are true over time; the person we are talking about is ambitious now and, we infer, will be ambitious in the future. Indeed, we will in all probability be describing the person in order to help our listener predict how the person will behave.

This 'common-sense' view of assessment and selection is encapsulated, then, in the following six assumptions.

(1) Attributes of individuals may be inferred from objective observation of their behaviour.
(2) These attributes are relatively enduring and unchanging; hence one can predict future behaviour in a variety of situations on the basis of our knowledge of those attributes which regulate such behaviour.
(3) Assessment of any given attribute can be made independently of the assessments of other attributes of the same individual.
(4) Assessments of attributes can be combined in rational ways to come to a decision regarding the overall suitability of the individual for employment.
(5) Jobs are relatively unchanging, and can be described in terms of the tasks they involve.
(6) The characteristics required to accomplish these tasks are specifiable, and may be matched to characteristics of the person.

Underlying these assumptions are certain yet more basic ones, regarding the nature and relationship of the major elements under discussion. We may characterize these more basic assumptions as follows:

(1) Behaviour or actions are the effects of causes.
(2) The primary causes are characteristics of persons.
(3) Characteristics of persons are psychological constructs, inherent in any description of the structure of personality and necessary to explain their behaviour.

1.2 THE CRITERION PROBLEM

While the above assumptions are embedded in our everyday language, they also form the basic tenets of the psychometric testing movement. Psychometric tests have provided the basic technology for operating systems of selection based on the above assumptions. The traditional psychometric procedure was first made explicit in the 1920s, and was the prevailing selection paradigm until the 1950s. It is well described by Brotherton (1980) and by Guion (1976). It assumes that the purpose of selection is to predict the individual's job performance. It is assumed that the preferred instruments are psychological tests, and that these should have predictive validity in the situation in which they are to be employed; that is, that they will predict some measure of job performance in the organization. It is further assumed that tests are the decisive data for selection decisions.

In recent years, however, this traditional procedure has been modified considerably; or at least, recommended practice has been modified; whether actual practice has taken account of these recommendations is another matter. Certainly in the UK, it is unlikely that even the traditional procedure is being adequately implemented. Very few organizations put the recommended procedure into practice. Sneath *et al.* (1976) found that 72% of the 281 UK companies who replied to their questionnaire used psychometric tests. Half of them only had tried to form estimates of the validity of these tests, and only 5% had employed statistical methods to do so. It has been one of the most basic tenets of the testing movement that empirical evidence should be obtained that the tests used for selection purposes predict some criterion of job performance; very few UK organizations apparently act upon this article of faith.

The revised procedure has been ably described by Guion (1976) as consisting of five stages of operations, all of which have to be followed in sequence if an appropriate selection system is being set up. The stages are as follows:

(1) *Identify clearly and with logical precision the important criterion constructs, basing judgement on data from job or situation analysis.*

The first step in the revised procedure, then, concentrates upon establishing what are the criteria for deciding whether a selection procedure is effective or not. It leaves open the nature of these criteria, thereby avoiding the assumption that the individual employee's job performance is the only appropriate measure. On the contrary, it permits criteria relating to overall organizational effectiveness to be considered. After all, it is hardly surprising that, as a major component of an organizational system, the selection procedure should have a major impact on the system as a whole. As Smith (1976, p. 750) states:

Criteria range from the description of actual behaviour, through evaluation of results, to estimates of the effects upon the organisation and society.

Ideally, of course, it would be these last estimates which we would hold in mind in doing any research on policy making. Organisational goals such as economic stability, growth, and flexibility, and societal goals such as contribution towards individual well-being and growth, economic and social vitality of the community, and general productivity are the kind of goals toward which our efforts are directed. But unfortunately, these are not always the dependent variables in which investigators are interested.

While Smith may be somewhat idealistic in her idea of organizational goals, she does stress the breadth of the outcomes upon which a selection system might be having an impact. We can quickly generate a series of criterion constructs, such as degree of innovation and degree of job satisfaction, which are easy to define operationally, once we have realized that organizational constructs as well as individual ones are legitimate criteria.

The other impetus for the broadening of the nature of the criteria permissible was not so much a wider perspective as a growing dissatisfaction with the quality of the measures of individual performance. Objective performance measures such as sales figures suffered from being subject to 'error' variance due to factors unrelated to the individual salesman. Subjective measures, such as supervisors' ratings of subordinates' performance, enjoyed higher reliability. They were, however, strongly criticized by Wallace (1974). Commenting on the fact that we are better at predicting what people will say about Bloggs than Bloggs' performance, he asks (p. 404): 'Is it possible that we have developed a system which measures and predicts some quality we might call the ability to make people say good things about oneself? Is this spuriously present in both our predictors and criteria?' Measures of individual long-term success within the organization gained much favour; these included measures of rate of promotion and salary rises. However, such indices may demonstrate merely the extent to which an individual succeeds in an organization, not the extent to which it benefits from his work. They may be 'deceptively predictable, dangerously reinforcing of the status quo, and demonstrably inappropriate to some of the broader social issues with which management in government and industry is confronted' (Wallace, 1974, p. 397). There is clearly a 'criterion problem', and psychologists are becoming increasingly aware of it.

1.3 OPERATIONALIZING CONSTRUCTS

The second stage of the revised procedure for setting up selection procedures is as follows:

(2) *Obtain operational definitions of these constructs, and be sure they exhibit satisfactory construct validity.*

The point being made here is that there is a distinction between a criterion and the method of measuring that criterion. Too often in the past, criterion measures such as turnover, annual appraisals, or end-of-training ratings had been employed because they were readily available rather than because they were adequate measures of a criterion. Hence, as so often in psychology, the ready availability of method determined the content of the investigation. In the revised procedure the criterion construct, or concept, has primacy, and its operational definition follows. The requirement of construct validity indicates that operational definitions should follow from criterion constructs in a theoretically coherent manner. It is, for example, no use assuming that turnover or absenteeism or a questionnaire are adequate indices of job satisfaction. The nature of job satisfaction as a theoretical construct has to be elucidated, so that the inference to a particular operational definition may be justified.

Stage 3 of the revised procedure reads as follows:

(3) *Postulate predictor and moderator variable constructs on the basis of informed opinion.*

Stage 3 reinforces the sequential emphasis; it is only when we have decided what are the organizational outcomes we wish to influence by our selection procedure that we can hypothesize what the predictor constructs might be. The inclusion of moderator constructs into stage 3 reflects the growing concern that selection procedures should take account of the nature of the populations from which the applicant sample is drawn. A moderator construct implies that the same psychological test or selection instrument

may be a better predictor for certain classes or subsets of persons than it is for others. For example, a given test may be a better predictor of criterion performance for men than for women, or a better predictor for applicants from a lower than for applicants from a higher socio-economic level. In these examples, sex and socio-economic level are known as moderator variables, since they moderate the validity of the test (Anastasi, 1982, p. 172).

Clearly, considerations of fair employment practice and legal requirements render moderator variables an important feature.

A further feature of the revised procedure exemplified in the wording of stage 3 is its scientific character. The procedure requires its practitioners to postulate constructs. That is, it requires them to engage in the scientific practice of forming hypotheses. The procedure is not the purely technical one of performing a job analysis, selecting appropriate tests, and establishing the degree of relationship between the two. On the contrary, the required statement of theoretical constructs, the derivation of an hypothesis, and the operational definition of the constructs for purposes of testing the hypothesis, are all elements of the revised procedure which bring it into the respectable boundaries of the scientific arena.

However, there is another very important phrase in stage 3. It is 'on the basis of informed opinion'. This phrase suggests that the relationships between predictor and criterion variables are to be hypothesized on the basis of previous experience: which predictor has been demonstrated successfully to predict which criterion in the working experience of personnel psychologists. While theory is not explicitly excluded from the idea of 'informed opinion', it is certainly not paramount. Rather, the implication is that relationships should be hypothesized which had been demonstrated to exist in the past. It is this excessive emphasis on the inductive rather than the deductive operations of scientific enquiry which has severely limited psychometric theory in the past. Few other scientists would expect to hypothesize a relationship between theoretical constructs primarily on atheoretical grounds. This hard-nosed empiricism has in fact resulted in the refusal of personnel psychologists to take account of theories developed in social and cognitive psychology. These offer the grounds for hypotheses which force a radical restructuring of selection theory and practice.

1.4 VALID PREDICTORS

Stage 4 of the revised procedure reads as follows:

> (4) *Select measures and find evidence upon which to infer their descriptive validities—content validity if the constructs measured on either side of the equation are defined as samples of the same universe of work behaviour, construct validity if the postulated relationship is quasi-theoretical.*

This stage again reinforces the distinction implied in stages 1 and 2 between a theoretical construct and its operational definition. A test of intelligence need not necessarily be an appropriate measure of intellectual aptitude in a particular selection procedure. The requirement in this case is to ensure construct validity; that is, 'the extent to which the test may be said to measure a theoretical construct or trait' (Anastasi, 1982, p. 144). Where the test is a job-sample test, the requirement is for content validity.

> Content validation involves essentially the systematic examination of the test content to determine whether it covers a representative sample of the behaviour domain to be measured. . . . Content must therefore be broadly defined to include major objectives, such as the application of principles and the interpretation of data, as well as factual knowledge. (Anastasi, 1982, pp. 131–132).

Thus construct validity is expected of a predictor variable, such as scores on an intelligence or personality test, which are assumed capable of predicting criterion variable(s). The underlying chain of inference is usually from job analysis to personal characteristics judged necessary for the job, and from these characteristics to measures of them. Content validity, on the other hand, is expected of a predictor variable consisting of a score on a job-sample or achievement test. There the underlying inference is merely that performance on a task will predict future performance on the same task.

The final stage in the revised procedure, stage 5, maintains that *only when stages 1–4 have been undertaken should empirical criterion-related validity testing be attempted*. That is, only when the predictor and the criterion constructs have been specified; when the relationship between the two has been explicitly hypothesized; and when satisfactory operational definitions of the constructs have been obtained; only then should the relationship between predictor variable(s) and criterion variable(s) be empirically discovered. Such a procedure would be in marked contrast to the shotgun approach, in which a large battery of tests are fired off to see whether any should chance to predict.

Traditionally, far more attention has been paid to predictor variables, especially psychological tests, than to criterion variables. However, as soon as attention is paid to criterion variables there is an immediate increase in the range of predictor constructs which are feasible. If the criterion constructs can be organizational as well as individual, and if the task is to predict the measures of these criterion constructs, then organizational as well as individual predictors are likely to be successful in accounting for criterion variance. As Guion (1976, p. 795) puts it:

Complex behaviour is in part a function of the characteristics of the individual, but only in part; it is also a function of the stimulus variables in the situation. We have been too long hung up on tests (i.e. measures of individual traits); if we turn our attention to the question of how best to predict a criterion, we would typically recognise potential predictors other than individual traits.

1.5 INDIVIDUAL PREDICTORS

Guion's call seems, however, to have been largely disregarded. The potential power of organizational climate and similar situational features to predict has been largely ignored by personnel psychologists. Most of them would probably subscribe to Dunnette's (1976, p. 488) confident statement: 'human attributes do indeed exist to a sufficiently consistent degree across situations so that the prediction of human work performance can realistically be undertaken on the basis of tested aptitudes and skills apart from situational modifiers'. Recent developments in personnel psychology suggest that the basic assumptions listed earlier in this chapter are still widely held to be true. Three approaches to setting up selection procedures will now be briefly described in order to support this assertion. Two of these approaches, those of Dunnette (1976) and McCormick (1976) depend upon sophisticated analyses of jobs. Typically, they result in the use of batteries of tests, thereby reducing the empirical objection that tests of aptitudes and personality do not predict job performance very successfully. Ghiselli (1966, 1973) had demonstrated that the correlation of individual tests with job performance measures was around 0.35 (0.45 with training success), but the correlations observed were only between single tests and criterion measures, not batteries. Dunnette (1976) describes his preferred technique as the analysis of the behavioural requirements of jobs, and that of McCormick as the behavioural description of jobs. Dunnette uses the well-known critical incident technique, whereby people doing jobs are asked to describe those incidents which led to successful or unsuccessful outcomes. The behaviours which led to those outcomes are also elicited from the respondents. Next, dimensions of behaviour which subsume these specific behaviours are inferred. These might include such dimensions as consideration towards subordinates, handling administrative detail, and organizing and utilizing manpower resources. Next, personal characteristics necessary to perform well on these behavioural dimensions are inferred. For example, the dimension of organizing and utilizing manpower resources quoted above was taken to require: dominance, supervisory quality, self-assurance, status orientation, initiative, decisiveness and work ethic (all the examples are from an investigation of the selection of supervisors in an insurance company, described by Borman (1973). Finally, tests are selected to measure these characteristics, tests which have each been previously validated descriptively as measures of the characteristic in question. Thus the overall sequence of inferences is from specific behaviours to behavioural dimensions to characteristics to tests of those characteristics.

McCormick's (1976) approach is to describe the behavioural tasks involved in a job exhaustively, rather than only those which are revealed by the critical incident technique. He lists 189 job elements in his Position Analysis Questionnaire (PAQ), which can be reduced to 27 job dimensions. Jobs can then be characterized in terms of which of these dimensions they contain, and to what extent. A job profile can be drawn up by which the job may be distinguished, both from other jobs in the same organization, and from jobs of the same title in other organizations. Tests may then be selected which have already been shown to predict performance along the behavioural dimensions which describe the job in question. They may be used to select personnel for the job, and they will each be given the relative weight which the dimension they measure has in the job analysis. Thus there is no need to establish the criterion validity of these tests (i.e. the extent to which they predict a job performance criterion within the particular organization). The method has generality, in the sense that the dimensions are assumed to be common over all jobs; it also has specificity, in that each job in each organization has its own dimensional profile.

Another development in personnel psychology is the abandonment of the lengthy chains of inference involved in the approaches of Dunnette and McCormick. One simply discovers those tasks which are involved in the job (or at least those tasks which predominate). Then one sets up tests of performance of these tasks (job-sample tests), and uses them to predict subsequent performance. This approach stems from a classic paper by Wernimont and Campbell (1968), where they argue that the validity of a test need not be established by a relationship between predictive *signs* and criteria.

Instead, *samples* of the criteria are better predictors, and there is no theoretical psychometric reason why they should not be employed in preference to tests of aptitudes or personality characteristics. Hence Wernimont and Campbell are recommending the use of one behaviour in one task situation to predict the same behaviour in the same situation. It would hardly be surprising if this procedure did not result in better prediction than the effort to use responses to a personality questionnaire to predict job performance (i.e. to predict different behaviour in a different situation). Asher and Sciarrino (1974), reviewing work sample tests, report that 43% of the motor work sample tests predicted job performance with a correlation of greater than 0.5, compared with 21% of verbal work sample tests. The verbal tests, on the other hand, were superior to the motor ones in predicting training success (39% and 29% respectively). These figures compare well with, for example, intelligence tests, where the figure is 28% for job performance. In addition, work sample tests have much less adverse impact than other forms of selection procedure, and are capable of reducing staff turnover dramatically (Cascio and Phillips, 1979). Robertson and Kandola (1981) report similar favourable outcomes.

A comparable degree of success has been obtained with trainability tests, a subset of work sample tests. Here, Robertson and Downs (1979), using large samples of UK semi-skilled employees, found that a test consisting of a sample of a training procedure predicted the actual subsequent training performance with considerable success.

Asher and Sciarrino (1974) dignify the underlying assumption that people will do well in the future at things they have done well at in the past with the title of 'point-to-point correspondence theory'. That is, the greater the number of behavioural features the sample and the criterion performance share, the greater will be the predictive power of the sample. This is no real explanation, however. The testees who score well might have had prior experience of the task in question. They may have possessed more of the more basic skills underlying this specific task. They may have well-developed strategies for coping with a new learning situation, thus learning faster while performing the test itself.

Whatever the explanation, the job sample test ignores the organizational context entirely. Moreover, it seldom claims to predict behaviours other than those tested, whereas measures of personal characteristics aim to predict a range of behaviours. Clearly, if the nature of tasks in the job changes, job sample (but possibly not trainability) tests will fail to predict job success. It is no accident that most work sample tests have been used in selecting for unskilled or semi-skilled jobs, and that the criterion measure employed in their validation has often been a further administration of the work-sample test itself. It seems hardly likely that such specifically behavioural predictors can serve to select managerial personnel in complex and rapidly changing organizations.

1.6 INTERACTIVE PREDICTORS

The purpose of describing the three recent examples of research and practice in selection procedures has been to demonstrate that the assumptions about assessment which were listed at the beginning of this chapter are all alive and well. They are embodied in these procedures, acknowledged for their sophistication as being the best current practice in personnel psychology. By contrast, research which uses organizational as well as individual characteristics as predictor constructs is very hard to come by. This is surprising, to say the least, since the effect of characteristics of organizations upon individual employees and their work is very well established in the field of organizational psychology (Katz and Kahn, 1978). Moreover, the now historical emphasis in social psychology upon interactionism (Hampson, 1982) seems to have passed personnel psychology by entirely. This is but one of the many advances in social and cognitive psychology which challenges the basic assumptions upon which psychometric procedures are founded. An example will hopefully elucidate the idea of interactionism for the present, although we will return to it in some detail in Chapter 3.

The idea of interactionism was originally based on the statistical notions of analysis of variance, although for several reasons this is a misleading analogy (Olweus, 1977). Let us suppose we are investigating the performances of middle managers in 20 organizations. We divide the managers into half: those who are more authoritarian and those who are less. We also divide the organizations into half: those which are more bureaucratic and those which are less (using, perhaps, such indices as number of levels in the hierarchy, degree of centralization of information and decision-taking, and degree of specificity of job descriptions). Suppose then that we obtained measures of job performance of all the managers (say, senior managers' ratings). We might find that, overall, there was no effect of authoritarianism; that is, over all 20 organizations, the higher authoritarian and less authoritarian managers performed equally well. Similarly, overall, the factor of bureaucracy might have had no effect. That is, managers in the highly bureaucratic organizations worked as well as those in the less bureaucratic ones. What we might well find, however, is a person-by-situation interaction; for example, there might be little difference between managers' performance in bureaucratic organizations, but in less bureaucratic ones, low authoritarians performed much better than highly authoritarian managers. In this case we would have demonstrated that characteristics of the person and characteristics of the organization interacted to produce an effect which neither factor would have demonstrated on its own.

There have been several very influential theoretical models in occupational and organizational psychology which have used this idea of interactionism effectively. Consider, for example, the theory of occupational choice proposed by Holland (1973, 1976a). He describes six basic personality types: realistic, intellectual, social, conventional, enterprising, and artistic. He describes environments by the same six categories, and proposes sub-types of each, such that a person or an environment can be described by the three predominant descriptors in order of their magnitude. Holland suggests that the extent to which the individual's personality and his occupational environment are congruent will predict his occupational choice, occupational stability, and vocational achievement.

Another well-received theory, this time in organizational psychology, which is interactionist in nature is the approach to motivation at work of Hackman and Oldham (1976). These authors do not describe characteristics of person and situation in the same terms, as did Holland. They do, however, relate the core dimensions of an individual's job, and the personal and work outcomes of that job (situational factors), to a personal characteristic, the strength of the employee's need to grow as a competent individual. It is the interaction of these variables together with the more specific psychological states such as the experienced meaningfulness of work, which predict the quality of the individual's work (among other things).

There are very few reports, however, of research specifically aimed at predicting performance of employees on the basis of personal and organizational characteristics. They are ably reviewed by Schneider (1978). All of them point to the potential fruitfulness of the interactionist analysis. For example, Forehand (1968) assessed whether the work climates of 120 government executives were group-centred or rules-centred. He administered tests of various cognitive factors of ability and obtained peers' assessments of the executives' degree of innovativeness. For group-centred climates, the cognitive measures predicted innovativeness, but in rules-centred climates they did not. Forehand concluded that some environments make a personal quality important for effective performance, while others make it irrelevant to, or incompatible with, effective performance. In similar vein, Bray *et al.* (1974) related eight different contextual features of jobs (e.g. what were the achievement models provided by the job occupant's superiors) and personal attributes as assessed at an assessment centre. They found that both job contexts and personal attributes predicted whether or not young managers achieved middle management positions within 10 years. Most important, so did the interaction between the two; congruence of context and attributes is clearly vital. As Schneider (1978, p. 291) puts it: 'assuming that the relevant ability or abilities for performance have been assessed, the critical issue seems to be to identify the facet or facets of the situation most likely to constrain or facilitate the display of that ability'.

These findings are of great importance. They force us to look at broader organizational factors when testing selection predictors against criteria. Interactionism also forces us to look at the selection process itself as a context of applicant behaviour, and to consider the possibility that applicants' performance may be a function of the interaction between their characteristics and the specific nature of the selection situation.

Thus we have seen in this chapter that, at least in terms of the ideal recommended procedures, greater emphasis has recently been placed upon organizational factors. Instead of the individual's performance being the sole criterion measure, broader indices of the effectiveness of selection procedures are coming into consideration. Consequently, some personnel psychologists are beginning to realize that a broader range of predictor variables is likely to be successful. If individuals' performance is not the sole criterion, measures of individuals' characteristics should not be the sole predictors. However, the idea that individuals' performance might be considered a function of both individual characteristics, organizational characteristics, and their interaction, appears to have made little impact. Instead, the preferred assumption is that the individual characteristics predict and are the cause of job behaviour. The individual's tasks expected of him in his job are assumed to be the operative situational factors. Such basic social psychological factors as the organization's image, and values and rules; the norms operating officially and unofficially in work groups; and the individual's perceptions of himself and his role, are all ignored. Instead we have a model of an individual with fixed characteristics being selected for a job with fixed tasks.

It may immediately be objected that this picture is not true of graduate recruitment. For a start, little emphasis is laid on psychological tests as predictors by graduate recruiters. Moreover, the suitability of the graduate for employment specifically in the recruiter's organization is a major consideration. However, it may be replied that in certain basic respects, the graduate recruitment procedures in the UK and the USA do resemble the psychometric model outlined above. In particular, they appear to make their assessment of the individual in terms of his characteristics. His past behaviour, as indicated by his record, and his present behaviour, as evidenced in the selection interview itself, are used as evidence for personal qualities. Application forms, interview, and exercises are used as though they were psychological tests, and inferences of characteristics are drawn. Suitability for employment in the organization is judged on the basis of these inferences; in effect, personal qualities are used to predict success or failure. Such practices do in fact imply most of the assumptions listed at the beginning of this chapter. The particular assumption that has come most under scrutiny in this chapter has been the assumption that characteristics of the person alone are adequate predictors of performance. The next chapter will indicate the basic weakness of the idea that it is in principle possible to assess individuals objectively.

2

Objective Assessment?

2.1 RATING SCALES

We have seen that assessment of an individual cannot be based upon individual characteristics alone. If past and present behaviour is to be explained appropriately, and if future behaviour at work is to be predicted, then situational interactions with personal features have to be considered. One of the basic assumptions of the personnel psychologist engaged in selection procedures has therefore to be challenged. Another such assumption is that attributes of individuals may be inferred from objective observation of their behaviour. Moreover, it is assumed that when attributes are assessed in this way, each attribute may be assessed independently of others. In other words it is considered possible to treat each task of assessing the extent to which the applicant possesses a quality separately from (a) other assessments that you have already made of other qualities in that individual; and (b) other assessments that you have made of other applicants already.

Assessments which are made during the graduate selection process tend, as has been stated, to be of personal characteristics. Good assessment practice would recommend that assessments should be made in a quantified way. Thus requests for references should ask the referee to quantify how often certain sorts of behaviour occurred, or how much of a particular quality the applicant possessed. Assessments of interview performance should be graded on rating scales. Exercises at assessment centres are rated in terms of the extent to which the applicant demonstrates various qualities in her performance. Good practice may be followed in some organizations. Others tend to write notes on the basis of the evidence which specify certain qualities which the applicant appears to possess to an above-average extent; for example 'Extraverted, go-ahead and ambitious, highly motivated to work for the company.' If it is shown that there are difficulties with rating scales, then, *a fortiori*, these less quantified judgements are similarly suspect.

As in the case of psychological tests, some personnel psychologists are coming gradually to the conclusion that rating scales too are some way from being objective indices of personal characteristics. They are nevertheless, particularly in the case of ratings by one's peers in one's present job, about as good predictors of future job success as psychological tests (Reilly and Chao, 1982). However, it has long been known that rating scales suffer from several shortcomings as psychometric instruments. As Saal *et al.* (1980) note, there are confusions in the definitions of these rating errors in the research literature. However, what is clear is that it is hard to attribute these shortcomings to the construction of the rating scales, but fairly easy to attribute them to the rater's judgements. Perhaps the best known of such errors is the halo effect, defined by Saal *et al.* (1980) as a rater's failure to discriminate among conceptually distinct and potentially independent aspects of a ratee's behaviour. A leniency or severity error has also been noted frequently, defined as a tendency to assign a higher or lower rating to an individual than is warranted by that ratee's behaviour (Saal and Landy, 1977). The error of central tendency is to rate around the mid-point of the scale, not using extremes, while restriction of range (the tendency to cluster one's ratings around *any* point of the scale) also occurs.

In an exhaustive review, Landy and Farr (1980) explore the possible contributing factors to these rating errors. They analyse the rating procedure as a system. The roles of the rater and the ratee, the rating instrument itself, and contextual features such as the type of organization and the purpose of the rating are inputs into the system. The actual rating process is its central feature, and the results of the rating—information and the uses to which it is put—are the output. In accordance with this analysis, Landy and Farr reviewed the extensive research literature, and revealed considerable effects of characteristics of the rater upon her ratings. For example, four studies showed that a rater favoured her own race. Raters low in self-confidence were less lenient, while those high in anxiety used more extreme response categories. Raters who were oriented towards high production within an organization were less lenient in their ratings; and so on. Indeed, one author explicitly defined a type of error in terms of rater characteristics: For De Cotiis (1977) the leniency or severity error is 'A response set attributed to "easy" or "hard-nosed" raters whose ratings are consistently higher or lower than is warranted, given some external criterion of known true performance level.'

When we turn to the characteristics of the ratee which affect ratings, there is considerable evidence of sex effects. For example, the sex stereotype of an occupation and the sex of the ratee interact in such a way that female ratees are rated less favourably on masculine occupations. Black females were rated worse than white females at an assessment centre, but subsequently performed equally well. The more white men there were among the raters in an assessment centre, the lower were black women rated. Hence there is much evidence that characteristics both of raters and of ratees which are irrelevant to the characteristics being rated in fact affect the ratings made, causing the types of error that have bedevilled rating scales from the start. Efforts to train raters to avoid these types of error have not been uniformly successful (Bernardin and Pence, 1980). Further, the evaluation of these training procedures has been in general so methodologically inept that it is hard to draw any conclusions as to whether they are in principle likely to be effective (Spool, 1978).

Far more effort has been invested in the attempt to develop more effective rating instruments. Much recent work has been carried out upon behaviourally anchored rating scales (BARS) (Schwab *et al.*, 1975). In such scales, the anchors that appear at different intervals on the scale are examples of actual behaviour rather than adjectives indicating levels of the trait in question, or simply numbers. Different groups of raters are required to develop dimensions of behaviour, to develop behavioural examples of those dimensions; and to assign values to these behavioural examples. Hence the development of BARS scales is a costly procedure and Landy and Farr (1980) have to conclude that 'although enthusiasm greeted its introduction, the BARS method has not been supported empirically' (as resulting in less errors than other rating instruments). Perhaps this is because of the way in which BARS scales are developed; the third stage of the procedure described above requires behavioural examples to be rated on a scale to discover the extent to which they are considered to reflect the behavioural dimension. Hence, ironically, BARS are developed employing the rating methods they were designed to supersede! Consequently comparison between BARS and traditional scales is confounded by the presence of traditional features in BARS. There may also be methodological weaknesses in the experiments comparing BARS with other rating methods (Kingstrom and Bass, 1981). Since BARS are often used in assessment centre procedures, these apparently esoteric discussions are very relevant to graduate recruitment and selection.

Part of the purpose of using BARS was to reduce halo effects. Each behavioural dimension or trait was anchored by different specific behaviours. Hence ratings of one trait would be expected to be independent of ratings on another, and indeed, the evidence suggests that BARS were effective in this respect. Procedural changes were also tried, whereby all individuals were rated in turn on a single trait, and on another trait and so on. This was in contrast to the more traditional method of rating each individual on all traits, then rating the next individual. Four studies found no superiority of the former method, however. Finally, efforts were made to reduce the halo effect statistically, by using factor analytic techniques. It was expected that the number of traits that were being rated could be reduced into a few factors. Possible confounding variables such as the individual's level in the organization could be partialled out statistically, thereby getting rid of some of the causes of halo errors. However, one is left with the key question which Landy and Farr (1980, p. 93) courageously raise: What do the factors obtained actually represent, 'behavioural patterns of ratees or cognitive constructs of raters'? They raise the issue which few organizational psychologists have tried to face: are the errors typical of rating scales behavioural phenomena governed by individual difference in raters rather than by properties of rating scales? Typically, only 4–8% of variance in ratings is explained by the format of the rating scale; over 20% by characteristics of rater and ratee which are irrelevant to the characteristics being rated. Landy and Farr (1980, p. 101) conclude: 'It is time to stop looking at the symptoms of bias in rating and begin examining potential causes.'

2.2 BIAS AND ATTRIBUTION

Even the most conscientious and professionally sound selection procedure is apt to depend very substantially upon judgements of personality, whether rated on a scale or noted in a qualitative rather than quantitative form. The more psychometrically virtuous an organization, the more likely it is to use rating scales; for it will have paid heed to the requirement to validate its procedures against ratings of job performance. Unfortunately, the idea that accurate and objective observation and assessment are possible is not only denied by the psychometric evidence reviewed above. It is also contradicted by a vast amount of evidence in social psychology regarding the way in which we form impressions and make judgements about people. Social psychologists have not concentrated upon the psychometric properties of judgements—their reliability and validity. They have rather tried to explore the cognitive processes which underlie them. Their interest has been in these processes of person perception in a wide variety of social situations, not merely assessment for selection or appraisal purposes. However, the data they obtain very often consist of ratings by subjects of others on scales measuring personality characteristics. Moreover, they would argue that the processes used in our everyday judgements of others do not suddenly atrophy when we are faced with the task of assessing them for employment. There is an interesting analogy in the history of experimental psychology. Students of verbal learning thought that by giving subjects nonsense syllables to learn (e.g. ZUP) they could study learning from absolute zero, without previous learning interfering with the experiment. They reckoned without the immense capacity of the human linguistic system to impose a structure upon practically anything! In the same way, the processes we use in other activities to help us to make sense of our social environment are bound to intrude upon our selection decisions.

In our examination of the evidence on rating scales, we saw that there was evidence of certain biases operating in a supposedly objective assessment. Social psychology indicates many more. For example, there is a tendency to place excessive weight on initial behaviour as evidence (Jones et al., 1968; Jones and Goethals, 1971). This is perhaps because one notices and attends to the person first, since she is the performing figure against the backcloth of the situation. Second, having formed an initial hypothesis, we try to confirm it rather than refute it (Snyder *et al.*, 1977), unlike a good Popperian scientist. In some selection procedures (e.g. the interview) we are actually in a position to elicit from the applicant the behaviour which confirms our initial judgement. Third, we form favourable judgements of those whom we like, or who are similar to us (Byrne, 1969; Ross *et al.*, 1977). All of these everyday biases are apt to intrude upon our judgements in selection procedures, and evidence that they do so will be reviewed in Chapter 6. Suffice it to say here that there are many reasons why we would expect such judgements to be flawed by subjective biases. They are ably reviewed in the introductory text on person perception by Cook (1979).

There are, however, more basic difficulties in the idea that the assessor can infer personality characteristics from observations. We saw in Chapter 1 that the personnel psychologist should be looking at characteristics of the organization as well as at those of the applicant in her effort to predict job success; she should also consider their possible interactive effect. Exactly the same is true of the way in which as individuals we form our judgements about the behaviour of others. In these everyday judgements we explain others' behaviour in a variety of different ways, some in terms of factors internal to the person (her motives, her character), others in term of factors external, in the situation. These processes are examined in the area of psychology known as *attribution theory*. By implication, if the principles of attribution theory are descriptive of our everyday judgements, they are possibly descriptive of our judgements in selection procedures.

It is not the intention here to review attribution theory. Simpler introductions are available in Eiser (1978), Schneider *et al.* (1979), and Cook (1979), and an up-to-date review in Kelley and Michela (1980). Rather, attention will be directed to the nature of the causal inferences people make about behaviour, and to some of the biases found to be operating in these causal attributions. It will be recalled that the psychometrician assumes that the observer can infer with accuracy personality characteristics from the applicant's behaviour which she has observed. Interactionists had urged that the situation in which the behaviour had occurred and the personality × situation interaction were also likely to be causes of the applicant's behaviour. Attribution theorists maintain that we ourselves are interactionists in our everyday life—we attribute the causes of others' behaviour to themselves, their intentions, motives and personal characteristics; to their situation; and to the interaction of these two. Thus the selector or assessor is urged by the psychometrician to ignore two of the three elements of assessing others' behaviour which come naturally to her. She is supposed to concentrate only on making judgements of personal characteristics.

Attribution theorists have made several important discoveries about the ways in which we make attributions to personal characteristics on the basis of observed behaviour, and how these personal attributions are related to situational and to interactive ones. Jones and Davis (1965) proposed the Correspondent Inference Principle. This states that the fewer distinctive reasons an actor might have for her action, and the less these reasons are shared by other actors, the more informative is the action for the observer in her purpose of inferring its causes. Hence, observers are apt to infer particular motives and characteristics only when such motives and characteristics are shared by few other people than the individual being observed. It is thus unusual causes of behaviour which are more likely to be inferred by the observer (Ajzen and Holmes, 1976). It is, furthermore, unusual behaviour itself which is apt to lead to inferences of personal characteristics. This is what emerges from Kelley's (1972) Discounting and Augmentation Principles: the Discounting Principle predicts that there will be less attribution to the actor as causing her behaviour when her behaviour is that expected in the situation than when the behaviour occurs in a setting free of situational demands. The Augmentation Principle states that there will be more attribution to the actor when her behaviour is contrary to that expected in a situation than when the behaviour occurs in a setting free of situational demands.

There is a wealth of varied evidence for these propositions; both are supported in an experiment by Himmelfarb and Anderson (1975). The implication is that as everyday assessors of others, we pay little attention to behaviour in social situations, except when the behaviour is unexpected. Using the terminology of role theory, in-role behaviour is attributed to the requirements and demands of the situation. It is only out-of-role behaviour that is attributed to the individual's characteristics—when the social rules are broken (Semin, 1980). I am likely to attribute the shop assistant's behaviour to the requirements of her job if she asks me what I want to buy; indeed, I probably will not even bother to infer a cause of her behaviour at all, since there is no reason to make such an inference. However, if she asks me whether I am saved or enquires solicitously about the state of my marriage, I begin to wonder just what sort of a person she is, and probably jump to some fairly immediate conclusions. The general point is that in everyday life one only tends to make judgements about others' personalities when they behave in some unusual way which breaks the rules, or when there are no rules operating as to how to behave. Otherwise we attribute the cause of the behaviour to the role requirements of the situation, if we attribute it to anything at all. In sum, on any occasion when we are assessing others' personalities from their behaviour, the two major factors taken into account are the extent to which the situation is a rule-governed one with specific role expectations of the actor; and the extent to which the actor's behaviour is in accordance with those expectations.

In general, the procedures involved in assessment for selection do not take these aspects of everyday assessment of others into account. Many observed behaviours would in everyday interactions be attributed to role requirements or to an interaction rather than to personal attributes. In the selection procedures this possibility is not catered for; all behaviour is evidence of personal characteristics. Moreover, different selection procedures differ in the degree to which they are rule-governed. There is probably a fairly specific set of rules governing the selection interview (for example, applicants are not expected to ask questions of the interviewer until invited to do so). A leaderless group discussion exercise, on the other hand, is likely to be a new experience with few rules. Assuming that our everyday modes of assessment affect our judgements in these two procedures, the procedures for making personality inferences are different in each; in the selection interview, rule-breaking may carry considerable weight (by the Augmentation Principle—Herriot, 1981), whereas in the group discussion all behaviour is taken as good evidence of personality, since it occurs in a relatively rule-free situation (by the Discounting Principle). Moreover, when it is rule-breaking that is used as key evidence, we have an interesting paradox; out-of-role behaviour is being used as evidence to predict how effectively the individual will subsequently behave in-role (in a job).

In summary, the selection procedures other than psychometric tests are likely to make inappropriate use of people's natural capacity for making assessments of others. People naturally make situational and interactional inferences from behaviour as well as personality ones. Yet the procedures require them to limit their inferences to personality ones only, with the consequent obvious danger that much applicant behaviour will be used inappropriately, as evidence for personality. Selection procedures and natural everyday assessment of others are also incompatible with respect to the nature of the behavioural evidence. We usually only find the need to make an attribution to personality when a person behaves *unexpectedly* in everyday life. In psychometric procedures, however, it is the expressed objective to make assessments of personality, so *all* behaviour is potentially grist to the mill. All-in-all, we may conclude that it was a bad mistake to assume that everyday modes of understanding others' behaviour would not intrude upon supposedly objective observations and inferences.

There is, however, one more feature of the way in which we attribute the causes of behaviour. It is so important that it deserves separate mention. This feature is an attributional bias, a bias so pervasive that Ross (1977) termed it the 'fundamental attribution error'. First discovered by Jones and Harris (1967) and subsequently observed in many other studies, it consists in attributing too much of the causation of behaviour to the actor's personality characteristics and too little to the situation in which it occurs. The tendency is, therefore, to pay too little attention to the role requirements of a situation, and to all the rules about what is appropriate behaviour. Instead, rule-governed behaviour is taken as evidence of character; for example, the good interviewee becomes the good applicant. It has already been pointed out above that all the pressure in the selection procedure is on the assessor to draw personality inferences rather than situational ones. When we add to this pressure the effect of such a profound bias in our everyday judgements, the dangers of using behaviour as evidence of personality become only too clear: we are apt to use many different types of behaviour as evidence of personality when they do not provide such evidence.

2.3 IMPLICIT PERSONALITY THEORIES

Selection procedures do not only involve the drawing of inferences about single personality characteristics from behavioural evidence. They also frequently require the assessor to infer several different characteristics from the same behaviours (for example, from behaviours in a group discussion exercise). Moreover, each procedure in the selection process is assumed to be independent of the others: the interviewer's judgements based on interview are not supposed to affect her estimate of the applicant's leadership qualities evidenced in a subsequent exercise. At the final stage of the typical assessment centre procedure (see Chapter 7) all assessees are rated on a large number of characteristics. These ratings are based on the evidence derived from every part of the procedure, and each rating is supposed to be independent of others. All of these aspects of selection procedures make the assumption that the only inferences that are made are those from observed behaviour to individual characteristics. They ignore the long-established findings of social psychology that people have *implicit personality theories*, whereby they relate different characteristics to each other. Inferences are made from personality characteristics to others; if we infer from her behaviour that a person is friendly, we may be likely to assume that she is also generous and kind. Thus our estimates of individual characteristics in assessment procedures are apt to be affected by such theories in our heads. We may make inferences from one characteristic to another when we are supposed to be assessing both characteristics separately and independently from a performance in an exercise. Or we may infer characteristic y from characteristic x evidenced in exercise 1, rather than from performance in exercise 2 which has been specially designed to reveal y. Now ratings of applicant characteristics are used both in selection procedures and in criterion measures of job performance. Thus it follows that, if implicit personality theories are operating in both sides of the prediction equation, any relationship between predictors and criteria is only valid to the extent that implicit personality theories are valid. Thus we need to look at the extent to which our implicit personality theories do intrude; and at how valid they are.

Such is the insularity of different branches of psychology that many applied psychologists are not aware of the developments in social psychology relating to implicit personality theory. The typical errors of rating scales are explicable in terms of the rater's own theories about the relationship between different traits in the overall personality of others. Hence ratings can never be entirely objective, since these subjective theories will inevitably be involved in judgements deriving from the observation of behaviour, and in the combination of those judgements. Of course this realization, which comes as a shock to psychometrically-oriented psychologists, is a truism in cognitive and social psychology. It is assumed in these branches of psychology that human information processing is a construction by the perceiver of evidence, not its veridical reception. The further inference, which we will pursue later, is of great interest: it is that judgements made subjectively are not therefore by definition wrong or useless. As with other aspects of cognition, subjectivity will include shared constructions of reality as well as individual differences in perceptions and judgements. There is no need to assume that these shared constructions are in some sense in error simply because they have been shown to be constructions. For the moment, however, we will explore some of the social psychological evidence regarding implicit personality theories. It will become clear that aspects of our implicit personality theories explain those effects in our ratings which are considered errors by psychometricians.

One interesting way in which over-interpretations of behaviour may occur has been discovered by Cantor and Mischel (1977). They theorized that people possess as part of their implicit personality theories prototypes of a typical member of a class or person. Thus, the typical extravert is talkative, sociable, self-confident, active, and so on. The organization of our implicit personality theories is hierarchical in nature (and parallels that of personality theories such as Eysenck's which consider types, such as extravert, to subsume traits, such as sociable). The possibility then arises that we infer that a person is an instance or example of this prototype after we have judged her to possess one or two of the traits associated with it. For example, a person appears talkative and self-confident, so we infer she is an extravert. From this inference we make a further jump; since she is extravert, she will also be sociable and active. Cantor and Mischel (1977, 1979) demonstrated this mode of inference in memory experiments, thereby showing that this effect occurred not merely when the information was received, but also when it was recalled subsequently after a passage of time. They used the standard experimental techniques of recognition memory and free recall. The material presented to their subjects in the recognition experiment was a set of descriptions of imaginary persons, in terms of the traits which characterized them. The traits were either those of the prototypical extravert or introvert, or else a set of unrelated traits. Subsequently, the subjects were given a list of trait names, and asked whether or not these had been presented in each of the original descriptions. Some of these listed traits had indeed occurred in the original descriptions, but others had not. These latter 'false' traits varied along a continuum of rated similarity to the traits actually presented. The analysis of the results concentrated upon the number and nature of those traits which were falsely recognized as having occurred in the original description when in fact they had not. It was found that the more related these were to the traits actually presented, the more likely they were to be falsely recognized as having actually occurred. These results were found *only* for those subjects who had originally been presented with a list of prototypical traits (extravert or introvert). Other subjects, who had been given a set of non-prototypical traits in the original description, did *not* falsely recognize more of the related than of the unrelated false traits in the recognition phase of the task. Hence we may conclude that the false recognition was not because the *individual* false traits were similar in meaning to the individual original traits. Rather, it was due to the *overall* super ordinate categorizing of the prototypical traits by the subjects. They falsely recognized related traits because they had themselves generated them from their encoding of the presented traits under an overall category.

Cantor and Mischel (1979) demonstrated the same sort of effect when the task was to recall as many of the traits as possible. More traits were remembered from a description of a 'pure' extravert or introvert than from a mixed description, where some of the traits presented were prototypical and others irrelevant. Least efficient recall of all occurred when the presented traits were contradictory—half introvert and half extravert.

The implication of these experiments for our understanding of the task of rating another individual on the basis of our memories of her immediate or long-past behaviour are considerable. The clear inference is that we are in danger of over-interpreting behaviour when it occurs, in the following way. Suppose that an individual subordinate or an acquaintance behaves in a careless way in one situation, and again shortly afterwards, in another. Here we have two pieces of evidence of what we could justifiably call carelessness, and so we attribute this trait to the individual. Suppose that on two other occasions we observe her breaking the recognized rules of the organization, and we attribute the trait of insubordination. On the basis of these two attributed traits, we may infer some sort of prototypical category of unreliability. When asked to rate this subordinate in an annual assessment along a variety of trait dimensions, we may consequently rate her low on punctuality and honesty as well as on carefulness and adherence to rules. Such ratings would be based on inferences from an inference from an attributed trait (behaviour → trait → prototype → trait)!

Research by Lingle *et al.* (1979) shows that these effects do not only occur when the superordinate category used in encoding is a prototype, the product of the rater's implicit personality theory. They can also occur when there are particular functions or purposes in the original encoding. Their subjects were given sets of traits suitable to particular occupations as descriptions of hypothetical applicants. Each set contained one half traits which were suitable for one occupation, and the other half suitable for an entirely different occupation. Subjects were asked to rate the suitability of applicants who demonstrated the list of traits. Some subjects were asked to rate their suitability for one of the occupations, other subjects for other occupations. Hence we have a situation where the same set of traits are presented, as a description of an individual, to all the subjects. Some of the subjects have encoded these traits in terms of their relevance to one occupation; others have encoded them in terms of their relevance to another occupation. The only difference is, therefore, in terms of the encoding by the subjects. The results demonstrated that more traits were recalled that were relevant to the occupation for which the subjects had judged the individual's suitability. The general lesson from this experiment is that other superordinate codings than personality prototypes may affect memory. The other, specific, implication is that a rater may infer the degree of trait possessed by an applicant from her knowledge of the traits typically considered necessary for the job.

2.4 ASSESSMENT AS CONSTRUCTION

The evidence from attribution theory, and that regarding our implicit theories which we have reviewed above, indicate that the assumption of objective observation and inference is a chimera. All of the procedures involved in selection require the selector to form judgements regarding applicants' characteristics. If our judgements regarding these characteristics are normally subjective constructions of reality rather than objective observation and measurement, there is no reason to suppose that selection procedures are any different. . . . Indeed, the evidence indicates that they are not. Personnel officers and selectors are perfectly willing to accept the idea that there are biases operating, and that some individual selectors are more liable to bias than others. Therefore, personnel officers either look carefully for the good judge of character who is skilled by nature and disposition, or they provide training courses which aim to make selectors aware of potential biases and of how to avoid them. However, they cannot come to terms with the idea that *all* assessments are perceptions, constructions of reality. Hence, there are no individuals who approach closer than others to the ideal of objectivity. There is evidence, however, which indicates that individuals differ in the way they do perceive others and form judgements about them. To this extent, personnel officers are correct, in that they may prefer some sorts of judgements to others, and therefore pick their selectors accordingly. For example, selectors' ideological preferences might be expected to be operative, even at the stage of encoding the actual behaviour and situation. One can imagine a Marxist attributing causes of behaviour predominantly to the environment, while a Freudian might attribute accidents to subconscious motives rather than to faulty design of equipment! More seriously, people differ in terms of the number of trait terms they habitually use and the number of distinctions they can make along a rating continuum of each (Bieri, 1966). They may also differ in terms of the nature of the evidence which they consider points to a particular trait. For example Wiggins *et al.* (1969) found that many of their subjects thought that industriousness was an indicator of intelligence. There is also some evidence that people will value highly those characteristics in others for which they themselves feel a personal need (Cantor, 1976).

Given the evidence presented thus far in this chapter, a graduate recruitment officer or selector might grudgingly admit that subjectivity inevitably intrudes into the practices she typically employs. The interview and the rating of performance in assessment centre tasks, for example, are unavoidably subject to bias. But she is still unlikely to admit that accurate, objective assessment is impossible. (We will leave aside for the moment the thorny problem of whether the characteristics and qualities being assessed actually exist at all!) The rest of this chapter will be concerned with demonstrating that *every* form of assessment is a construction. Therefore there is no evidence against which the accuracy of an assessment can be judged. There are simply different constructions originating from different points of view, which can be used for different purposes. Each type of assessment is based upon different psychological processes from other types; rating scales require the rater to use mental processes of memory and judgement which are different from those required to complete a psychological personality test questionnaire. Both these activities require different processes again, from ratings of oneself, one's own past achievements, present characteristics, and future plans. None of them can be treated as objective truth, as a criterion which the other modes of assessment approach more or less closely. Some psychometricians would like psychological tests to be treated as such a criterion. However, as an account of relevant research in social psychology will show, no mode of assessment can achieve such status.

Social psychologists have used rating scales for quite another purpose than as evidence of the personality of the ratee; ironically, they have used them as clues to the nature of the implicit personality theories of the raters! A typical social psychology experiment is that of Passini and Norman (1966). They asked members of small groups to assign other members of the group to one end or the other of 20 personality trait scales. However, the subjects of the experiment had merely sat with each other for 15 minutes, and had been forbidden to talk to each other. Hence, in effect, the raters were rating individuals who were strangers to them; they had little more than appearance to go on. They certainly did not have access to the behavioural data which are available to supervisors rating subordinates, to referees providing character references, or to assessment centre staff rating assessees. Nevertheless, the ratings obtained in this way were very similar to ratings obtained after much longer acquaintance; they were also similar to the results of personality questionnaires answered by individuals being assessed. The similarity lies in the underlying structure of the ratings as revealed by factor analysis: in all cases a similar number of factors emerges, and their descriptions appear to be overlapping. Thus, for example, Eysenck and Eysenck (1969) derive three basic factors from their test data: extraversion–introversion, neuroticism–stability, and psychoticism. Passini and Norman's (1966) study revealed five factors, labelled extraversion, agreeableness, conscientiousness, emotional stability, and culture. Factor analysis of ratings in other personality rating studies normally reveals the three basic factors of evaluation, activity, potency first delineated in Osgood's (1962) semantic differential. While the labels of the factors are somewhat different, inspection of the traits and descriptive adjectives which described the rating scales suggests considerable overlap. For example, emotional stability and conscientiousness (Passini and Norman) overlap with stability–neuroticism (Eysenck) and activity (Osgood). Hence the underlying structure of personality as evidenced by personality questionnaires, and the structure of implicit personality theories as revealed by judgements based on little or no behavioural evidence, are similar.

Not only so; it is not merely that tests and implicit personality theories describe personality similarly. It is also the case that our natural language itself describes personality in exactly the same way. D'Andrade (1965) asked his subjects simply to rate a set of trait adjectives for the degree of similarity in meaning between them. Mulaik (1964) obtained ratings of trait names (not people) on a large number of adjectival scales. In both cases the same factor structure emerged as in the personality tests and personality ratings. Thus in a situation where language itself was being rated, rather than behaviour or appearance, the structure of personality theory remains the same.

One could put a wide variety of interpretations upon these findings taken together. Our native language could have formed both our own implicit personality theories and those of the psychometricians who devised the tests of personality. Or there could exist an underlying structure of personality recognized in our language, in our implicit personality theories, and in our tests. Or our implicit personality theories could have determined both the language we use to describe people and the items we put in our tests. These different explanations are not capable of proof or disproof on the basis of the evidence available. What the evidence has shown is that the search for veridicality is vain—all assessments of personality are constructions. Implicit personality theories and attributional processes are not unfortunate subjective biases distorting objective observation of the truth. They are part and parcel of any attempt to understand the behaviour of others.

3

Process and System

3.1 SELF-ASSESSMENT

Instead, therefore, of treating subjectivity as a bias and an intrusion in assessment, in this chapter we will treat it as a resource. The overall strategy involved is that of using man's naturally developed capacities to the full. We will look at the psychological processes involved in making assessments. Such an analysis will point to the strengths and weaknesses of the respective modes of assessment, and hence to their most appropriate use.

First, let us consider a mode of assessment which has as yet hardly been mentioned in this book: self-assessment. Its omission is no accident. Psychometricians have searched for objectivity, and the probability of objectivity in one's description of oneself appears to be considerably less than in the description of others. Attempts have nevertheless been made to treat self-assessment as a psychometric tool, researching into its reliability and validity as though it were a test.

As Heneman (1980) has noted, it is a singularly pointless exercise to assess the potential usefulness of self-appraisals by discovering how highly they correlate with psychometric test scores or with supervisor ratings. Their usefulness is not to be considered in terms of whether self-assessment can be substituted for other modes of assessment. Rather, we must examine whether self-assessment, because of the peculiar processes involved, can add to what other modes have to offer. Low correlations with test results may be due to the two types of measures measuring different but valid variance (Reilly and Chao, 1982). This point can be made more clearly with the aid of an example. If we wish to use a rating method to discover which single employee from among a group merits promotion to a more senior position in competition with his fellows, we would not expect to use a self-assessment. When employees rate themselves in their organization, we may not be surprised to learn that 40% place themselves in the top 10%, and 1 or

2% place themselves in the bottom 50% (Meyer, 1980). When one's peers nominate the member of the group who is best at particular job behaviours or dimensions, however, such nominations correlate highly with 'objective' measures of job success and possess a high level of inter-rater reliability (Kane and Lawler, 1978). Obviously, self-interest and self-esteem are likely to render self-appraisal less than useful for such purposes.

On the other hand, a consistent finding has been that, in comparison with other sorts of ratings, self-ratings suffer less from halo (and horns) effects. That is, the ratings of each trait predict the ratings on other traits less in the case of self-ratings. The implication is that the discovery of a profile of strengths and weaknesses is suitably attempted by means of self-ratings (Meyer, 1980). In his comprehensive review of 22 studies of self-appraisal, Thornton (1980) also stresses this important function. When compared with supervisors', peers', and subordinates' ratings, self-appraisals show more leniency errors but less halo effect. The lack of correlation and these other differences with other forms of assessment indicate that self-assessment may require different psychological processes and be useful for different purposes. There are one or two other hints in the psychometric literature on self-assessment which suggest that this may be the case. When they reviewed 55 studies which related self-ratings to measures of achievement, Mabe and West (1982) found that closer relationships were found when the self-raters were of high IQ, high achievement, and had an internal locus of control. This suggests that self-assessment is a skilled intellectual activity, and is related to the individual's view of himself as an active determiner of his fate. Previous experience of having rated oneself also helps.

It is only when we turn to social psychology, however, that we can obtain some evidence about the processes underlying self-ratings. There are very interesting pieces of evidence which lead us to suppose that our self-ratings are based on different evidence from ratings by others. The first is the well-established finding (Shrauger and Schoeneman, 1979) that our self-perceptions correlate highly with how we believe others perceive us. They do not correlate so highly, however, with how others actually do perceive us. This result argues against the symbolic interactionist theory that we gain our notions of the sort of people we are from the way other people behave towards us. On the contrary, we may well use our own self-perceptions to infer the way we think others perceive us (though correlation need not imply causality). This suggests that we have alternative evidence for the sort of people we are; one strong candidate is our observations of our own past behaviour.

The second significant finding leads us further. It is well established (Jones and Harris, 1967; Jones and Nisbett 1971; Nisbett et al., 1973) that individuals are less liable to the fundamental attribution error when assessing the cause of their own behaviour than when assessing that of the behaviour of others. They are more likely, in other words, to take situational factors into account when judging their own behaviour. A wide variety of explanations has been offered for this phenomenon. For example, it has been treated as purely perceptual in nature. The actor does not concentrate upon himself acting; he pays attention to his situation and the people in it. He is more likely to attribute causality to that to which he has attended. When he is forced to observe himself behaving by video feedback (Storms, 1973) or even merely to imagine himself in the other person's shoes (Wolfson and Salancik, 1977), he attributes more of his behaviour to his own characteristics and less to the situation. Another explanation is that people believe that their own actions are typical and usual (Ross *et al.*, 1977), and therefore they do not use them to infer personality characteristics (since we use unusual behaviour as evidence of personality). We can more plausibly explain the finding, however, on the grounds that people have a great deal more evidence to go on when considering their own behaviour than do others considering that same behaviour. The outside observer sees the person behaving in a certain way in a situation, and encodes that behaviour as an instance of a certain characteristic. He has insufficient information, however, to be able to do so; he may well have no information about how the actor has behaved in similar situations in the past, nor about whether he has exhibited the same sort of behaviour in different situations. Contrast the actor himself; Kelley (1972) proposes that the actor will only infer that he himself possesses a certain characteristic if he knows that he usually acts this way in this situation, *and* that he acts this way in other situations as well. These sorts of information are not often available to outside observers. Observers tend to assume that these conditions are met more often than they are, whereas the actor knows how infrequently they are met. It is not often that his behaviour is consistent across situations. Hence he is less ready to make personality attributions about himself, whereas the observer over-interprets, in the absence of further evidence. These differences would also explain the psychometric findings that there is less halo error in self-ratings: trait ratings are less predictive of each other because each trait is more likely to have been assessed separately on the basis of evidence, rather than inferred from other traits via implicit personality theory.

This is not to say, however, that self-ratings are based on veridical memories of one's past actions. Memories of one's own actions are cognitively structured, just as are memories of others' actions. The major implicit personality theory in this case, however, is one's theory about oneself—one's self-concept (Gergen, 1971; Wylie, 1974; Markus, 1977). Like our personality theories about others, our self-concept has a strong evaluative component, our self-esteem, which affects our description of ourselves and any comparisons of ourselves with others which we may make. More important, however, our self-concept is itself a predictor of our actions. Thus, since we are likely to be more aware than anyone else of our self-concept, we are more able to predict those actions which are predicted by that self-concept.

A very important experiment by Bem and Allen (1974) illustrates this latter point. They asked subjects to rate themselves in terms of how consistently friendly they were across situations. The subjects were divided into two groups: those who rated themselves more consistent, and those who rated themselves less so. This rating was independent of how friendly they believed themselves to be—it was self-perceived consistency either in friendly or in unfriendly behaviour which was assessed. The subjects also rated themselves on how friendly they thought they were; they were rated by their parents and a friend; and they were rated by observers of their behaviour in a group discussion. The important finding was that for those subjects who believed themselves highly consistent, there was a close relationship between self-ratings of friendliness, others' ratings, and observer-rated behaviour in a group. For those who considered themselves inconsistent across situations with respect to this trait, only low correlations were obtained between the other three measures. Hence self-perceived consistency acted as a moderator variable: it predicted the relationship between perceived friendliness and friendly behaviour. The experiment demonstrated, therefore, that the individual is perfectly capable of stating whether or not he possesses a trait—that is whether he behaves in a certain way consistently across situations or, at least, whether he is perceived to do so.

The self-concept is beneficial in another way also. It assists the individual in his account of his past development (Bandura, 1978). The self-concept contains aspects of the individual's roles; part of our self-definition consists of occupational and social roles such as secretary, wife, and mother. These roles are incorporated into the self-concept as they are forced upon us at different stages of our lives; as Super (1980) notes, there are some periods of our lives, such as young adulthood, when new roles are thrust upon us in rapid succession: thus our self-concept contains features which are constant reminders of our past, and of how we responded to the onset of new expectations and new demands. The self-concept is, therefore, a valuable and potential cue to our memories of those periods of change and transition in our lives. It can help us chart the course of our life thus far, and enable us to recall the nature of our response to novel situations. It also offers in summary form our assessment of our present performance at the major roles we play.

However, the self-concept does not merely have past and present dimensions. It also contains elements of the sort of person we think we are becoming or would like to become. The self-concept may, therefore, not only be a useful predictor of shortly subsequent behaviour but also of major developments and transitions. Permitting an individual to predict his own future might appear to be a highly risky and psychometrically invalid procedure. Consider, however, the information the individual has available to help him. He has an overall view of his previous achievements and adaptations to the changing demands of his previous environment. And he has a clearer view than others of his future objectives.

The capacity of the individual to review the past, present, and future with the help of the self-concept has been rarely utilized in personnel selection. A review of the past career of an applicant by both the applicant and interviewer in discussion is rendered easier by the availability of the application form as a basis for discussion. More frequently, however, it seems that the application form has been used as a source of biographical data which predict future performance statistically (Owens, 1976); alternatively, it has been used as an informal clinical predictor of job success. Perhaps such a clinical approach is preferable to the actuarial one, since the selector can take account of the applicant's opportunities and background in evaluating his achievements hitherto. It seems surely more appropriate, however, that the application form should form the basis of an interview in which both parties review the past, present, and future in an effort to predict the likely outcomes if the applicant joins the organization. A self-appraisal, as Downs *et al.* (1978) maintain, can be 'a convergence of selection and guidance'.

The evidence that self-descriptions and expressed plans and intentions for the future are potentially of great use is reviewed in detail in Chapter 9. Here it suffices to quote Tullar and Barrett (1976), who state (p. 373): 'While a great deal of research has focused on the biographical information blank, which is past oriented, a viable complement may be a measure of future orientation.' They asked 36 sales trainees to write their future autobiographies in the course of a more orthodox selection procedure. The element of these future autobiographies which significantly predicted 10 criteria of subsequent sales success was agency—'the extent to which a person sees himself as the prime agent in determining the course of his future life'. This is clearly the personality dimension of internal versus external locus of control (Rotter, 1966). Whether this is a fundamental personality dimension (Phares, 1978) or merely a reflection of the current ethos (Sampson, 1977) is a matter for debate. What is to the point in the present discussion is that perceived locus of control is an element of the self-concept which can be used to predict future activity.

Another indication of the value of the concept of the future self is available in the occupational choice literature (which will be reviewed later). Suffice it to say here that one's occupational concept and one's self-concept may be very closely related—'occ talk becomes psych talk', as Starishevsky and Matlin (1968) put it. Hence one's concept of one's future occupation expresses part of the future aspect of one's self-concept. Research evidence bears this idea out. Time and again students' statements of the occupation they intend to enter are the best single predictor of the occupation they actually do enter (Holland and Whitney, 1969: Gottfredson and Holland, 1974; Richards, 1971).

Of course, many psychometric tests of personality are in fact self-reports. Typically they ask questions of an individual about his habitual behaviour (e.g. sleeping and digestive habits), his preferred activities (e.g. parties or reading), and attitudes towards various issues or classes (e.g. the death penalty, homosexuals) (Eysenck and Eysenck, 1969; Cattell, 1973). Hence they tap a person's memory of his own behaviour: what he has normally said and done in the past and continues to say and do. Their standardized procedure, and the existence of norms, ensures their relative efficiency in comparing individuals along these dimensions. They mostly appear to direct the respondent's attention to aspects of his behaviour which would generally pass without much attention being paid to them. Hence they tap the sort of evidence upon which we do not normally base our personality judgements. Instead of out-of-the-ordinary responses to ordinary situations, or adaptive responses to new situations in the individual's experience, personality questionnaires mostly tap habitual responses in frequently experienced situations. To be more specific, personality questionnaires are apt to ask about such things as health, eating, and sleeping, not about an outstanding performance at football nor how well one coped when one broke a leg or started a new job.

Given the different nature of the behaviours being sampled by tests and by self—or other—ratings, it is hardly surprising that tests and ratings have different psychometric properties. Specifically, test scores show a high consistency over such periods of time as 7 years within the same individual (Schaie and Parham, 1976). They also demonstrate the same factor structure and roughly similar scores for cross-sections of young, middle-aged, and older adults (Eysenck and Eysenck, 1969). Hence they present a picture of continuity over one's life-span, with the strong implication of a major hereditary contribution to personality (Eysenck and Eysenck, 1980). The continuity is one of reported habitual behaviour, attitudes, and preferences, and there is no reason to suppose that these self-reports are inaccurate accounts. Much of the behaviour sampled by personality tests is likely to reflect precisely those patterns of regular and unconscious biological adaptation which remain constant over time.

Self-reports and the observation of others, however, are likely to lead to a perception of discontinuity. This is primarily because we use as evidence our non-habitual behaviour in habitual situations, or our reactions to new situations. Hence the major transitions in life are perceived as occurring when new environmental pressures make themselves felt. As far as students are concerned, for example, entry into the world of work, independence from parents, and establishing adult relationships with others are all societal expectations which are thrust upon them around the same time in their lives. It is their reactions to this battery of role expectations which students observe. It is also the changes in their self-concept which are consequent upon adopting these new roles. Hence the individual has two sources of information peculiar to himself—a great deal more evidence of his own behaviour and its effects than anyone else has; and potential access to his own self-concept.

3.2 ASSESSMENT BY OTHERS

Self-assessment and psychological tests are the two forms of assessment which have been discussed thus far in this chapter. It now remains to attempt an analysis of ratings of others as a form of assessment. It will be recalled that this mode is the most frequently used in graduate recruitment. It is very important, therefore, that the processes which underlie it are differentiated from those which underlie the other modes, and its particular advantages and disadvantages are indicated. The following account owes much to the incisive analysis of Hampson (1982), as do previous chapters.

It is useful first of all to review what we have already discussed regarding ratings of others. In Chapter 2 it was demonstrated that these ratings depended upon attributions made from behaviour to character, where such attributions might be appropriate. It was also shown that implicit personality theories could result in ratings of one characteristic affecting ratings of another. However, little effort was made to detail the specific sub-tasks involved in making a rating; nor were more fundamental questions raised regarding the nature of trait terms.

Essentially, the rater's task is a cognitive one. It involves the processing of information over time, and its subsequent recall. The information concerned is the behaviour of the ratee. This behaviour might be that observed over a long period by a referee, in which case many different actions in a variety of situations would be the data-base. Similarly, it might consist of the behaviour at work of a subordinate when the rater is the supervisor making an annual appraisal. In the context of specific selection procedures the behaviour observed might be that exhibited during an interview; during a specific exercise; or during the assessment centre procedure as a whole.

The important question that has to be answered is how these events are perceived and encoded in memory by the rater while they are occurring. We have seen that attribution theory suggests that only some behaviour will be attended to and encoded in memory. This is likely to be out-of-role behaviour; or behaviour in which, in comparison with some reference group, an individual behaved in an unexpected way; or behaviour in unusual situations, such as emergencies, where individuals' responses become crucially important. Attribution theory indicated that strong emphasis would be put upon the actor, the individual being rated, in such situations. Further, the fundamental attribution error would suggest that yet more emphasis would be placed upon the individual since the situational constraints would be devalued. Implicit personality theory predicts that once it is coded into terms of behavioural attributes (e.g. carelessness), a behaviour might also be associated with a more general superordinate category coding (e.g. unreliability). From this superordinate category, a further category may derive (e.g. insubordination). By this time the memory of the specific action may have become submerged in a more general judgement of the individual who was careless.

Let us consider a specific example. An employee fails to parcel up goods to be delivered properly. As a consequence his supervisor receives a complaint from the customer. The supervisor will code the employee's behaviour into memory. He will do so because the behaviour has had noticeable functional consequences. The coding itself will consist of abstract elements of meaning (Underwood, 1969; Herriot, 1974). These elements will depend entirely upon how the supervisor has construed the event. He may have construed it in terms of the individual's identity, the nature of the error made, and the extreme pressure of work at the time. Alternatively, he may have attributed the cause of the event to the subordinate's characteristic carelessness, relating it to previous actions which could be described as careless and to other instances of unreliability as well. In both these examples of the supervisor's construction of the event, elements of what we mean by the word 'careless' will have been coded. In the first example, these meanings will have justifiably been used of the action; in the second, they will have been used of the actor.

It is of extreme importance how the event has been encoded into memory, since it is only those codings which have been used in the encoding stage which can be employed to retrieve the memory. This is known as the principle of encoding specificity, and states (Tulving, 1972, p. 392): 'no cue . . . can be effective unless the to-be-remembered item is specifically encoded with respect to that cue at the time of storage'. Now a rater is faced with a memory task. He is being asked to retrieve from his memory a set of actions, which exemplify the characteristic he is being asked to rate. Only when he can recall actions which demonstrate care or lack of it can he rate a subordinate for care and attention to the job on the basis of behaviour. Otherwise his rating will derive from a judgement of personality only, a judgement which may be inferred from other supposed characteristics rather than from observed behaviour. Thus if a rating is to be of behaviour rather than of character, specific events will have to be recalled.

Tulving (1972) distinguished episodic from semantic memory. Episodic memory refers to the remembering of specific events, whereas semantic memory refers to the cognitive structure of general past experience. Thus, if I remember when I scored 50 runs at cricket, I am tapping episodic memory, whereas if I try to recall the details of the rules regarding leg-before-wicket dismissals, I am tapping semantic memory. It has been demonstrated repeatedly, that for specific events to be retrieved from memory, codings of the situation in which they occurred have to be used as memory cues. Thus, for example, lists of words learned by deep-sea divers when submerged are better recalled subsequently when they are underwater than when above the surface! The assumption is that they coded aspects of the situation when they learned the lists, and those codings were reinstated by their being submerged. Consequently, they were able to use these coded elements of the situation as cues to help them retrieve the word list.

The implication for rating scales is obvious. If rating scales simply ask the ratee to rate a personal characteristic or quality, then they are merely reinstating one element of the coding of the original event. The element reinstated is in fact the least appropriate for the recall of the event, since it is that part of the coding created by the attributional and implicit personality theories of the rater. If the event is to be recalled, then elements of the situation which obtained when it occurred must be reinstated. The implication for practice is that rating scales should be *situationally* anchored. The difficulty is that little is known about how people encode situations into memory, and therefore it is not clear what specific elements of the situation should be used for this purpose.

The basic point is that our knowledge of our language and culture enables us to categorize actions in terms of various verbal labels (e.g. careful). Since we share these labels and their meanings with others, we can refer to various types of actions and communicate successfully about them. As Hampson (1982) notes, these labels actually imply situational as well as personal elements of meaning. For example, a 'kind' action implies the existence of another person(s) beside the actor to whom it is possible to act in this way. The danger is that the use of these labels as characteristics of the person, encouraged by attributional processes and implicit personality theories, swamps the situational elements of meaning. Thus the potentially valuable information regarding actions which is available in principle from the observer and rater is not retrieved, although it could be. We simply fail to access it because we use the wrong retrieval cue.

That this is the case is indicated by the considerable success of references which are responses to specific situationally-based questions about the applicant. For example, Jones and Harrison (1982) asked head teachers to recall the achievements of pupils in various settings, and the resulting references predicted the training success of those pupils when they were commissioned as officers in the Royal Navy.

The contrast with those references which permit the referee to express his implicit personality theories in vivid free-ranging prose is spectacular (Muchinsky, 1979). Similarly, as Hulin (1982) has recently observed, it is perfectly reasonable to expect so-called halo effects in ratings if the above analysis is accurate. For halo effects need not imply the erroneous inference of presence and quality of one trait from another (Landy and Farr, 1980). Rather, they may reflect the fact that the names of the characteristics share certain elements of meaning, while being different in respect to others. Thus rated characteristics are not independent entities, but words which overlap to a greater or lesser extent in meaning. Ratings of the behaviour which related words describe will therefore be themselves correlated.

In summary, it would seem that rating scales may be of use once we take account of the psychological processes involved in their use. They in principle permit general categories of behaviour of an applicant to be recalled by an observer. The more occasions such a category of behavior has occurred, and the wider the variety of situations, the more confident one may be in predicting future behaviour of this category. On the other hand the behaviour being rated is, as we have seen, prone to very considerable over-interpretation at the encoding stage and, therefore, at recall. Furthermore, ratings are often based on a highly circumscribed sample of behaviour (e.g. behaviour in a selection interview, itself a situation involving specific rules of procedure and unlikely to be repeated in the job).

Overall, however, ratings are potentially important evidence if they are based on a range of behavioural evidence; if the raters are reminded of the behavioural and situational context; and if the standards of comparison according to which they are to operate is made clear. All of these conclusions have only become evident after we have considered the nature of our normal modes of remembering the actions of others and forming judgements about them. It is when we use our cognitive and social capacities in the ways for which they have become adapted that they are useful in the selection procedure. Different modes of assessment, sampling different sorts of evidence and using different psychological processes, are useful for different purposes. If we wish to predict the long-term and stable mode of adaptation of the individual as a biological organism, we will employ personality tests. If we wish to predict how he will respond to new role expectations and create roles for himself, we will obtain his own and other's views of him. If we wish to predict level of performance at particular tasks, we will test performance at those tasks. The crucial addition of self-perceptions as part of the selector's armoury is likely to have profound effects upon the selection process. Suffice it to state here the two most important. First, self-reports lead to inferences of developmental change in the individual, and hence to the need to mesh the organization's procedure with the individual's prospective development. Second, self-reports include the applicant's account of his own preferences and plans; the fact that he too is making a decision in the selection procedure becomes explicit.

3.3 ANY ASSESSMENT?

Thus far we have had grave doubts about accepting many of the initial set of assumptions listed in Chapter 1. The idea of objective assessment of unchanging characteristics, each capable of independent assessment, has come under severe scrutiny in the light of theory and findings in social psychology. The idea that all assessments are to some extent subjective, and are none the worse for that, has been enlarged upon in the present chapter—we have noted that assessments from different sources have different advantages and disadvantages attached, consequential upon the different psychological processes involved in making them. There is, however, a far more radical approach which we will take from here on. What if the very act of assessment itself is an inappropriate way of setting about the graduate selection process? There is, it will be argued, another more appropriate model than that of the organization assessing the applicant and rejecting or accepting him on that basis. The theoretical grounds for the rejection of the total idea of assessment are incorporated in a critique of the most basic assumptions noted in Chapter 1. These were as follows: (1) behaviour or actions are the effects of causes; (2) the primary causes are characteristics of persons; (3) characteristics of persons are psychological constructs, inherent in any description of the structure of personality and necessary to explain their behaviour. In Chapter 1 it was argued that aspects of situations and interactions between persons and situations, were also determinants of actions. Assessment procedures implicitly make the same assumptions regarding a linear causal model, in which personal characteristics and situations are assumed to determine job performance. Even psychometric psychologists, such as Eysenck and Cattell, permit situational as well as personal determinants of behaviour to be taken into account (Eysenck and Eysenck, 1980). But they do so by creating another intervening variable, that of psychological states. Traits, they assert, are long-term dispositions of the individual, whereas states are transient and the result of the interaction between personality and environment. However, the point is that all of these psychological models, whether interactionist or psychometric, assume that behaviour is a consequence of these other factors. The difficulties with this assumption can best be appreciated by a consideration of the critique of interactionism which arose from within that approach.

A crude interactionism suggests that the statistical procedure of analysis of variance is a good model for the effect of person and situations upon actions. Each of these two is taken as one of the factors in a two-factor design, and if each singly has an effect, then the outcome is two main effects in the statistical sense. The hypothesized finding, of course, is the interaction effect between the two main factors. The example on p. 10 of authoritarianism (person factor) and bureaucracy (situation factor) makes the statistical analogy clear. Indeed, in the early interactionist research in social psychology, experiments using analysis of variance designs were carried out, and a lot of results where statistical interactions were found were taken to support the theory (Bowers, 1973). However, it was soon realized (Olweus, 1977) that the analysis of variance was an inappropriate model. In analysis of variance, each main factor has to be independent of the other(s), otherwise any interaction obtained may be artifactual rather than the reflection of a real interactive effect between two separate factors. Hence the person factor and the situation factor should be independent, but in fact are not. In their magisterial review of interactionist theory, Magnusson and Endler (1977) point out that it is the individual's perception of the situation, not the situation *per se*, which more reliably predicts. Moreover, people select the situations in which they act, probably because they expect to be able to act in certain ways in them. Magnusson and Endler (1977) also point out a yet more basic difficulty with the analysis of variance model. It is that we cannot conceptualize behaviour as the dependent variable caused by persons, situations, or their interactions, since behaviour instantly changes the situation which is supposed to be causing it. The characterization of situation as the independent variable and behaviour as the dependent variable is therefore purely arbitrary (Mischel, 1977). Indeed, since situations are selected by actors because of the actions they expect to be able to perform in them; and since those actions change the nature of situations; then it may well be more appropriate to describe situations in terms of the actions which may be expected to occur in them.

It seems clear that instead of the linear model in which person and situation cause behaviour, a systems model is far more appropriate. Such a model implies a reciprocal relationship between constituent parts and has been proposed by (among others) Bandura (1978). The title of Bandura's influential paper was 'The self-system in reciprocal determinism'. This points to the centrality of the self in the system of interaction between the individual and his environment. As Bandura emphasises (1978, p. 348): 'In social learning theory, a self-system is not a psychic agent that controls behaviour. Rather, it refers to cognitive structures that provide reference mechanisms and to a set of subfunctions for the perception, evaluation, and regulation of behaviour.' In line with the remarks on self-assessment earlier in this chapter, Bandura allocates the function of self-observation to the self. In case this sounds like an advanced case of contemplation of the navel, it is necessary to stress that it is one's past and present behaviour that are the object of one's observations. We notice such features of it as its originality, and what its consequences are. Having observed our own behaviour, a judgemental process may follow. We compare it with our personal standards, the social norms operating, and then make personal or situational attributions. Having made such judgements as these, we respond by evaluating ourselves in a certain way, and by applying these processes to our consequential actions. Thus the process is one of observing one's own behaviour, evaluating it, and responding to these observations and evaluations. It is a process view of the self—the self is a system for monitoring and regulating one's intercourse with one's environment (physical and social). It is a sub-system of the superordinate system of individual-in-environment. Moreover, according to Bandura, the self is an articulated and an adaptable system. Criticizing psychologists such as Rogers, he insists 'A global view of what people think of themselves cannot possible account for the wide variations they typically show in their self-reactions under different situational circumstances, on different activities, and at different times' (Bandura, 1978, p. 348).

The implications for selection of this systemic approach to the relationship of the individual with his environment are profound. Of particular importance is the centrality of the self-concept to the model; for it implies that, in the relationship between individual and organization, it is the self-concept that is responsible for regulating the individual's response to the expectations of the organization. Thus it is the self-concept which is likely to predict the way this relationship develops in the future. Therefore, it is the applicant's self-concept which should be the prime 'object' of investigation in the selection procedure. Since the applicant himself has privileged access to his self-concept he is likely to be the most reliable source of information about it. Thus the conclusion is inescapable; it is that far more responsibility for selection should be invested in the applicant than is presently the case. Self-selection for an organisation, as well as selection by an organization, are necessary.

3.4 ROLE THEORY

At this point practitioners will give up in disgust, if they have come thus far! This is the point to promise that the case for the self-concept has a lot of evidence to support it, and that this will be reviewed later in the book. Our next task, however, is to characterize further the dynamic reciprocal model which describes the relationship between individual and environment. As far as this book is concerned, the environment is mainly the organization, which is a social rather than a physical environment. Therefore we are looking for a theoretical account of the relationship between the individual and his social environment. The other essential feature of such an account is that it permits the self-concept a central position. Such a theory has long been available in social psychology; it is the theory of roles (Biddle, 1979).

A social role consists of the categories of behaviour expected of a person in a particular position. This definition hints at some of the advantages offered by role theory. First, it stresses the overall context of social behaviour—the person's position is set in a sub-system of a system (e.g. in a department of an organization). Second, it implies an immediate inter-personal context, since expectations of behaviour have to be communicated by others, perceived by the actor, and acted upon (or not, as the case may be). Third, the definition indicates a dynamic process rather than the static matching of individual to job. This process is operating at two levels (at least). First, the overall system, the organization, is itself interacting with its environment. As a consequence it will change its expectations of occupants of positions; bank clerks may have to become computer operators. The second level of process is that of interpersonal communications; the individual occupant of a position will engage in a process of negotiation regarding the extent to which he is willing to respond to others' expectations. His behaviour will signal this extent, and their response will indicate whether they are willing to change their expectations.

The fourth advantage of role theory is that it is capable of incorporating the self-concept into its formulation; for it is the self-concept which is responsible for monitoring the individual's response to other's expectations. If these responses are incompatible with the individual's memories of his past behaviour, with his own internalized values and norms, or with his expectations for the future, then he may not respond in accordance with expectations. Not only so; the self-concept serves another function as well. It permits the expectations of others to be internalized as part of itself. Hence the role performance of the individual does not depend upon the communication of expectations by others; rather, it is self-regulated. Of course, such internalization itself has to be seen as a part of the process; for internalized expectations by definition become part of the self, which then starts evaluating new and different expectations. An example may help make this last point clear. A middle-aged manager may have internalized his organization's expectations of loyalty, so that he himself would not dream of leaving his job before retirement. However, the organization's expectations of him may change: it might wish him to leave long before retirement is due. Hence he will have to evaluate this new expectation in the light of his existing self-concept: that of a loyal and valued employee.

The final advantage of role theory, and perhaps the most basic of all, is that it forces us to take a much broader view than before of the relationship between individual and organization. We are not selecting individuals for the specific tasks detailed in a job description. Rather, we are choosing an individual, and he is choosing himself, for the way in which he will respond to a multiplicity of expectations at different levels. The organization will expect him to represent its image, and take over for himself its values and norms; his supervisor will expect him to work effectively and efficiently; his colleagues and subordinates may expect him to temper his enthusiasm so as not to show them up. Above all, the relationship between individual and organization is based upon how expectations and responses to them may change and develop in the future (Frese, 1982).

4

Organizations and Roles

4.1 ORGANIZATIONS AS OPEN SYSTEMS

Having considered the overall advantages of role theory as an explanatory device, we must now examine more closely its application to the organizational context; otherwise, the term role will become synonymous with job, and these advantages will be lost. The literature on organizations and their analysis offers a bewildering array of theoretical accounts. Instead of trying to review these, we shall select one particular approach to the study of organizations: the open system approach. This is probably the modal model, and is clearly and fully explained in the authoritative work of Katz and Kahn (1978). The following account depends heavily upon their work, just as previous chapters have relied upon Hampson (1982).

Open systems theory can be characterized by three features. First, it states that the parts of a system are interdependent, and hence that changes in one subsystem will have effects upon others. Open system theory tends to move in its search for explanations in the opposite direction to much of psychology. Instead of trying to reduce the level of analysis down to constituent elements, it looks for its explanations to higher levels of the system. As Katz and Kahn put it (p. 63): 'The first step should always be to go to the next higher level of system organisation, to study the dependence of the system in question upon the supersystem of which it is part, for the supersystem sets the limits of variance of behaviour of the dependent system.' The second distinguishing feature of open systems theory is its insistence that the organization as a system is open to its environment and has to adapt to it if it is to survive. Third, the system has inputs (of all sorts: information, people, raw materials), throughputs, and outputs. The outputs affect the environment, and these effects are part of what the organization has to adapt to; hence there is a feedback loop to assist adaptation.

The basic dynamic of the organization as an open system is the tension between the organization's need to adapt to its environment and the need to maintain its own structure. There is a clear similarity with Piaget's concepts of the organism's accommodation to its environment and its assimilation of the environment to its own structures. Piaget stressed that organisms continually strive to maintain equilibrium. Organizations, on the other hand, may have lengthy periods when their need to adapt overrides their concern to maintain; and vice-versa.

Maintaining the functioning system involves ensuring that various cycles of events occur and recur. These events are the activities of people; or of people and machines. They may have as their function the production of goods or services; the procurement of raw material or clients; the disposal of the product; the tying of people into their roles; the provision and maintenance of machines. These cycles of events have to be coordinated to ensure that they occur regularly and in sequence. First they have to be divided into sequences of tasks; tasks have to be specified and responsibility for their completion allocated to individuals. Hence individuals acquire a task role (though it is unlikely that this is the only role they will play within the organization). Coordination then requires the establishment of routines, the setting of priorities, and the scheduling and synchronizing of activities so that objectives may be attained. The close relationship of one task role with another ensures that the individual's role is expected of him not only by management, but also by other individuals who depend upon his successful performance.

There are other way of making sure the system is integrated. Not only are specific task requirements expected of the occupants of particular positions in the organization. There are also more general expectations which tie all the members of a system to their roles, and which ensure some level of uniformity of practice across the organization. In some service organizations, for example, it is expected of all employees that they will greet potential customers in a friendly manner. Such norms, or general expectations, may be justified, encouraged, and expressed as a value priority: 'The company places the highest value upon customer relations.' The value may also be incorporated into a self-conscious company image: 'The caring, sharing Co-op'. What is important to note here is that all these devices serve to tie individuals' behaviour into their functional roles. While the more abstract devices such as values and image are potentially highly ambiguous, they have a major advantage: they can become incorporated into the individual's self-concept, especially if they reinforce value priorities and aspects of the self-concept already existing. This possibility involves more of the person in the organization; there is relatively little of the person involved in the fulfilment of a highly specific and delimited task role.

It is important to distinguish norms from rules. Norms may include general expectations of employees by other employees which may be inimical to the organization's supposed objectives; the norm that it is all right to use the company's telephone to make extensive personal calls is an example. Rules, on the other hand, concern the implementation of decisions. They give authority to a particular position in the organization, and define the limits of that authority and the ways in which it may be exercised. Rules, too, may be internalized; the individual can use them to monitor and control his own performance (Harré and Secord, 1972). Rules are another mechanism of integration; they legitimize the authority of those who have to regulate the system's function.

The maintenance dynamic, then, sustains the organization. The system of interlocking roles assists the necessary cycles of events to occur reliably; and the various externally generated ways of integrating the organization are sometimes internalized into the person. A task role becomes expected of oneself rather than expected by others. Standards and norms of performance become internalized as evaluative features of self-esteem. Value priorities and company-image may be integrated into the most central structures of the person (Rokeach, 1973). Hence the organization's survival is tied closely to the individual's—a powerful bind. The individual needs the organization's existence to permit her to express what are now some of her own values. As Katz and Kahn (1978, p. 407) put it: 'The reward is not so much a matter of social recognition or monetary advantage as establishing one's self-identity, confirming one's notion of the sort of person one sees oneself to be, and expressing the values appropriate to this self-concept.'

But organizations cannot survive on the basis of the maintenance dynamic alone. They have to adapt to their environment, which is itself continuously changing. Technological change and social and political value systems march hand-in-hand, economic and legal structures follow suit, often after much delay. Organizations are structured so that certain of their subsystems carry a heavy responsibility for adaptation. Maintenance subsystems, on the other hand, 'face inward; they are concerned with the functioning of the organisation as it is rather than with what it might become. The risks of concentrating attention and energies inward are directly proportional to the magnitude and rate of change in the world outside the organisation' (Katz and Kahn, 1978, p. 54).

The subsystems are often characterized in terms of their position in organizational space. Central in that space is the original function which the organization was set up to perform; for example, manufacturing cars, teaching children, or devising computer programs for clients. The subsystems serving these central functions are concerned with technical efficiency; making good cars, using effective teaching methods, producing elegant programs. They may be so obsessed with technical proficiency that they are less effective than they might be; the computer programmer is so concerned with elegance that he gives little thought to communicating effectively with the client. Moreover, radical change in the basic process is difficult to achieve, partly because of the effort that has been invested in improving it in its present form. Other subsystems are also oriented towards maintenance, and the support of the central function. Administrative subsystems define roles formally by devising job descriptions on the basis of job analysis. They tie people to their roles in the central function by setting up detailed systems of rewards and sanctions. They select and train people so that they understand and perform their roles adequately. Procurement subsystems ensure raw materials or clients are available so that the production or service subsystem can keep functioning. They may even take over suppliers to guarantee supplies, with the consequence of growth and greater formalization of the organization. Sales and marketing subsystems ensure that output is satisfactorily injected into the environment, permitting the basic production process to continue smoothly.

On the other hand, both procurement and sales and marketing subsystems are further away from the central function. They are boundary subsystems, because they have direct exchanges with the organization's environment. Thus they have a potential for adaptation, since they can feed into the organization important information. However, there seems to be a tendency for these subsystems to strive to maintain ideal conditions for the central subsystem rather than to be agents for change. Procurement subsystems will try to change laws when conservationist rulings prevent the continued acquisition of natural resources. Sales and marketing will spend far more in trying to persuade people into buying what they do not need than in discovering what they want.

Some subsystems, on the other hand, are expressly concerned with adaptation. Research and development, for example, is evidently involved in creating the technological changes which will influence the organization's products or services; or at the least, it seeks to discover those changes in products or services which technological change created elsewhere will make necessary. Such development will require structural changes in the central subsystem; new cycles of events imply new task roles, and possibly new norms, values, and image. Top management, too, has a potentially adaptive function, when it is not busy sorting out quarrels between subsystems or between organizations within the organization (a maintenance function). Top management has to plan policy in the light of intelligence about the environment—information gained from the organization's research and development, market research, and financial analysts, and from its own contacts with outside organizations and institutions. Decisions about policy changes, and how to effect the structural change which they imply, rest usually upon top management. One of the major policy benefits of worker participation in policy decisions is that the structural changes consequent upon a policy adaptation are part and parcel of those decisions; hence those whose roles will be redefined are partly responsible for the redefinition.

It should be noted, however, that even those subsystems with an overtly adaptive function may not actually fulfil it. For example, there are many scientists in research and development departments whose loyalty is not towards the organization but towards a group of scientific peers world-wide. To use Gouldner's (1957) terminology, they are cosmopolitans, not locals.

Hence their scientific or technological achievements are not necessarily intended to enable their organization to anticipate change and act on it; rather, they are aimed at achieving a reputation amongst the scientific community. Thus, while certain subsystems may be more motivated towards the adaptation rather than the maintenance dynamic by their very function, there is no guarantee that they will be effective in enabling the organization actually to adapt. It is hardly surprising that many organizations hire teams of experts to work on a single specified project (Toffler, 1970). They assume that such experts are concerned with solving the task and working with each other, having little loyalty to the organization: technological soldiers of fortune.

The relative balance of adaptation and maintenance in an organization will determine the nature of the roles allocated to its members. This is likely to happen in two ways. First the adaptive organization will place more emphasis upon, and devote more resources to, those subsystems which perform primarily adaptive functions; similarly with maintenance-oriented organizations: second, the overall degree of structure, control, and formalization will be determined by the relative influence of adaptation and maintenance dynamics, and this will be expressed in the definition of roles.

The empirical research on organizational structure offers some support to these generalizations, although the use of a variety of descriptors of organizations does not help. Organizations have been characterized in the research literature in terms of their size, climate, technology, and environment. Obviously, some of these features bear no very direct relation to the maintenance–adaptation balance. We might argue, for example, that large size reflects a maintenance dynamic, since it implies that the organization has taken over some of its sources of supply, and perhaps its competitors. On the other hand, size may equally well be the consequence of an adaptive response which has diversified products or services in the light of information about future market trends or social needs. The most useful characteristics of organizations to study are those which most clearly relate to the balance between adaptive and maintenance dynamics. There are several studies which examine the technology of organizations and of their environment, and these reveal clear relationships between type of technological environment and the nature of the roles allocated to members. Clearly the relationship is a complex one; external technological development will have resulted in the adoption by the organization of an internal technological system, and it is this system which plays a large part in the determination of the nature of roles. If the external technology is changing rapidly, however, then internal systems will probably be more capable of adaptation to this change. The prediction would therefore be that the more subject to change an area of technology is, the more flexible both the internal technical systems and the roles associated with them will be.

The latter part of this prediction is supported by the pioneering work of Woodward (1965). She clearly demonstrated that the type of technology employed within an organization affected the nature of the role structure. She categorized technology into three types: small batch and unit production, mass production or large batches, and process production (e.g. chemicals). These types (unit, mass, process) differed in the number of levels of authority, the ratio of managers to total personnel, the number of explicit rules, and the delegation of authority.

The mass production organizations delegated authority less, and had more rules than the other two types. Mass production is usually characterized by heavy investment in plant which renders major changes in the product difficult; apparently new models of cars are often new combinations of old components. Hence we would expect mass production to be a preferred technology of organizations which did not need to adapt. The car industry relied on its capacity to control popular taste until political events and environmental legislation forced adaptation. Similarly, many educational organizations still employ the equivalent of mass production technology even when they face overwhelming evidence that individuals differ in their modes of learning. Educational organizations have largely controlled their environment, however, by keeping control for themselves of the examination system, supposedly the means of assessing whether learning has occurred.

More direct evidence comes from studies which have related the degree of change in their environments to the role structure of organizations. Burns and Stalker (1961) and Lawrence and Lorsch (1967) all found that the more change in the environment (technological and market) the less formal was the structure. Specifically, there was more communication between individuals at the same level of responsibility, more delegation of authority to take decisions, and less clearly defined roles, with more informal relationships. Interestingly, these relationships were contingent upon effectiveness—it was the effective organizations which had structures appropriate to their environments. It must be stressed that effective performance resulted from having a type of role structure appropriate to the environments. Lawrence and Lorsch, for example, found that organizations manufacturing containers where the environment was steady, were more effective with a formal structure. In the light of more recent developments, however it is worth asking whether any organization can be said to have a relatively stable environment. Recent changes in information technology are part of the environment of every organization. So are global political and economic developments which affect supplies of raw materials, transport, and finance. So too are huge social changes regarding work values and the rights of minorities.

A further finding of Lawrence and Lorsch which is important for the present discussion is that different departments within organizations differed in terms of the formality of their role structure: those departments more concerned with adapting to the environment had less formal structures. What is more, these differences in formality of structure are perceived by employees. Norwegian employees saw their organization as living, responsive, flexible, and dynamic when the production technology was small batch; and static, inflexible, and fixed when it was mass production. Mass production employees are more likely than process workers to feel isolated at work. They think poorly of their foreman and see him as having no influence over higher management. They are more likely to have a competitive orientation in industrial relations, and to devalue the company and their own prospects within it (Fullan, 1970).

Organizations and departments, then, differ in terms of their role structure. Degree of specialization of role; the extent to which the tasks expected of the individual were specified; the number and restrictiveness of rules; the degree of hierarchy of authority; the amount of information available; and the levels of those with whom the individual might communicate all differed. In more formal systems and subsystems, there is a strong tendency to divorce planning and coordinating from performance roles.

The dangers of drawing conclusions regarding the psychological *consequences* of these differences in roles are considerable. On the one hand, much of the literature reviewed above also points to decreased job satisfaction when organizations are large and formal. On the other, there is a considerable body of research demonstrating the stressful effects of uncertainty regarding what one's role really is. It is not our purpose here to review these consequences, however, but rather to explore further how these differences in roles relate to the individual's self-concept. It is also important to examine how the process of communicating roles to the individual by others in the organization is affected. It is important to continue the analysis in social psychological terms, for it is at this point in the argument that trait terminology becomes extremely attractive to the would-be selector. For example, authoritarianism has already been quoted (p. 10) as an example of a trait which might interact with formality of role-structure; more authoritarian persons perform better in more formal systems. It is worth stressing once again that the term 'formality' includes under its umbrella a wide range of dimensions (number of rules, role specificity, etc.), each of which in its turn encompasses a large number of behavioural situations. As was argued earlier, such trans-situational consistency of behaviour is rarely found; it depends not so much upon traits as upon self-perception of consistency.

Rather, we must consider the social *process* of communication of roles, norms, and values by others to the individual; the individual's understanding of this communication; her continued negotiation regarding which roles, norms, and values she accepts as consistent with her self-concept; and her incorporation of those she accepts into it. It is *this* process, ably described by Graen (1976), which we must analyse in the light of the likely differences in the type of role expected by different departments and different organizations.

4.2 ROLE SENDING

First let us consider how roles are likely to be communicated to the individual member of an organization. In some organizations different individuals will inform the newcomer of her duties and obligations because of their office in the organization. A member of the personnel department might inform her of the nature of her formal contract and job description, and also of her rights and obligations. Her immediate superior or supervisor will also communicate expectations to her, and so will the others in her work group. In a formal organization there are likely to be incompatible differences between these messages, and the newcomer will be faced with recognizing the gap between the organization's espoused policy and its practices. This dilemma may be resolved by throwing in her lot with the working group and thereby ruling out for some time the possibility of any strong identification with the organization as a whole; or it may result in role conflict, with the individual suffering stress as a consequence of receiving incompatible role expectations. Less formal organizations may not present such overt differences, but the possibility of role conflict is still present. This is because expectations will be communicated by each of those who are dependent upon the newcomer's successful fulfilment of those expectations; and each may believe that his own function is more vital than that of the others. Also, in an informal organization, communication will more likely be on a personal footing rather than a role footing; someone tells the newcomer what is expected of her because she wishes to help her as an individual, not because it is her duty to do so.

What will be communicated to the newcomer? In formal organizations she will be told what her job is by means of a relatively complete job description which is specific as to what actions are included in the job. Sometimes such descriptions also include explicit statements about what is *not* expected, but more usually non-role behaviour is implied rather than spelt out. The consequence of this may be that newcomers are hesitant to exercise initiative, even where such action is of obvious benefit to the organization. What is probably intended as a minimum set of expectations becomes a maximum. Other properties of detailed job descriptions are also of importance. First, they are apt to contain certain prescriptions regarding methods and procedures, as well as tasks and objectives. Such prescriptions will reflect the accepted beliefs about how things should be done, and hence inhibit the development of new methods; perhaps it is the newcomer who is most likely to perceive the need for methodological change. Second, detailed job descriptions, by their very lack of ambiguity, make discrepancies between the communications sent from different sources more obvious. As a consequence it is more difficult for the newcomer to fudge over these discrepancies and make comfortable adjustments. Finally, the formal organization is more likely to be cautious in the degree of responsibility for decisions which it gives to a newcomer. Hence the newcomer has little personal credit to gain from successful outcomes, nor does she have the chance of gaining the respect and confidence of those who are dependent upon this success. Large responsibility implies independence from close monitoring supervision, but it also implies interdependence with many others who depend upon the responsible task being accomplished. There is considerable evidence that early responsibility leads to better performance, promotion, and less turnover (Berlew and Hall, 1966; Buchanan, 1974; Kaufman, 1974).

There are other messages being sent, apart from expectations about the job done. Some of these involve the mapping out of the organization's space for the newcomer's information and benefit; and often the sender's benefit as well. In formal organizations, departmental boundaries will be pointed out, and demarcation between the functions and responsibilities of departments clearly defined. Vertical as well as horizontal boundaries will be made clear—levels of authority and their respective responsibilities and status, and the signals which indicate membership of different levels. Of particular importance to the newcomer are the functions formally allocated to her immediate supervisor. Again, the more detailed and specific is the description of these functions, the harder it is for the supervisor to perform other functions. These may include mediating between the expectations of others in the organization and the newcomer and, in the longer term, acting as a mentor in the early stages of her career (Levinson *et al.*, 1978). Moreover, tight definitions of authority and responsibility may inhibit the newcomer from going for help to those who are most able to aid the solution of the problem; such individuals may not be those formally invested with supervisory responsibility. Finally the newcomers are likely to be carefully informed about where the organization ends and the outside world begins—where the boundary of the organization itself lies. Such information is likely to be especially stressed in the case of those in boundary roles—sales staff, research personnel, and the providers of service to the client. The more formal and maintenance-oriented the organization, the greater is the stress laid on the recognition of this boundary line and the importance of remaining loyal within it. The interests of the organization and those of the client are thus apt to be distinguished, and those of the organization made paramount; such a distinction may, in the longer term, be inimical to the organization's real interest. So may the constant monitoring of boundary employees, which results in their going by the book so as not to break the rules (Adams, 1976).

This leads on to the next set of messages which are sent to the newcomer—those concerned with integrating her into the organization. To use Piaget's terminology, these messages are intended to assimilate the newcomer into the organization, not to accommodate it to her. She will be informed of the rules of the organization, in particular those relating to procedures, authority, rewards, and sanctions. The norms of the organization may also be communicated overtly: 'we believe that the rules of this organisation should be applied without fear or favour, and that justice should be seen to be done'. Such explicit statements anticipate the newcomer's judgements of what the truth is in these matters, and render any shortfall doubly dangerous. The same is true of overt communication of the organization's supposed value priorities—the statement of guiding principles for the future and rationalization of the past and the present. Finally, corporate image may be stressed early in the newcomer's career with the organization. Again, the danger is that the image often fails to correspond to the image it actually possesses in the outside world. The discovery of such discrepancies early in her organizational career is apt to render the individual alienated from the organization rather than integrated within it.

Overt communication of this sort as an initiation is more likely to occur with formal than informal organizations. Covert communication of norms and values, on the other hand, is likely to occur in all sorts of organizations. The setting of rates of production in working groups is a well-documented norm relating to task activity. The important question to ask in this connection relates to the relative importance placed by the individual upon the different norms and values that are communicated to her. Is her primary reference group her work group, her professional peers, her union, her department, or the organization? Of course, if the norms and values of these different groups do not diverge excessively, then the division of her loyalties does not matter much. The danger of overt communication is of subsequent disillusion, and arousing instant suspicion as to the motive of the organization in communicating in this way. Why are they so keen to present the official version first—to convince and persuade before reality obtrudes?

It is also important to note how the various expectations are communicated to the newcomer. Formally, various situations are set up to enable tasks, rules, norms, values, and image to be made clear. The first such may be a job preview; real time in the organization, or by means of films, literature, and talks by representatives. The second may be the selection interview. If selected, the individual may undergo an initiation ritual stressing her new loyalties, and an orientation programme. A graduate may undertake subsequently a general management training, which will involve moving round considerably within the organization. Informally, all sorts of situations will permit communication between members of the organization and the newcomer. The main difference between formal and informal situations is that informal ones permit of greater trial and error. Members can try out different ways of communicating expectations to see if the newcomer understands and acts upon them. The newcomer can similarly try out the limits of the role to discover what is acceptable and unacceptable, and what might become acceptable. Formal communications may not permit this sort of trial and error, and tend to be one-way rather than two-way processes. For example in the orientation programmes, newcomers are told what the organization thinks they need to know; they are not always asked at the beginning what it is they want to know. In training programmes the individual is not always consulted regarding what she considers to be her training needs.

What is most important in terms of the communication of role expectations, however, is that both formal and informal situations are what Argyle *et al.* (1981) term '*episodes*'. That is, they are sequences of events in time which each have their own rules as to what is and what is not permitted behaviour within them. These rules are not often made explicit—the applicant is not told she should wait to be invited by the interviewer to smoke, nor is the trainee warned in advance not to challenge the expertise of the trainer. The newcomer, therefore, needs to know these rules and act on them. The same is true of informal situations—newcomers are expected to accept teasing and even ridicule without fighting aggressively back because these are recognized ways of communicating expectations and norms. To perform effectively in such episodes the newcomer needs to know the repertoire of behaviours that are the elements of the episode in question. She also needs to have the social skills to choose the appropriate behaviour from the repertoire and perform it. In a word, she needs to know what to do, when to do it, and how to do it. The interviewee, for example, knows that she has to provide accounts of her past record and demonstrate interest in the type of work and organization for which she is applying. She also knows that she should wait until asked before she volunteers such accounts. The newcomer being teased by her colleagues knows that she has to accept it in good part, and to have various ways of showing that (a) she does not take it personally, (b) she knows what the message is, and (c) she will act on it or indicate why she will not.

Thus the newcomer to the organization has to possess or acquire the skills to act upon the expectations of others; but before she can do so she has to discover what those expectations are, and this discovery *in itself* requires her to know various social rules and act upon them. In order to become and remain part of an organization, an individual has to demonstrate much, much more than technical task competence or potential.

4.3 ROLE NEGOTIATION

However, we have concentrated hitherto only upon the communication by others of their expectations to the individual. This is part of the process, which has several stages. Assuming that the newcomer has attended to and understood the messages she has received from several sources, she has yet to decide whether to act upon them (Crites, 1976a). It is here that the social psychological distinction between compliance, identification, and internalization (Aronson, 1981) comes in very useful. Compliance refers to behaviour attributable to the expectation of reward or the threat of punishment. An individual may possess different values and norms from the organization, but still accept its expectations regarding the task. She will do so because of the rewards which permit her to express her values in activities outside work. Such an orientation has been termed 'instrumentalist' by various English sociologists (Goldthorpe *et al.*, 1970; Cotgrove, 1972). While earlier theorists suggested that it was monetary rewards which operated to produce compliance, there is considerable evidence that it is the perceived equity of rewards in general, relative to comparison groups, which can motivate compliant behaviour (Stephenson, 1978). Whatever the nature of the reward, the point to be made is that the work behaviour is compliant, a response to the expectation of reward. Discrepancy between the values and norms of the organization and the individual is therefore irrelevant—the individual is devoting merely a small part of her person to her work. Hence formal organizations need only make clear to newcomers the precise nature of their jobs and the rules, especially those regarding reward systems. Such compliance may be bought at cost of repeated disputes regarding rewards and working conditions.

Both the other forms of social influence, identification and internalization, have implications for the individual's response to the communication of expectations by the organization. Identification implies the assumption by the individual of another person's or an organization's norms and values because the individual admires and wishes to be like the other. The corollary is that as soon as this admiration ceases the norms and values are discarded. Both compliance and identification are therefore contingent forms of social influence—desired behaviour is conditional either upon expectation of reward or upon admiration of a referent individual or group. Hence an organization which initially presented a particular image to the newcomer, but which subsequently failed to live up to its espoused values, would risk losing the benefit of the norms and values which she had accepted. A chief executive or departmental head who embodies for the new recruit the organization's identity, but then moves on, is in danger of achieving the same effect.

Before such identification can occur, however, or before more permanent internalization of norms and values can take place, we must assume some sort of *comparison process*. The newcomer must compare the expectations which she realizes the organization has of her with, first, her own anticipation of what those expectations would be; and second, her view of herself. The latter comparison may actually occur more often first in time. That is, the individual considers the image of an organization as expressed in the media, in its publicity material, in its repute among her friends, and compares it with her view of herself. Tom (1971) had students rate organizations in terms of their attractiveness. For the more attractive organizations there was a higher degree of relationship between organizational image and student's self-concept than for the less attractive ones. However, there is some evidence that only students of high self-esteem choose organizations similar to their self-concept (Behling and Tolliver, 1972; but see Mansfield, 1973).

Such a comparison may well be in terms of possible futures as well as in terms of the present; not only whether presently held norms and values are compatible, but whether an individual can see her future development in the context of the organization as it too may change. If this comparison results in a judgement that there need be no incompatibility in principle, the individual may consider applying to the organization. For example, an electronic engineering student may apply to an organization aware that she will be engaged in research on defence contracts, or an arts graduate to a local authority knowing that social workers are treated as convenient scapegoats for the tragedies resulting from inadequate resourcing of services.

Hence at selection interview and subsequently, the newcomer will already have various anticipations about the organization and what it will expect her to do. The communications which she subsequently receives may contradict those anticipations. Now, since the anticipations were congruent with the self-concept, these communications may be inconsistent with the self-concept too. Such inconsistency may be hard to cope with, since it may be considered a betrayal, a denial of those earlier messages which induced the individual to apply and commit herself to the selection process. One way of adapting to the inevitable mismatch is to negotiate, to modify one's own expectations of the organization in return for some change in the organization's expectations for oneself (Dansereau *et al.*, 1975; Crites, 1976a).

Before we consider this negotiation process, however, it is worth exploring the different expectations, norms, and values which may be communicated by different organizations. Some will persuade the newcomer that her effort will be rewarded; effort will result in visible achievement, for which the newcomer will receive recognition and rewards which meet her needs or wants. Maintenance-oriented organizations will stress the norms of keeping rules and following procedures, of observing boundaries, and referring decisions to the correct person. They will stress the importance of certain values; for example, those of loyalty and equity. Loyalty will involve staying with the organization, not questioning its ends, and, often, not questioning its methods of achieving those ends. Equity refers to the fairness with which rules are administered, and to the demands which the organization may fairly make of an employee in return for the rewards it gives her. The inroads of an employee's work into her home, leisure, and social life may be related to her position in the organization. Adaptation-oriented organizations, on the other hand, may well value other types of achievement—creativity or the cultivation of contacts in other organizations.

To return to the negotiation process, the newcomer may respond to the messages sent by others in different ways. In some organizations there may be very little scope for negotiation at all; the job description and other features of work have been laid down by following agreed procedures in considerable detail. There is little possibility of changing a role to suit an individual. Other employees may be unwilling to adapt their roles to fit in with the changes the newcomer desires in hers. Further, the power is normally so firmly in the hands of the organization that the individual is chary of appearing to challenge it in any way. Hence, rather than state overtly that she is unwilling to fulfil one or two specific expectations, she merely omits to carry them out. Such a response may be misinterpreted—the senders may believe that the newcomer cannot do these things, whereas in fact she will not do them. Such attributional error may result in attempts to train the individual to accomplish those expected actions which she does not wish to learn to do. The individual may signal her unwillingness in terms of jokingly saying that to do such a thing would be 'not me', making explicit the incompatibility of the expectation in question with her self-concept. However, such attempts at defining and negotiating roles are typically rebuffed with the encouragement that the newcomer will be surprised to discover what she is capable of doing. Violation of personal norms or values is thus presented as a possible chance for self-development. On the other hand, behaviour by the newcomer which breaks the rules is quoted as feedback for her by maintenance-oriented organizations: adaptive ones may well concentrate on telling her how successful she is becoming in benefiting the organization.

The persuasive influence of the organization and its members upon the individual can thus result in the internalization of the organizational norms and values. The values currently held by the individual may actually change to accord more with what she currently finds herself, for whatever reason, saying and doing. This classic process of the reduction of cognitive dissonance (Aronson, 1981) would explain why, the longer the service with an organization, the greater the individual's commitment to its basic values (Hall *et al.*, 1970). On the other hand, those with a set of values derived from their occupational or professional membership rather than their organizational membership may stay only a short while with organizations. Thus, for example, research scientists, typically boundary people, have multi-organizational careers (Hall and Schneider, 1972; Gouldner, 1957). To the extent that adaptive organizations foster and promote boundary roles and relationships, they would be expected to place less emphasis upon such integrating factors as organizational values. Research scientists and technologists, engineers and systems analysts, even trainers and selectors, may place a much higher value on solving interesting problems than on maintaining the organization which employs them. They need no justification of an ideological nature for spending their working lives in this way, or if they do it may well be couched in more general terms such as the increase of knowledge and benefits to mankind resulting from their professional skills. It is those who have devoted, or who intend to devote, a large part of their lives to an organization or an institution who need to have incorporated its values into themselves. Then there is no inconsistency between their work role and their self-concept; they have a satisfying explanation for their past loyalty and the opportunity to express themselves in their work in the future.

Of course, such an equilibrium may not always occur. If an organization has continued to use the individual's need to achieve in order to motivate her, the discrepancy between the expectations for herself which she has been permitted to retain and the discovery that she will never get a seat on the board may be shattering. Moreover, even if an organization succeeds in persuading individuals of the value of loyalty, such loyalty may not be expressed in behaviour that is in the organization's interests. It may be better for an individual to leave or retire than to remain loyally with the organization; it might be better if she were not so convinced of the sanctity of existing procedures and policies that she fights to retain them when they are inappropriate.

It must be stressed again—it is the process of communicating role expectations and receiving them, acting upon them and observing others' reactions to these responses, adapting both one's actions and one's values to others' expectations but seeking to modify those expectations as well, that defines an individual's part in an organization. This process is a continuous one, repeated in episode after episode, more frequently perhaps near the beginning of an individual's reception into the organization, but continuing throughout her organizational career. It is as part of this process that individuals are selected.

We would, however, be guilty of a naive view of the distribution of power in an organization if we assumed that the new recruit on her own stood much chance of achieving her objectives in these negotiations. As Frese (1982) observes, there are several prerequisites for any attempt to improve work situations. These prerequisites include perceived collective control and solidarity of other colleagues; the knowledge of such matters as legal obligations on the part of the employer; and the realization that the work situation can only be changed in collective ways, since roles are interdependent. In a word, the relationship is not one solely between the individual and her employee with the negotiation being concerned with her career development. It is also between the individual and her colleagues; and their collective relations with the organization.

5

Graduate Selection: Application

5.1 SELECTION AND SOCIAL NEGOTIATION

The selection procedure is itself a part of the organizational system. We have characterized the social influence that the system exercises upon its individual members as a continuous process of role communication and negotiation. Hence the selection process must be construed as a series of episodes within this social process. Like all other social episodes, selection episodes have rules which the parties know and follow; they have repertoires of skilled actions which they must perform. Moreover, like other parts of the social influence process, the selection process involves the mutual sending and receiving of messages. The objective of each party is to discover whether it is worth continuing with further episodes of social exchange, thereby further committing themselves to each other. The key feature of selection episodes, therefore, is that they constitute the most convenient and recognized point at which to break off the social exchange process. Neither party has so far committed itself to the other, although the applicant probably stands to lose more in personal terms since she may lose self-esteem if rejected. She has, after all, presented herself for assessment.

The key *elements* in the episodes of the selection procedure are therefore the same as those in any other episode of social exchange. They are, first, the rules and repertoire of the episode itself; second, the organization's expectations, its norms, values, and image, and the applicant's understanding of these; and third, the applicant's self-concept in terms of her past, present, and future, and her own expectations regarding the organization.

The key *events* in the selection procedure are also apparent, given the analysis in terms of social exchange. They are, in order: (1) the initial communication of organizational expectations, norms, values, and image by means of publicity material or advertisements; (2) the understanding of these by the potential applicant, and the comparison process whereby she matches them with her self-concept; (3) the decision whether or not to apply, and the communication (in the form of her application) of her own self-concept and her willingness to enter negotiations; (4) the organization's comparison of this self-presentation with its own expectations, and its decision whether or not to continue the selection process. Events 1–4 above may be considered one episode in the selection procedure. The next event is (5) the interview, in which both parties have the opportunity to reveal more of themselves and to discover more of the other. The chance to negotiate is also present for the first time; each party may possibly be willing to adapt expectations in the light of similar concessions by the other. Comparison and negotiation will result in a decision whether to cease the social exchange or whether to continue it. This event clearly represents an episode in itself. (6) The final process is the final selection episode. Here the organization's expectations may well be communicated much more explicitly, for example in assessment centre exercises which sample the job. Moreover, the applicant will meet more representatives of the organization, in an organizational setting. Similarly, the applicant will be given varied opportunities for self-presentation: exercises, interviews, and tests. Again, decisions will be made based on the same comparison as before, but with greater understanding of the other's expectations. While the organization has not yet made any real commitment to the individual, the individual's own commitment of herself by this stage has been considerable. Hence rejection by the organization may well damage her self-esteem; and rejection on her part of an offer from the organization will be difficult: she has invested so much already that she has to convince herself that it has been worthwhile. Hence she may reduce the gap between organization and self by changing her perception of the organization. ('They don't only make cigarettes, and they're trying hard to make safer ones.') Acceptance of a job offer at the end of an arduous selection procedure may, therefore, not be too good a predictor of long-term commitment.

Throughout this sequence of three episodes, then, there are decision points consequent upon a comparison between self and organization. At each comparison point there is the possibility for either party to opt out of the exchange process; or to continue with it. The decision to continue may be based on an actual negotiation, which has decreased the gap between the two parties, with one, the other, or both changing expectations; or it may be based on the judgement that future negotiations are likely to be successful, and that the other party is flexible enough to change.

What, then, are the factors which lead to successful outcomes of these episodes? Before answering this, we must briefly address the thorny question of what constitutes a successful outcome. However far we venture into social exchange theory, the 'criterion problem' still raises its hoary head! In social exchange terms the criterion of success is that social exchanges and mutual adaptation continue to both parties' satisfaction; or that if they cease it is because it is in both parties' perceived interests that they should. Just as the organization adapts to and adapts its environment, so does the individual adapt to and adapt the organization. The process cannot be conceived of as a one-way influence of the organization upon the individual, for the following reason. The organization, in adapting to its environment, will as a consequence change its expectations of its members, since it will require them to perform new tasks, accept new norms and value priorities, and even help to project a new image. On the other hand, the individual members will be changing too, and not only in response to the organization's expectations. They will be responding in other social exchanges with their families and friends and with other organizations or institutions of which they are members. Thus successful social exchange between organization and individual will always be a two-way process; the organization will need to modify its expectation of the individual in the light not only of its need to adapt to the environment, but also of the individual's personal development.

The *selection* episodes in this social exchange process are more likely to prove successful if the following conditions are met:

(1) The parties should be aware of the rules governing each of the episodes of the selection procedure, and follow them. Similarly, they should possess the repertoire of behaviours necessary to carry the episode through. Only if these conditions are met will adequate communication be possible. Social knowledge and social skills are therefore necessary conditions for a successful selection procedure (Argyle *et al.*, 1981).

(2) The organization should present an accurate picture of its expectations, norms, values, and image in its publicity material. It is this information which provides the basis for the first comparison between organization and self which results in the decision whether or not to apply. Hence the applicant has already made a personal commitment on the basis of this information. If subsequent messages are inconsistent, applicants will need to change already-formed beliefs: they will also have developed mistrust of the organization, a major impediment to social exchange.

(3) The interviewer should present an accurate picture also; she should remember that the applicant will take not only what she says, but how she behaves, as evidence of the nature of the organization. There is a delicate balance to be struck between what the recruiter thinks the applicant needs to know and what the applicant wants to know.

(4) The applicant should present an accurate account of her self-concept; how she construes her past experience and achievement, her present attitudes and values, and her future intentions and ambitions.

(5) The apparent discrepancies between self-concept and organizational expectations should be declared and discussed. The discrepancies may appear different to the two parties. Alternatively, the possibility of negotiation, present or future, may become apparent. Parties may indicate the size of the discrepancy which would persuade them to withdraw from any further social exchange.

(6) Comparisons should also be made between estimated future self-concept

and estimated future organizational expectations; for the purpose of the selection procedure is to predict whether fruitful social exchange will be possible then, or whether the discrepancy will be so great that parties will withdraw.

It is only by discussing discrepancies that decisions can be reached which both parties accept. Social exchange and negotiations are episodes which are brought to a conclusion by mutual agreement. Agreement to continue further, the making and acceptance of a job offer, involves a mutual commitment which will cement future exchange.

This conception of selection as a social exchange process does not require the development and use of many new tools for selection. Rather, it involves the use of presently available tools in different ways. In the next three chapters the selection procedures employed in graduate recruitment are reviewed. It will become evident that employers tend to operate more on the basis of psychometric assumptions described in Chapter 1 than on the lines of the social exchange model outlined above.

5.2 THE APPLICATION FORM

5.2.1 Procedure

A graduate normally will have to write to an organization to obtain an application form (known in the USA as a resumé). However, in the UK there is also the possibility of employing a standard introduction form for application to several organizations. Where organizations send their own forms this is usually because they wish to obtain certain additional information which is not required on the standard introduction form. In the UK there are no very remarkable differences between forms; the major variation is in the amount of opportunity given to the applicant to write discursively about such topics as what he feels about his degree course, how he sees his career developing, what are his assets and liabilities as an employment prospect, and so on. Common to all forms are requests for various items of biographical data, such as academic record, schools attended, home address, date of birth, job experience, etc.

The initial function and stated purpose of the application form is as a pre-selection device. This is the first stage of what is normally a three-hurdle course: pre-selection, milk-round interview, and final selection procedure. At pre-selection the overall number of applicants is reduced, often by more than 50%. There is huge variation, however, for some organizations will have a much higher selection ratio than others; further, some applicants (e.g. those with computer science or electronic engineering degrees) may be more in demand than others (e.g. those taking courses in sociology or modern languages). Such an initial sift is performed on the basis of the application forms alone, and it is the main purpose of section 5.2 to discuss the basis for this pre-selection and how it is actually carried out.

However, it must be emphasized that the application forms have considerable influence upon decisions at all three hurdles of the overall selection procedure. The applicant who has passed successfully through the pre-selection sift will then have his form scanned by the milk-round interviewer before the initial interview. This will probably be a different individual from the one who has made the favourable pre-selection decision. The pre-interview scan is likely to predict the outcome of the interview itself. Herriot and Rothwell (1983) found that judgements of suitability of applicants by interviewers made after scanning the application forms, but before interview, correlated $r = 0.40$ with post-interview judgements. There are many reasons why this might be the case; the interview may have been used to confirm judgements about the applicant made on the basis of the application form; or the questions posed by the interviewer may have been based on information on the form, in order to find a topic to discuss.

Suppose that the applicant successfully passes through the initial interview, and moves on the third stage of the selection procedure. This sometimes takes place at one of the organization's sites, and is very likely to involve the employee destined to the applicant's supervisor if he obtains the job with the organization. The application form, together with the interviewer's report, is likely to have been sent on to the site. It will also be employed if the organization conducts an assessment centre for selection. Hence, at least three individuals (and perhaps others) will base a judgement at least partly upon the application form. It is usually the only information at the pre-selection stage, and it is the first information considered at the other two stages. Given people's propensity for basing judgements upon first impressions, it is hard to over-emphasize the probable influence of the application form.

5.2.2 Validity of biodata

The application form is in principle a source of the most valid predictors of job success yet discovered: biodata. Biodata will be defined here, with Asher (1972), as historical and verifiable pieces of information about an individual. This definition rules out measures of attitude and also memories of such vague items as emotional climate of the home, which feature in some of the research literature on the topic. Biodata are extremely reliable, in the sense that responses to 200 items were almost identical 2 months after first administration of the questionnaire (Owens *et al.*, 1966). Whether biodata are reliable in the sense of being accurate, however, is not so certain. Goldstein (1971) and Weiss and Dawis (1960) all found that groups who had good reason to falsify certain data (e.g. amount of previous salary) frequently did so.

The criterion validity of biodata as predictors of various measures of job performance, and also of employee turnover, is extremely impressive. Most of the research uses concurrent validity measures; that is, biodata and job performance are measured and correlated simultaneously. Few studies have employed predictive validity, in which subsequent performance of those previously selected is studied. Nevertheless, as Owens (1976), Reilly and Chao (1982) and Asher (1972) remark, validity is well above that for other methods of selecting employees. Asher, for example, summarizing studies between 1960 and 1970 which used measures of job performance as the criterion, and which were cross-validated, found that multiple correlation was greater than 0.50 for 55% of biodata validity coefficients. Only 28% of IQ validity coefficients exceeded 0.50.

This extremely rosy picture must be qualified, however. It is not established that biodata will predict equally well on subsequent occasions despite high validity found on a previous occasion. Specifically, when the regression weights discovered on the first occasion are used to score biodata for a new sample, the validity drops dramatically. Using female clerical employees as subjects, and turnover as the criterion measure, Wernimont (1962) lost a tremendous amount of validity over 5 years (from 0.61 to 0.07); while, with merely 1 year's gap Dunnette et al. (1960) found a drop from 0.61 to 0.38. However, these studies predict turnover among female clerical employees. Performance and turnover in life insurance agents hired between 1969 and 1971 was predicted with some success by biodata scoring key developed in 1933 (Brown, 1978).

There are some indications that the biodata weights obtained from a certain population can be applied to a different population. Buel et al. (1966) found that regression weights derived from the biodata of a sample of petroleum scientists satisfactorily predicted measures of job performance in pharmaceutical scientists employed by NASA. However, when we compare more diverse occupations, such as chemist and psychologist, the same biodata do not always predict. Chambers (1964) found that while the same 16 biodata items discriminated between successful and unsuccessful chemists and psychologists, there were 10 additional items significant for chemists only, and four for psychologists only. On the other hand, there is a considerable agreement in the biodata which predict success in the same occupation in different countries. Salesmen's success can be predicted across European national boundaries (Hinrichs et al., 1976), and so can that of managers in general (Laurent, 1970).

5.2.3 What do biodata predict?

When we consider studies which deal with occupations typically staffed by graduates, we can discover which particular biodata items are predictive of job performance. It is first of all worth noting an imbalance, however, in the criterion variables which are predicted in biodata studies. Studies which predict job performance are overwhelmingly conducted with men in middle-class professions as the subjects. The criteria employed are typically supervisor's ratings of job performance or more objective measures such as sales performance, number of patents registered, etc. Studies which predict turn-over, on the other hand, are usually conducted upon woman employees, mostly in clerical or unskilled manual jobs. Specifically, of 29 studies predicting performance, 27 were conducted, as far as could be determined, upon male subjects and 2 on subjects of both sexes. Of these 29 studies 11 were of scientists, 5 of sales personnel, 4 of managers, 3 of divers, 2 of army officers, and 4 of miscellaneous occupations. Not all of the studies reviewed stated which specific biodata items were statistically significant predictors in their own right. However, from those that did, the following items were mentioned as significant, listed in order of frequency of occurrence: level of education reached; amount of professional activity (e.g. membership of societies, attendance at conferences); undergraduate academic achievement; health; postgraduate academic achievement; school academic achievement; father's occupation; age; athletic participation; birth order; financial responsibility (mortgage, insurance, etc.); time at present address; number of hours spent on academic work at college; number of previous jobs (negative relationship); number of part-time jobs during education; number of family responsibilities; mother's educational level attained.

Too much weight should not be placed on this order of frequency, however. This is because very few studies list all the items which were tested; they only list those which proved statistically significant predictors. Hence we do not know the proportion of the times it was included in a questionnaire that any item proved significant. Nevertheless, we can be reasonably confident that the items listed above are likely to be predictive if applied to certain occupations usually staffed by graduates, and when the criterion measure is job performance. The obvious question to ask is why such a diverse set of biographical data should predict job performance.

5.2.4 Why do biodata predict?

Little attention has been given to explaining the validity of biodata. Indeed, Korman (1968) criticizes the 'brute empirical approach, where items are utilised according to the specific level of correlations involved in the specific situation, rather than to the meaningfulness of the variables and the possible psychological constructs which could lead to an effective theory' (p. 308).

All the attempted explanations are partially successful. Asher (1972) and Asher and Sciarrino (1974) suggest that those biodata items are successful which share elements of the behaviour being predicted. Thus, for example, high academic grades in graduate school, where vocationally relevant education is given, predict job performance. A moment's perusal of the list of predictive items above, however, demonstrates that this 'point-to-point correspondence' theory cannot cope with the majority of them. Why, for example, should academic performance at high school predict job performance on this theory, let alone such items as birth order (eldest children do better)?

Another explanation is the developmental one proposed by Super (1980) and Jordaan and Super (1974). Developmentalists postulate a set of developmental tasks typical of particular stages of development. Tasks at one stage bear little overt resemblance to tasks at a later stage, since different role expectations are held of individuals at different stages. However, success at the tasks of any stage predicts success at those of later stages. This permits an explanation of why academic and athletic prowess at high school are predictive. However, it fails to account for such items as age, father's occupation, birth order, and mother's educational level.

These latter items suggest very strongly the operation of the opportunity structure, both within the nuclear family and within society. Parental occupation is the major determinant of access to educational and occupational opportunities.

There still remain certain predictive biodata items which are not explained by any of these theories: financial responsibility, time at present address, number of previous jobs, number of family responsibilities. These could perhaps be represented as stability of commitment. In terms of the theory of Levinson *et al.* (1978), they represent the extent to which the role requirements of young adulthood have been met and maintained. Clearly, they are inapplicable to most graduate applicants.

The failure of a simple-minded learning theory, a developmental theory, or a sociological theory of opportunity structure to explain all the predictive items is hardly surprising. An individual's achievements can only be seen in the light of his social identity: the social context and his subjective construction of his self within that context. What is important is how the biodata available from application forms are used. If nothing else, the previous sections have demonstrated that biodata are powerful predictors. Hence, if the psychometric virtue of validity of a selection procedure is desired, biodata should be of immense use.

5.2.5 Decision-making and biodata

It is not clear, however, either that the biodata obtained on application forms are so used; or, if they were to be, whether such use would be desirable; adverse impact on minority groups is evidenced in some cases (Reilly and Chao, 1982). It is worth detailing the concurrent validity procedures which need to be followed if application forms are to be used in this way. First, the biodata of a large group of graduate employees who had joined the organization in previous years would need to be gathered from their application forms and related to their subsequent job performance. This would preferably be measured by a variety of criterion measures, e.g. success at training courses, rate of promotion, supervisors' ratings. The relative weights of items should be observed for each year's subsample of recruits, to discover whether these were changing over time or relatively constant. If the latter is the case they could be used for the pre-selection of the next set of graduate applicants. Each biodata item would be scored in such a way as to give it the weight already established by the previous analyses. Hence the sifting of the application forms would be a routine actuarial exercise.

The writer can say, on the basis of wide contacts with graduate recruiters in the UK, that very few organizations indeed use application forms in this way. Most take subjective rather than statistical decisions, using a variety of decision dimensions. For example, even between interviewers within the same organization there may be differences in the way in which information is utilized in coming to a decision (Valenzi and Andrews, 1973).

It is likely, however, that there are yet more general features of decision-making along which recruiters differ. They may employ different strategies overall. For example, some may employ linear additive models—adding favourable and unfavourable items of information, then comparing the final 'sum' with some ideal requirement, or with other current applicants. Other recruiters may employ cut-off items—the presence of which in an application form indicates an immediate select or reject decision without the need to consider any further information. Yet others may place particular emphasis upon those items which best differentiate applicants; that is, those items on which applicants differ most. Other recruiters, again, may have an overall picture of the sort of person they are looking for. Once they have read sufficient items to suggest that the applicant fulfils this stereotype they may take a decision, ignoring possible later disconfirming items of information. Recent techniques for analysing the tape-recorded 'think-aloud' protocols of decision-makers have made it possible to discover all these strategies and more. The application of such analyses to the initial sift of graduate applicants has only just begun, but preliminary results indicate a variety of strategies in use.

5.2.6 Judgemental biases

The evidence regarding the presence of biases when application forms are being assessed is somewhat ambiguous overall. One thing that is clear is that recruiters differ as to how favourable or unfavourable particular items of information about an individual are (Mayfield and Carlson, 1966). Some items (e.g. those referring to stability versus variety of experience) have a U-shaped configuration, with recruiters treating them as either very favourable or as very unfavourable. It is not only the dimension of favourability along which recruiters differ, but also that of importance: what are the relative weights to be attached to particular items of information? Hakel *et al.* (1970) found that real-life interviewers and student judges differed in the relative importance they attached to academic standing, level of experience, and interest factors. This difference was found both within and between the two groups. Valenzi and Andrews (1973) also found wide individual difference in the weight attached to different items. They discovered in addition that there were differences between how judges thought they were weighting items and how they actually were. However, the applicants in their research were secretarial staff, not students. Although Mayfield and Carlson found little evidence of any strategy other than the linear additive one, two of the four interviewers imployed by Valenzi and Andrews used configural rather than additive strategies to a certain extent; that is, they made additional holistic judgements about the applicant which were inferences from the information provided.

There is some evidence that selectors pay differing attention to favourable and unfavourable items of information. However, while Bolster and Spring-bett (1961) maintain that this is because too much attention is paid to unfavourable items, Hollman (1972) suggests that it is because they do not weight favourable information strongly enough. Either way, negative information is considered more important than positive. Perhaps, as Webster (1964) proposes, this is because recruiters only get feedback from organizations about their mistakes. They learn a great deal about the shortcomings of these 'false positive' choices, and so build up a detailed stereotype of the sort of employee the organization does not want. Similar feedback of their successful appointments is not likely to be offered, so they have less opportunity to form a stereotype of the desirable employee. There is the additional possibility that early stages of the recruitment and selection procedure concentrate on eliminating false positives more than selecting true positives. That is, recruiters take care to reject those they think may be a costly mistake as far as the organization is concerned. This is particularly true where there is a favourable selection ratio with large numbers of well-qualified applicants. Another factor affecting decisions is whether the recruiter is keeping up with his schedule for filling vacant posts. If he is behind schedule he is apt to offer more; if ahead, less, as one might expect (Carlson, 1967).

5.2.7 Other factors

There are certain other features of the information-processing task which do not seem to have clear effects on decisions, however. Unlike the interview, application form judgements do not seem to show very clear order effects, either within each application form or between forms. Hence, within the form, some investigators find a primacy effect, with early items of information carrying more weight in decisions (e.g. Springbett, 1958). Others find a recency effect (Farr, 1973), while yet others find no effect at all (Peters and Terborg, 1975). These somewhat artificial experiments (some of them using neither real application forms nor real recruiters) have conflicting results, then, but the conflict may perhaps be resolved by the consideration of when the judgement or decision is made. If judges have to make repeated judgements throughout their reading of the form, they have to pay more attention to later items; whereas if they merely have to make one judgement at the end, they can afford to pay less attention to them (Farr and York, 1975).

When we consider between applicant order effects the position is similarly confused. Again, unlike the selection interview, the order in which the recruiter reads the application forms or resumés does not have a large effect on decisions. While Carlson (1970) and Hakel *et al.* (1970) found negligible effects, Landy and Bates (1973) failed to find one at all.

The common-sense assumption that more information about the jobs for which the applicants are being selected would help selectors in their evaluation of the application forms is supported by research findings. Such job information removes order effects (Peters and Terborg, 1975), reduces the effect of irrelevant information on decisions (Wiener and Schneiderman, 1974), and increases inter-rater reliability between recruiters and discriminability among applicants (Langdale and Weitz, 1973).

In sum, then, as one might expect, the decisions based on application forms, when taken subjectively, demonstrate the wide variety of decision-making strategies employed by recruiters, and also some biases.

5.2.8 Reference reports

Another aspect of the application form which can reduce any validity it may possess yet further is the reference report which is sometimes requested in addition. Applicants are asked to give the names and addresses of persons to whom reference may be made, and the organization may take up these references. In the case of graduate applicants, referees may well be members of university staff who have taught them. Requests for reference may be in the form of a straight request; a request together with some instructions regarding how to write the reference—what points are relevant etc.; a checklist of traits to be rated plus a space for comments; and a checklist only. According to Muchinsky's (1979) excellent review, employers use the reference to check on data in the application form, or, slightly more often, to obtain additional information. The reliability of references is very low; even when a standardized form, the Standard Employment Questionnaire (Mosel and Goheen, 1958) is used, reliability across different types of raters (for example acquaintances and supervisors) is very low. Eighty per cent of reliability coefficients were less than 0.4.

Validity, too, is very low indeed, both for skilled workers and professionals, averaging 0.13 across a range of studies, with the criteria the summated scores of job performance on several factors. The most predictive ratings were those of mental ability, with the more social virtues such as cooperation, consideration, and reliability least predictive. Perhaps this is due to the tendency to damn with faint praise (Peres and Garcia, 1962). However a far higher degree of validity may be possible: Carroll and Nash (1972) gave referees a forced-choice form to complete, with 24 pairs of statements presented. Each pair of statements was equated for social desirability, but one had been shown to be related to job success, the other not. Deprived of the opportunity of painting a favourable picture, referees' ratings predicted job performance with a correlation coefficient of 0.64. Validity was particularly high when the referee had observed the individual for a long time, was of the same sex, race, and nationality, and when the job on which the applicant was being rated was similar to that for which he was applying. Jones and Harrison (1982) enjoyed an encouraging validity coefficient when using head teachers' reports to predict the training performance of applicants for naval officer. The reference form moves from requests for factual information (e.g. about sports participation) to judgements of personal attributes.

These studies, however, are the exception. In general, validity ranges 'from unacceptable to mediocre' (Muchinsky). The mean corrected validity coefficient for eight recent studies against a criterion of supervisors' rating was 0.18 (Reilly and Chao, 1982). As Muchinsky notes, this is hardly surprising when referees may wish either to get rid of the applicant as an employee or get him or her a good job as a friend. Applicants select a referee usually because of his prestige or because he feels favourably towards them. Hence the referee is the applicant's choice, and is unlikely to have been selected because he is an accurate judge or is well acquainted with the applicant. Thus, although in principle the reference report could be a psychometrically valid predictor, its present mode of use reduces its validity to negligible proportions. Furthermore, there is no reason to suppose that organizations would use reference reports in an actuarial procedure, applying previously established statistical weights, even if they were valid. Just as with biodata, recruiters will prefer to make decisions on subjective assessments of the evidence. There is little evidence available as to the validity of such subjective decisions based on the application form and on references; but a considerable amount of research derived from other situations indicates that actuarial prediction is almost invariably superior. Hence we have the paradoxical situation that biodata, the information which is potentially the most valid data upon which to base selection decisions, are used for that purpose in less valid ways. On the other hand it is also possible to argue that the application form should not be used as a psychometric device at all.

5.2.9 Application forms and the self-concept

Instead, the application form can be used as a form of introduction. It represents a statement of where the applicant stands at the moment; not a bald list of past achievements, but rather an account of the sociocultural and family context of his upbringing; the educational influence of his schooling; the success he has enjoyed at the variety of developmental tasks with which he has been presented; his present stage of occupational maturity, and his view of his occupational future. In sum, the application form can introduce the applicant, not as an individual character disconnected from his past, present, and future context, but as a social person who has ideas about who he is. Its function is not in this case that of psychometric assessment for purposes of selection. It is rather to present to the organization and its representative the applicant's self-concept. The application form is the third event in the first episode of the selection process. It is the applicant's response to his understanding of the organization's expectations. Having compared this understanding of the organization with his self-concept the application form is the graduate's indication that he wishes to continue the social exchange further. If the organization is to treat this response with the respect it deserves, it will have to compare very carefully this picture of the applicant's self-concept with its expectations for that applicant, estimating the probability of continued fruitful exchange and mutual adaptation.

Note, however, that for this episode of application to be used successfully the necessary conditions for the success of any episode have to be met. That is, both parties have to know and understand the rules of the episode, and both have to possess the repertoire of skills required. Organizations have to discover what graduates wish to know about their expectations of graduate employees, their norms, values, and image, and the lifestyle involved. Then they have to be able to present this in their recruitment literature in a truthful way. Graduates have to understand this presentation, which implies some knowledge of the nature of organizations and what is important about them. Graduates then have to be sufficiently aware of their self-concept to be able to match it with these features of the organization. Having made a judgement regarding the probability of future fruitful social exchange with the organization, they decide whether or not to apply. In order to complete the application form appropriately, they need to be capable of expressing clearly in writing the past, present, and future aspects of their self-concept. Such expression has to follow the constraints of the questions in the application form. Finally, the recruiter has to understand the completed application as an expression of the self-concept, not as an 'objective' measure of achievement. He then has to match it with organizational expectations, and decide whether he wishes to continue or terminate the exchange. If the appropriate skills are not present in both parties for the application episode to be conducted, then its objective will not be achieved. Communication between parties will not occur satisfactorily, and decisions to continue or terminate social exchange may be taken for the wrong reasons.

6

The Graduate Selection Interview

6.1 THE INTERVIEW AS A PSYCHOMETRIC DEVICE

The interview is a focal point in the recruitment process. It is probably the first occasion when the graduate and the organization make personal contact with each other. Hitherto the organization has sent messages to the graduate in the form of recruitment literature, and the graduate has responded with her application form. Now, for the first time, there is the possibility of dynamic, two-way communication. Such dialogue makes possible the discovery and clarification of areas where parties want more information. It also provides the ideal arena for negotiation. Hence the selection interview is an extremely appropriate situation for social exchange to occur. This opportunity has, sadly, often been missed. The interview has been treated as another psychometric tool for assessment purposes. Research into its use has been conducted almost entirely within the psychometric tradition, and in complete disregard of the findings from other areas of psychology. Arvey and Campion (1982) put it thus:

> In reviewing recent research, one is struck by the almost complete lack of attention which has been paid to the person-perception literature by researchers in this area. It is almost as if industrial and organisational psychologists have studied the employment interview in isolation from the rest of psychology, perhaps even ignoring the fact that the phenomenon under investigation is essentially a perceptual process. . . . The price has been somewhat shortsighted and situationally bound research, without the guidance of broader based theories (pp. 312, 313).

Yet again, a recent review of a major area in organizational/industrial psychology has courageously concluded with a confession of insularity of outlook.

The research literature on the selection interview has been ably reviewed, to 1975 by Schmitt (1976) and from 1975 by Arvey and Campion (1982).

The purpose of this chapter is not to provide an exhaustive review. Rather, it is to demonstrate how the research which points out the interview's inadequacies as a psychometric tool also points towards its conceptualization as a social episode.

If the interview is to be considered an adequate psychometric selection device, then by definition it has to possess the psychometric properties of any psychological measure: it has to be both reliable and valid. A selection interview might be considered a reliable measure if the same judgements were made by the same interviewer of an applicant upon different occasions; or more usually if different interviewers made similar judgements of the same applicant. It would be considered valid if the judgements derived from the interview predicted behaviour in the job. The criterion variables employed have ranged from voluntary leaving or staying in the job, through objective measures of performance, to supervisor ratings of the employee's effectiveness.

It is worth recapitulating in greater detail the sequence of stages of assessment implied by the use of the interview as a psychometric device. First, it is assumed that a job analysis has been carried out, and that the personal characteristics necessary for that job's successful performance have been identified. Second, it is assumed that evidence regarding the degree to which the applicant possesses these characteristics can be obtained. It is supposed that this evidence will consist of historical data regarding the applicant's experiences and achievements, obtained both from the application form and from the interview itself. It will also consist of the applicant's appearance and behaviour during the interview. Third, the interviewer is considered capable of inferring from these data the degree to which the target characteristics are present in the applicant. Finally, she is assumed to combine these assessments of characteristics so as to come to a decision (usually, whether to reject the applicant or pass her on for the next stage of the selection procedure). Hence there are, in sum, four stages: job profile, data collection, inferences to characteristics, and decision-making. It should be noted that some investigators (e.g. Landy and Trumbo, 1976) recommend that the final stage should be carried out by statistical procedures rather than by the interviewer. They advocate taking the interviewer's ratings of characteristics and applying statistical weights to them in proportion to the relative importance of each characteristic for job success.

Judged by the acid test of psychometric efficiency—that is, its validity—the selection interview is a miserable failure. Review after review of the literature has indicated that the degree of validity is lower than that obtainable by means of appropriate psychological tests, and much lower than for biodata. Ulrich and Trumbo (1965), for example, reviewed the low reliability and validity coefficients obtained, but pointed specifically to judgements of interpersonal skills and motivation as having somewhat higher validity than judgements of other characteristics. Mayfield (1964) in a similarly comprehensive review, singled out judgements of intelligence as most valid, but pointed out that even these never improve on tests of the same characteristic. Few recent studies have even attempted to test validity. The mean predictive validity coefficient of the 12 which have is 0.19 (Reilly and Chao, 1982). The only type of interview in which increased validity has been found is that of the board interview, where several interviewees interview the applicant simultaneously (Rothstein and Jackson, 1980; Anstey, 1977). Mayfield, (1964) also makes the important point that validity is low even when there is high reliability. Therefore the weakness of the interview as a psychometric device cannot be attributed to the fact that it is technically impossible to have high validity when there is low reliability of predictor or criterion variables. We must look elsewhere for an explanation.

The immediate response to these difficulties was to search for shortcomings in the interview as a psychometric device. The implication was that, just as psychological tests can be refined by eradicating sources of measurement error, so the practice of interviews could be improved so as to make judgements more accurate. As a consequence of this optimism the interview has continued to be the most widely employed selection device, recommended with a greater or lesser degree of confidence (Fear, 1978; Shouksmith, 1978; Bayne, 1977). An alternative response to the low validity of the interview, of course, is to question its utility as a psychometric device at all; this response will be developed later.

Since the mid-1960s research into the interview has concentrated upon exploring different aspects of the procedure in order to try to discover where the inaccuracies or biases creep in, distorting 'true measurement'. The list of possible culprits is immense. In the absence of any theoretical account of the interview at the time, Webster (1964) attempted the Herculean task of identifying the sources of error. He and others found, for example, that interviewers do not assess each applicant independently of other applicants; the quality of previous applicants affects judgements of subsequent ones (Heneman et al., 1975; Schuh, 1978); first impressions carry disproportionate weight (Blakeney and McNaughton, 1971; Springbett, 1958); interviewers favour applicants similar to themselves (Rand and Wexley, 1975); they match candidates against stereotypes of idealized successful applicants, rather than against job requirements (Hakel et al., 1970); and so on. Practically minded researchers set about trying to remedy these unfortunate biases. Finding that a staggering 80% of the variance in the ratings of an average applicant was accounted for by whether she was preceded by two highly or two lowly qualified applicants, Wexley et al. (1977), warned their interviewers that this might happen, and gave them special cues to help them avoid such gross contrast effects. Only a slight improvement resulted. It was only after a week-long workshop that the bias was eliminated. Given the number of possible biases, the number of weeks' training required to eliminate them seems a large chunk of a personnel officer's life! Moreover, there were some investigations which failed to find the biases discovered in others; and many investigations were extremely artificial.

Returning to the sequence of four stages in the psychometric model above, it is possible to explore more systematically the theoretical possibility of error. First, it is possible that the job profile is inaccurate, or even misguided in its very conception. The job may not need the set of characteristics postulated in the proportion suggested, or it may not be independent of its incumbent. That is, the individual may adapt the job to herself (Katz and Kahn, 1978); hence it is inappropriate to look for a very specific set of qualities.

Second, the data themselves may be inaccurate. Historical data may not be accurately reported on application forms (Goldstein, 1971), nor in interviews, (Weiss and Dawis, 1960), especially when the applicant has good reasons to present herself in a favourable light. Not only may the data be inaccurate; they may also be a biased sample of the population of behaviours upon which the judgement is supposed to be based. This is particularly likely to be true of the behaviour produced in the interview itself, where self-presentation is of prime concern. Confusion may be worse confounded when the applicant believes that the interviewer is looking for different characteristics from those she actually is looking for, although evidence is conflicting here. Fletcher (1981) finds several differences, whereas Posner (1981) discovered that faculty, students, and recruiters all considered communicative ability and future potential to be the most important characteristics.

Not only may the data themselves be inaccurate or misleading; there is very likely to be error involved in the inferences from behavioural data to characteristics of the applicant. Recent advances in the theory of personality and in the study of person perception and attribution reviewed in Chapter 2 have pointed up the complexity of these processes. The potential hazards in attributing traits of character to an individual are numerous, and will be reviewed again briefly here. First, there is the general theoretical difficulty of attributing past and present behaviour and achievements to aspects of character alone, when both psychological theory and everyday practice attribute them to an interaction between the individual and her environment. It is not enough to 'make allowances', to attribute a little more intelligence and motivation to an applicant who has achieved a high academic perform-ance at a non-academic school. This fails to do justice to the complexity of the interaction; persons do not have qualities independent of their social environment. Rather, they develop as part of that environment. Their iden-tity is a social one, and their own development is part and parcel of their social exchange within their society.

Related to this theoretical difficulty is an empirical finding from the litera-ture on attribution theory. Attribution theory, as was indicated in Chapter 2, is concerned with discovering how people come to their understanding of the causes of behaviour, both other people's behaviour and their own. The most basic bias, so widespread that Ross (1977) calls it the fundamental attribution error, is to attribute too much of the causation of behaviour to the actor's disposition, and too little to the situation within which the behaviour occurred. This bias was first observed by Jones and Harris (1967), and has since been found in a wide variety of contexts. When we apply it to the selection interview the implication is that the interviewer is likely to place too much emphasis on the individual's personality in explaining both her record and her behaviour at interview. Interview behaviour is particularly susceptible to this bias: the applicant is taken to be behaving in a certain way at interview because she has certain characteristics, not because she is attending an interview.

Another attributional bias is that of seeking to confirm rather than disconfirm one's initial judgements about an individual. Again, this propensity has been evidenced in a wide variety of situations (Ross et al., 1977; Snyder et al., 1977). As Karl Popper has pointed out, scientists themselves are not immune from this bias. The interviewer is especially tempted, since she is usually in charge of the way in which the interview progresses. Hence she can direct her questioning towards topics which will provide further evidence of characteristics which she has already inferred. Recent evidence that this bias occurs in interviews is provided by Snyder and White (1981).

A final potential source of bias derives from the implicit personality theories of the interviewer; that is, from the ways of thinking about others which direct her inferences. For example, having inferred one characteristic from the behavioural data, the interviewer may infer from that another characteristic, this time without data. The applicant may be considered strongly motivated to work for the interviewer's organization; she may be inferred to be highly ambitious also, simply because it is assumed by the interviewer that a person who is strongly motivated in one respect is also strongly motivated in another area of her working life. In this case the inference would have been from one personality trait to another of a similar range of application (Rosenberg et al., 1968). However, the inference may instead be hierarchical in nature; the inference may be from a trait (e.g. cheerfulness) up to a more global personality type (e.g. extraversion). Further inference may be in the downward direction again—if she is extraverted, she will also be talkative and impulsive (Cantor and Mischel, 1977). Alternatively, the interviewer may have a certain prototype in mind—'the ideal engineering graduate employee for this company', for example. Once certain aspects of this prototype have been inferred, others will follow; this is because the applicant has, at a certain point, been identified as fulfilling the prototype. The rest of its features are then assumed to be present. There is every reason to suppose that global and hierarchical modes of thinking of this sort are occurring in the selection interview.

However, inferences from the presence of one trait to the presence of another *within the interview situation* may not be the worst hazard. As Hampson (1982) has pointed out, these inferences may well have some validity. This is because the traits which are inferred do in fact have some overlap in meaning. If the interviewer uses the words 'sociable' and 'talkative' of an applicant, she may well be inferring both traits from a common set of behaviours, since both words share certain elements of meaning. It is not so much the inference of one trait from another that we need to be concerned about. It is rather the prediction of subsequent behaviour on the basis of traits inferred from behaviour in an entirely different situation. Of course, some will say that a trait is by definition trans-situational. This may be true, but the evidence reviewed in Chapter 2 suggests that there is little evidence to support the idea that such predictions are successful. In brief, the interview is likely to provide poor behavioural evidence on which to base inferences of job-relevant traits, partly because it is a situation little resembling future employment.

Thus the final, decision-making stage of the psychometric model is at risk. Given the existence of the implicit personality theories described above it is hardly likely that the interviewer will conclude the interview with a set of estimates of personality characteristics which are independent of each other. Indeed, they are often highly correlated with each other (Hakel, 1971). Rather than subsequently combine them in either a subjective or a statistical weighting procedure, she is far more likely to have come to an implicit decision much earlier (for example, in deciding how close the applicant is to a prototype). Thus her judgements are likely to have been interactive and inferential rather than linear and additive.

6.2 SOME EVIDENCE ABOUT THE SELECTION INTERVIEW

Given the very considerable number of possible biases in judgement, it is hardly surprising that graduate selectors do not show any marked additional prowess in the predictive validity of their judgements to other interviewers. They seem to achieve reasonable success at some of the classic stages of the psychometric procedure, but such partial success is not sufficient.

Let us consider first the selection of those characteristics which are to be considered relevant to jobs. Hakel and Schuh (1971) employed Hakel and Dunnette's (1970) checklists for describing job applicants. They asked interviewers for jobs in seven diverse occupations which attributes they considered favourable; some of the entrants to some of these occupations are habitually graduates. They found that universally important, favourable, and frequent were two clusters of attributes: a personal relations cluster, and a good citizen cluster (dependability, conscientiousness, stability, etc.). Thus in broad terms, very little difference is evident in the characteristics which are considered appropriate to different occupations. However, when we look at detailed stereotypes of e.g. 'a good electrical engineer', there is hardly any inter-recruiter agreement (Shaw, 1972). Looking specifically at graduate recruiters in the USA, Campion (1978) found academic achievement and participation in social and professional activities at college were preferred. For a British sample of graduate recruiters, on the other hand, there was marked agreement between recruiters when they were asked to rate the relative importance of twelve characteristics for a wide variety of jobs

(Keenan, 1976). The key characteristics were, however, different from those discovered by Hakel and Schuh, incorporating in the British case four main factors: achievement motivation, knowledge about the job and the company, quality of references, and academic performance. Interviewers who were personnel managers placed more emphasis on the first two of these than did non-personnel interviewers, but less on academic performance. Thus we find, admittedly on the basis of only four studies, no evidence that different jobs or occupations are seen to require markedly different characteristics, some dissimilarity between UK and US interviewers, and differences due to aspects of the interviewer.

Moving on to the second stage, let us consider the drawing of inferences to particular characteristics from behavioural evidence. There is some research bearing upon the evidence derived from the application form, and its effects upon post-interview judgements. If the appropriate psychometric assumptions are made, then there should be no difference in the weight given to data obtained from the application form and those which happened to be acquired in the interview. This appears to be the case according to the evidence of Okanes and Tschirgi (1978). Their recruiters made pre-interview judgements of 'probably recommend', 'unable to determine', and 'probably not recommend', on the basis of information about college grade, job experience, campus activity, and faculty references. They then re-sorted applicants after the interview. There were shifts from the 'unable to determine' category, suggesting that more information had been received which permitted decisions to be made; further, most shifts were to the 'probably not recommend' category, indicating that the major intended junction of the interview was to reduce false positives.

However, there is other research which suggests that less psychometrically virtuous judgements are being made. Specifically, it seems possible that interviewers use the application form to make general impressions of the applicant, then use the interview to confirm these impressions. For example, Tucker and Rowe (1979) had students read 10 transcripts of interviews in which an applicant's past achievements were reviewed. In five of the transcripts the achievements were successful, in the other five failures. Prior to reading the transcripts the students had read either favourable, unfavourable, or neutral references for each of the applicants. The results indicated that the interviewers who had read the unfavourable reference were likely to give the applicant less credit for her past successes and more responsibility for her failures. Although this research had students rather than real recruitment officers as judges, this fault is not present in the work of Tullar et al. (1979). They gave experienced employment counsellors data regarding the quality of graduate applicants (grade point averages, etc.). The counsellors were then instructed to come to a select or reject decision as soon as they felt they had received sufficient information to do so from a video recording of a staged interview. Ratings of suitability were negatively related to decision times for the high-quality applicants, positively for the low-quality ones. In other words, little time was needed to confirm the impression based on the initial information, whereas a lot of time was needed to disconfirm it.

Dipboye and Wiley (1977) demonstrated a reverse effect: recruiters were shown video recordings of two applicants, one male and one female. While the content of the interview was held constant, the non-verbal behaviour was manipulated to give the impression of either a passive style or a moderately aggressive one. The latter resulted in a greater probability of being invited for a second interview, and of ultimate recommendation for hiring. More to the point here, the moderately aggressive applicants were judged to have better academic qualifications, experience, and training, despite the fact that their application forms had been identical! In other words, behavioural data from the interview had distorted biodata. Further evidence of how such data can interact is provided by Tessler and Sushelsky (1978). The job being applied for in this case was one requiring self-confidence, but the 'interviewers' were undergraduate students and the interview was a laboratory analogue. The applicants engaged in continuous, partial, or no eye-contact with these 'interviewers', who were led to believe that the applicants were either college educated, or high-school educated only. Those applicants who were college educated were rated as better suited for the job, as were those who used more eye-contact. Most interesting, however, was the finding of an interaction effect: those of college education who made no eye contact were rated as having very little self-confidence and therefore being highly unsuitable for the job.

In sum, information is not processed independently in a linear additive way to arrive at inferences about characteristics. Moreover, there is evidence that the inferred characteristics themselves are not independent of each other, particularly when the data are the non-verbal behaviour of the applicant at interview. Using personnel managers as interviewers, McGovern and Tinsley (1978) showed four video recordings of simulated employment interviews. Applicants employed either a low level of non-verbal behaviour or a high level (eye-contact, energy and affect levels, fluency), with verbal content held constant. Interviewers rated applicants on 10 dimensions previously identified as critical in influencing decisions. Ratings on almost all of these qualities were superior for those applicants who demonstrated a high level of non-verbal behaviour. Moreover, the evaluations on these dimensions were highly correlated with each other, suggesting an overall impression, rather than specific inferences about characteristics. Sterrett's (1978) failure to obtain similar outcomes using similar procedures should be noted, however.

One possibility is that interviewers are affected by applicants' non-verbal behaviour in the same way as they would be in an ordinary conversation. That is, in addition to consciously using the applicants' non-verbal behaviour as evidence for their level of social skill, they also form overall impressions of character as they would, often unconsciously, in ordinary social intercourse. Forbes and Jackson's (1980) evidence that interviewers are often unaware of the fact that they are basing their judgements on non-verbal behaviour supports this supposition. We will return to the idea that the interview is more appropriately considered as social intercourse in the next section.

We must also, however, enter a note of warning against exaggerating the effect of non-verbal behaviour upon decisions. Several of the experiments which demonstrated its powerful effects were laboratory studies, which held other factors, such as verbal content, constant. When Hollandsworth *et al.* (1979) looked at real-life campus recruiting, they discovered a different overall picture. They employed discriminant analysis to discover which of seven rated categories of behaviour best predicted final decisions. The decisions were 'not a chance', 'probably not', 'probably', and 'definitely', and the seven categories could be defined as follows: articulatory (fluency, loudness of speech), non-verbal (dress and appearance, eye-contact, posture, composure), verbal (appropriateness of content). Appropriateness of content, fluency, and composure, in that order, were the categories which discriminated best between decision groups. Hence, relative to other aspects of behaviour, the non-verbal category is not excessively influential. It really does matter what you say.

It remains to consider, however, some evidence which suggests that the final stages in the classic psychometric model are not so biased in the case of the interview as has hitherto been maintained. Using graduate recruiters and real applicants Keenan (1977) found no evidence for a halo effect. Considering both the intelligence and the likeability of applicants, the recruiters' overall evaluation of them did not confound these two characteristics. When the effects of likeability on the evaluations were partialled out statistically, intelligence was still moderately related to evaluations. Rothstein and Jackson (1980) achieved more remarkable results. Their interviewers showed an astonishingly high level of agreement in inferring a set of characteristics from observed interview behaviour. Moreover these inferences were 'accurate' in that they agreed with the applicants' ratings of themselves (although, obviously, there is the danger that self-ratings are related to self-presentation, which in turn affects interviewer ratings). Again, Rothstein and Jackson found that there was high inter-rater agreement regarding judgements of suitability for jobs in engineering or accountancy. These judgements were reliable, not based on a global desirability stereotype, and unique to each target occupation. Finally, Mayfield *et al.* (1980) demonstrated validity coefficients of around 0.6 when selecting insurance salesmen by interview. This was due to asking specific questions regarding past experiences which were relevant to the job. The same applies when applicants are only evaluated on specific and relevant job dimensions (Osburn *et al.*, 1981).

Despite these latter pieces of research, however, and despite some benefits of training interviewers (Latham *et al.*, 1975; Keenan, 1978), the overall judgement of the interview as a psychometric device for the selection of applicants must be an unfavourable one. There is an alternative strategy to identifying and eliminating sources of bias, however. It is to admit that the interview should not be conceptualized as a psychometric device at all.

6.3 THE INTERVIEW AS A SOCIAL EPISODE

Interviewers are encouraged to establish rapport with applicants, to help them to relax and treat the interview more as a conversation. The assumption underlying this strategy is that applicants are more likely to behave 'naturally', in ways more typical of their everyday conversation. Hence they will give more evidence of the sort of person they really are. They will be able to 'do themselves justice' (presumably in the direction both of favourable and also of unfavourable judgements), since they are less inhibited by anxiety caused by a formal occasion. The motives underlying this strategy are admirable; the interviewer is trying to obtain more reliable data upon which to base her judgements, and she is anxious to enable the applicants to reveal the range of their competences.

However, the actual outcome of such a strategy is possibly the opposite of that intended. It may result in yet more confusion regarding the rules of the interview itself: how is one expected to behave oneself, and how can one expect the other person to behave? It is only when we start considering the interview as a social episode with somewhat ambiguous rules that its poor validity as a psychometric device is fully explained. The interviewer's strategy of pretending that it is really just a friendly conversation between new acquaintances adds to this ambiguity; so do several other features of the graduate selection procedure.

First, however, it is necessary to indicate how the selection interview is best analysed as a social episode, with rules operating and reciprocal roles being played. One way of demonstrating the existence of social rules is simply to list some of them and discover whether the reader agrees that they represent some of the assumptions she makes about a selection interview.

In general, the interviewer is supposed to be in control of the interview. She is expected to ask questions of the applicant, and the applicant is expected to answer them truthfully but with the understanding that she will be wishing to show herself in a good light. The interviewer will be expected to offer the opportunity to the applicant to ask questions in her turn; such opportunity will be expected to occur towards the end of the interview. The termination of the interview will also be under the interviewer's control.

The topics covered will also be governed by unspoken rules. The applicant should expect to be questioned about her academic prowess, her educational experience, and her extracurricular interests. She may also be asked about the organization to which she is applying—evidence of the care she has put into preparing for the interview and hence of her motivation to work for the organization. While her attitudes on social or political issues of the day may be within the permitted areas the applicant may feel confident that her personal life will not be touched upon, except in so far as it affects her potential mobility. The increasing doubt in the reader's mind regarding these last few rules indicates the fuzziness at the boundaries of what is permissible and what is not; one may also expect cultural differences in this regard. The range of topics about which the applicant may ask the interviewer is much narrower: the organization, the specific job offered, career prospects. The applicant is not expected to ask the interviewer about his life, although to ask about his experience with the organization which he represents may be acceptable (and, indeed, taken as evidence of initiative).

Interview manner and behaviour, too, has its limits. The applicant is expected to be confident where he has reason to be, but not brash; to be polite, but not sycophantic; lively and interested, but not voluble or manic; to answer the question and keep to the topic, but to volunteer occasional additional information; to demonstrate a certain degree of nervousness, given the importance of the occasion, but not to remain visibly anxious throughout the interview. There may even be specific behaviours which are considered appropriate or not; applicants are not expected to smoke unless invited to do so. They are expected to be tidy and clean in appearance, although the particular items of clothing (e.g. dress or slacks, suit or jacket) may have some leeway.

The point of quoting these rules is not to demonstrate that they all play a large part in decisions which are arrived at as a consequence of the interview. It is rather to indicate that there is a wide range of rules which exist, some of them relating to apparently quite unimportant aspects of behaviour. Appropriate behaviour, moreover, does not merely involve knowing the rules and obeying them. It also requires the playing of reciprocal roles. The applicant must not only cover the right topics and display the expected non-verbal behaviour; she must do so *in response to* the interviewer's behaviour. The appropriate answer must be given to a question; laughter should be in response to a joke! In brief, the process is a dynamic one, where parties must synchronize their behaviour. As in ordinary social conversations, turns must be taken, and conversational flow maintained. But there are the additional requirements of the interview: the need to defer to questioning, to await the signal for questioner and respondent roles to be reversed, and so on.

The interview, then, can be seen to be a rule-governed social episode in which the parties play reciprocal roles. Given such a conceptualization, attribution theory attempts to provide an account of how judgements about other persons are made in social episodes of this nature. It runs as follows. Two of the earliest generalizations of attribution theory are the Discounting and Augmentation Principles of Kelley (1972). The Discounting Principle predicts that there will be less attribution to the actor when her behaviour is that expected in the situation than when the behaviour occurs in a setting relatively free of situational demands. The Augmentation Principle states that there will be more attribution to the actor when her behaviour is *contrary* to that expected in a situation than when the behaviour occurs in a setting relatively free of situational demands. The evidence supporting these general principles, and subsequent theoretical developments, are ably reviewed by Kelley and Michela (1980).

It is evident that, when applied to the selection interview, these principles suggest that the interviewer will be making judgements about the causes of the applicant's behaviour. The Discounting Principle should mean that the interviewer will consider these behavioural data in the light of the situational constraints operating. Data from the applicant's past history, for example, may suggest that the family pressure from an engineer father was the context of the applicant's choice of engineering as a university subject. In this case the interviewer may be unwilling to attribute the choice of subject to the applicant. The interviewer may reason in the same way about behavioural data obtained from the interview itself. If she considers the interview is in itself a constraining situation (as our previous analysis suggests that it is), then she will not be very willing to attribute the applicant's behaviour at interview to her character, but rather to the situation. Unfortunately, of course, the fundamental attributional error, of placing too much causal emphasis on the actor and too little on the situation, may bias the operation of the Discounting Principle. It will lead the interviewer to infer personal characteristics from situationally-determined behaviour—and after all, the inference of such characteristics is probably what the interviewer's objective is anyway.

Applying the Augmentation Principle, the interviewer is to be seen as paying particular attention to behaviour which is unexpected in the interview, or which is unusual in the life history of an applicant. From such behaviour she will be able to make inferences about personal characteristics; for the behaviour is contrary to situational constraints and therefore cannot be attributed to them. An applicant, for example, may have taken up engineering in the absence of any engineering tradition in her school or family. Similarly, an applicant at interview may ask exceptionally detailed and well-informed questions about conditions of employment; or she may ask a barrage of questions before being invited to do so.

These attributional principles therefore provide an account of which behavioural data the interviewer may be using to infer personal characteristics in the applicants, and how she does so. If the interviewer were to operate in this way, and were additionally to avoid the fundamental attributional error and other biases, then there is no reason why the interview should not be a reasonably valid procedure. Indeed, there is some evidence that interviewers do operate according to the Augmentation Principle. Constantin (1976) presented a taped interview to students of organizational behaviour. Two factors were varied: whether the applicant had a normal or deviant profile of grade scores, and whether these scores were, overall, high or low. The applicants who had high but deviant scores were rated most suitable, and the ones who had low but deviant scores were rated least suitable. Thus it was deviance from the norm which resulted in more extreme judgements.

Similarly, in the experiment of Tessler and Sushelsky (1978) already described on page 75, it was the highly qualified applicant who, unexpectedly, showed least eye-contact, who was rated unsuitable.

Although the interviewer may operate along these attributional lines, the psychologist analysing the interview as a social interaction cannot do so. She cannot think in terms of mutually exclusive internal (character) and external (situational) determinants of behaviour. At the very least, the psychologist has to be an interactionist; that is, she has to suggest that people of certain types of disposition are going to behave in an interview differently from persons of different dispositions. However, the *major* emendation that the psychologist has to make in attribution theory before it can become her own explanation is as follows. She may not accept that the situation, the events external to the person, are the cause of that person's behaviour. The social psychologist maintains that it is the person's *perception* of her situation, her own construction of social reality, which she uses to regulate her behaviour. Hence we may say that it is the applicant's received *role* which regulates her behaviour in the interview, unless she steps outside it. It is the definition of role which is important here: the applicant's received role is how she thinks she is expected to behave at the interview. She may choose to behave as she thinks she is expected to; or she may choose to behave outside that role. Thus the applicant's received role may be different from what the interviewer believes the applicant's role to be (the sent role). Putting it another way, the applicant may think the interviewer expects her to behave differently from how the interviewer actually does expect her to behave. Both the applicant's received role and the interviewer's sent role may differ from the general rules of the game which people more or less agree (see above). However, the received role is perhaps likely to differ more from the generally held view than the sent role, because the applicant has had less experience of the interview situation than the interviewer. Also, more important, she may have differing objectives in the interview from those of the interviewer, and also from those generally assumed to be the purpose of selection interviews.

What might the applicant's objectives be? One key determinant will be the extent to which the applicant has responded to pressures to think and act about her future. She may be trying to discover more about the nature of work and jobs in general, the nature of particular occupations, what selection interviews are like, or the characteristics of the organization to which she has applied. All of these objectives imply different degrees of progress in occupational development; none of them is identical to the universally assumed objective of an applicant: obtaining a job.

There is quite a lot of evidence that the applicants have learning objectives for themselves. Alderfer and McCord (1970) found that MBA students had positive attitudes towards interviewers who confronted them with technical questions in their area of interest. That is, they accepted the traditional function of the interview as a selection device, and assumed that the criterion for selection should be technical expertise. However, they also valued highly interest and concern from the interviewer, and the chance to discuss the careers of other MBAs in their company. The interviewer's behaviour plays a crucial part in the applicant's decision whether or not to accept a job offer: according to Glueck's (1973) respondents, in over one-third of cases the recruiter was the major reason why they chose a particular company, while for two-thirds the recruiter was a major influence. When Keenan's (1978) applicants liked the interviewer they were more likely to accept job offers; and according to Fisher *et al.* (1976), job incumbents are perceived to be more knowledgeable and trustworthy sources of job information than professional recruiters, and are more likely to secure acceptances of offers. Schmitt and Coyle (1976) found that perceived interviewer personality, manner of delivery, and the adequacy of the job information provided affected student applicants' evaluations of the interviewer and of his company, and also their intentions of accepting a job if offered one. Rynes *et al.* (1980) stress the importance of these findings as indicating that there are two parties making decisions in the interview. The processes whereby applicants evaluate the organization are a matter of conjecture; they may treat recruitment procedures simply as evidence of how attainable a job is with that organization; they may use them as evidence of the nature of the organization—is this the way it typically behaves towards it employees? Or they may use the recruitment procedures in general or the interview in particular as the only feature which discriminates between very similar jobs in different organizations.

Whatever the decision-making process, the point to be stressed is that applicants may have many different purposes, but that common to them all is the need to obtain information about the organization's expectations. Given that the objective of the interviewer is also to obtain information of a different sort (Schmitt, 1976), interviewer's and applicant's objectives are different, and may clash. As Keenan and Wedderburn (1980) point out, applicants may be disappointed because interviewers do not provide what they expect. The most absurd situation is where applicants ask about the organization in order to find out about it; interviewers ask about the organization in order to discover whether the applicant has done her homework! Recent research by Herriot and Rothwell (1983) demonstrates that the two parties do indeed have different expectations of the interview. Interviewers expect applicants to talk more than applicants expect to, and applicants expect interviewers to talk more than interviewers expect to. Both parties, in other words, expect to obtain more information from the other party than the other party expects to give. More important, however, was the finding that disappointment of expectations actually predicts decisions, particularly for the interviewer. The lower their experiences of the amount covered in the interview, the less likely were the interviewers to consider graduate applicants suitable for the job.

This finding is an indicator of a major reason for the low validity of the selection interview. The problem is not mainly one of bias in interviewer judgement. It is one of confusion about roles and objectives. Applicants have different objectives from interviewers; they may have different ideas as to what is appropriate behaviour. It is these confusions which cause misperceptions and misjudgements. Consider an interviewer who is trying to form a judgement about an applicant. The interviewer will be paying little attention to the applicant's standard role behaviour. The applicant appears tidy, waits to be invited to sit down, and appears reasonably relaxed. However, within a very few minutes the interviewer finds herself being questioned repeatedly. She has hardly covered the applicant's educational experience when she is interrupted and asked about the career prospects. The interviewer is apt to draw inferences from this behaviour about the applicant's character, and they may not be favourable ones. This is because, as far as the interviewer is concerned, the applicant has acted out of role; this is good attributional evidence for a dispositional rather than a situational inference. This is an impatient and forward young person, she concludes, who will not permit me to obtain the information which is the main objective of the exercise. Of course, this behaviour may be within the bounds of the applicant's own received role; what *she* expects to do and thinks is expected of her. Hence behaviour which is in role as far as she is concerned is out of role for the interviewer and taken as evidence of character (Herriot, 1981).

What can we conclude about the selection interview? The evidence that has been reviewed here suggests that it is a poor psychometric device, confounded by biases. When analysed as a social episode the confusion of purposes and hence of roles make it clear why inferences based upon it are so hazardous. It is only when rules and objectives are agreed beforehand that it can become a fruitful episode of social exchange; and it is only when the interpersonal and communicative skills necessary for the carrying out of the episode are available to both parties that its success is possible. The success of the initial interview, like that of the application episode, cannot be construed in psychometric terms. Rather, we must consider whether it has been successful as a social negotiation. Is the applicant clear what the organization expects? (Is the organization clear what it expects?) Is the organization clear about the nature of the applicant's self-concept? Have the two parties had a chance to discover the extent to which these are congruent, and to negotiate about reducing incongruence?

7

Assessment Centres

7.1 WHAT ARE ASSESSMENT CENTRES?

Many organizations used to employ an interview as their method of graduate selection at the final stage of the procedure as well as at the second stage. This was often conducted by the individual who would be the applicant's supervisor if he were appointed. This procedure was less likely to be valid than at the second stage, since the supervisor was less likely to have received training in interviewing than the milk-round interviewer (who is often from the personnel department). In recent years, however, many organizations have started using the assessment centre technique for selection purposes. While the term 'assessment centre' is American in origin, and emerged in the late 1950s, the practice was prevalent previously under the title of 'extended interview'. It was begun by the German army in the 1930s, and developed in the British and American armed services during the Second World War; the UK Civil Service Selection Board procedure was based upon the same principles. Huck (1973) gives a more extended historical review.

The term 'assessment centre' covers a multitude of sins. As Finkle (1976) observes in his review article: 'Despite the popular common label, there is no such entity, but only a variety of programs, each of which must be evaluated in the context of its own objectives and circumstances' (p. 885). The features distinguishing assessment centres from other forms of assessment seem to be as follows, according to Finkle. First, the assessees are in groups; second, the assessors are in groups, and are often managers from within the organization; third, there are multiple methods of assessment, including tests, exercises, and interviews; fourth, unlike many assessment procedures, assessment centres are favoured by managers, perhaps because they have high face validity.

Examples of the exercises, which are the novel element in the selection methods, are the in-basket exercise and the leaderless group discussion. The following description of an in-basket exercise is taken from a recent article (Dulewicz and Fletcher, 1982):

> This exercise simulates the in-tray of a senior manager in STC; almost all of the 27 items were gathered from the in-trays of senior managers in STC, with suitable amendments to maintain confidentiality and to fit into STC 'Geo-Systems Division' in which this, and some of the other exercises, take place. The participant is asked to stand in for the Division's General Manager and has two hours in which to deal with various memos, letters, reports and other documents as he sees fit. He is then asked to fill in an action sheet on which he summarises how he dealt with each item. He is then interviewed by an assessor and asked to explain why he took the various actions, and encouraged to clear up any outstanding issues.

As Finkle (1976, p. 864) says: 'Such activities are more or less standardised exposures of one or more assessees to one or more assessors under conditions and performing tasks believed to simulate work exposures or at least to elicit performance that generalises to the work environment.' Thus the Civil Service Selection Board sometimes have applicants draft a reply to a letter of complaint; the Royal Navy have them devising a plan of how to transport men across an (imaginary) yawning chasm, and then leading a team putting the plan into operation.

Another feature of the assessment centre is the way in which the information derived from the different assessment methods is used. A group of assessors reviews all this data, and discusses it. Each assessor then rates the assessees on a number of personal qualities, and on the basis of these ratings, allocates an overall assessment rating (OAR). These ratings and the OAR are discussed, and group ratings and OARs are arrived at. Thus the final OAR is (a) both an individual and a group product, and (b) only indirectly derived from the data, being filtered through the ratings of qualities.

Here is a list of the qualities rated in the IBM assessment centre: self-confidence; written communications; administrative ability; interpersonal contact; energy level; decision-making; resistance to stress; planning and organizing; persuasiveness; aggressiveness; risk-taking; oral communications. Such lists of qualities are normally those hypothesized to be of importance to the individual's success. Clearly, they are derived entirely from consideration of the job, and not at all from consideration of people. For example, the qualities tested in the pioneering ITT Studies by Bray and Grant (1966) were derived from a review of the literature and from discussions with managers in the company. The lists of qualities rated by different organizations differ considerably, and yet the sets of exercises employed differ little. One might assume that particular exercises were selected in order to test particular qualities; for example, the in-basket exercise to test administrative and organizational skills, and the leaderless group discussion to test interpersonal communication skills. However, it seems clear that organizations use exercises that are already available as evidence for whatever set of qualities they are looking for.

'Whatever the labels and definitions are for the selected variables, therefore, the meaning of variables within a program is strongly a function of the choice of instruments available to provide input for the judgements made' (Finkle, 1976, p. 873). The suspicion that the ratings of the qualities might be dependent upon the exercise from which they were derived was supported by the research of Hinrichs and Haanpera (1976). They tested 369 pre-management candidates for one organization in eight different countries. Candidates were given six typical exercises, and were rated on 14 personal characteristics on the basis of each of the six exercises. The correlation of ratings of all 14 qualities across six exercises was 0.49. Certain qualities taken individually correlated very poorly; administrative ability not at all, and written communications and planning and organizing 0.22 and 0.25 respectively. In order of increasing correlation across exercises, the other qualities were: decision-making, resistance to stress, creativity, interpersonal contact, energy level, analytical ability, mental alertness, persuasiveness, aggressiveness, self-confidence, and oral communications (0.73). These, of course, are precisely the results we would expect if we took account of the social psychological findings regarding the difficulty of predicting behaviour across situations.

Summarizing the last two paragraphs, therefore, we learn that the same exercises are used to test different qualities; that exercises are probably selected because they have been developed and are available; and that ratings of the same quality taken from different exercises agree little for many qualities. The conclusion must be that the availability of an exercise partly determines the score on a particular quality of an applicant.

7.2 HOW ARE ASSESSMENT CENTRE DECISIONS ARRIVED AT?

One of the reasons for the rating of personal qualities is the variety of uses to which assessment centres are put. They are very frequently used to decide whether an assessee is qualified to be promoted to a particular level of job, e.g. middle management. Thus the middle management posts in question might have been analysed to determine the qualities required, and the qualities to be rated selected accordingly. Similarly, when assessment centres are used, as they sometimes are, to discover the individual employee's training needs, a profile of qualities is useful. However, the use in which we are particularly interested here is for selection, and the rationale is that the assessment centre method can identify long-range potential. In this case the OAR is the appropriate predictor, and ratings of qualities are irrelevant.

It is possible, indeed, that the ratings of qualities detract from the predictive power of the OAR by making the inference of OAR from the data more indirect. Very few assessment centres adopt the procedure found to be most predictive of future performance by Sawyer (1966). This procedure involves collecting all the usual data, including qualities. Then, however, these data are treated statistically, and the final rating and decision are based on the previously established predictive power of each of the types of data. To quote an example; it might have been found on the basis of research that psychological tests were the best predictors of long-term promotion prospects, followed by interview ratings, with exercises third, and ratings of qualities last! The scores obtained by applicants on each of these measures would then be weighted proportionally, and an overall score arrived at. This overall score would represent the best statistical summary of the evidence in terms of its predictive power.

Assessment centres do not typically employ this procedure, however. Instead, the final stage is judgemental. The assessors weigh up the data, arrive at ratings of qualities, and derive OAR. They may be unaware, when making these judgements, of the proven relative predictive power of each of the measures. Or they may have been informed, but trust more to their 'clinical judgement'. Given the face validity and immediacy of exercises compared with tests, the obvious danger is that a disproportionate emphasis may be placed upon exercises as evidence. Interesting hints that this may indeed be the case are provided in Gardner and Williams' (1973) account of the Royal Navy's Admiralty Interview Board. The stated aim of the Board is to predict success in training, and research had demonstrated that the best predictors of this are tests of spatial and mechanical aptitude ($R = 0.45$), and civil service written examinations ($R = 0.38$). However, these predictors either hardly predicted the Board's OAR at all (tests) or were negatively related to it (exams), and the OAR predicted training success only $r = 0.22$. Thus the proven best predictors were largely ignored in arriving at the OAR. Exercises, on the other hand, have variable success in predicting training, but carry heavy weight for the OAR. Similar evidence is provided by Wollowick and McNamara (1969). Ratings of qualities, test results, and exercise performance taken together predicted promotion $R = 0.62$, whereas OAR predicted promotion $r = 0.37$. The insistence of assessors on exercising their judgement appears, then, to result in a considerable loss of predictive power.

How does this reduction occur, and why are assessors so insistent on retaining the final decision themselves? The immediate and obvious hypothesis for a social psychologist to entertain regarding the first of these questions is that of the effect of group processes. Decisions taken by groups have been shown repeatedly to differ from those taken by individual members of those groups, and it will be recalled that the OAR is arrived at after group discussion. However, research by Schmitt (1977) and Jones (personal communication) indicate that OARs and ratings of qualities made after group discussion do not differ greatly from those arrived at by individuals before it. Indeed, Sackett and Wilson (1982) found that assessors agreed on 77.6% of their ratings of qualities; where they disagreed, the outcome could be well predicted by taking the mean or the mode of the individuals' ratings.

The explanation must lie in the nature of the judgements made by individual assessors. These could differ from the statistically optimal decisions simply because the assessors attach different weights to the different measures employed. However, they could also differ because the assessors were adopting entirely different modes of decision-making. Instead of summating data from different sources, they could well be assessing the applicant against a positive stereotype—the ideal civil servant, middle manager, naval officer, etc. Judgements of success or failure to match up to this stereotype might be made during earlier parts of the procedure, affecting judgements of subsequent parts. Such judgements of acceptability might be arrived at when certain of the qualities in the stereotype are adjudged to be present, and others inferred as a consequence (see Chapter 2). A negative stereotype might also be present in assessors' minds. Given the anxiety of selectors not to perpetrate a 'false positive' error (selecting someone who should not have been selected), it is quite likely that only one or two of the features of this negative stereotype need to be inferred before an unfavourable judgement is arrived at.

It is difficult to know what sort of evidence could prove that such processes were at work. If it could be shown that those selection methods which offer most scope for such stereotypes predict OARs and also long-term promotion, then there are some grounds for maintaining the use of stereotypes as a tenable hypothesis. Anstey (1977) for example, reports better prediction of long-term promotion on the basis of the Civil Service Final Selection Board (an interview) than on the basis of the Civil Service Selection Board (a complete assessment centre procedure). Hinrichs (1978) found that managers' reading of personnel records was a better predictor of long-term promotion than an assessment centre. Huck and Bray (1976) found that black women received lower OARs than white women. These are just hints, however; and the lack of research on the processes by which decisions are made prevents firm conclusions from being drawn. Nevertheless, at last the users of, and researchers into, assessment centres are becoming aware that the social psychological processes of person perception and attribution are involved (Borman, 1982).

7.3 HOW VALID ARE ASSESSMENT CENTRES?

In terms of the psychometric properties of validity and reliability, the research is relatively weak when the widespread use of the assessment centre method is considered. The validity evidence is reviewed by Huck (1973), who points out that the data are derived from only four major USA organizations (ITT, SOHIO, IBM, and Sears). In addition, longitudinal data relating to the Civil Service Selection Board and the Royal Navy have been published in the UK. The seminal research was carried out by Bray and Grant (1966). Young junior managers were rated on 25 dimensions and also on an OAR. The situational exercises carried the heaviest statistical weight in predicting the

OAR, and also in predicting the criterion. The primary criterion measure was promotion to middle management within 7 years of assessment. For junior managers who had been recruited from college, the OAR correlated 0.44 with promotion, and for non-college managers, 0.71. Similar results were obtained by Kraut and Scott (1972) using a similar sample. Comparable degrees of validity were reported by Albrecht *et al.* (1964) and Bentz (1968) using supervisor and peer ratings as the criterion measures.

It is long-term advancement within the organization which is the favourite criterion measure, however, and here there is a very interesting finding: the relationship between OAR and degree of promotion or salary achieved actually increases over time. This holds true for a 30-year follow-up of senior civil servants (Anstey, 1977), an 8-year follow-up of sales staff (Hinrichs, 1978), and a 5-year follow-up of managers (Mitchel, 1975). Thus there is *prima facie* support for the idea that it is specifically long-term potential which assessment centres are measuring.

It is important to notice at this point that criterion measures do not necessarily correlate highly with each other. For example, Bray and Campbell (1968) used as their basic criterion measure of performance the observation of actual sales contacts made by the salesmen they had rated in the assessment centre. There was good prediction of this observed job behaviour on the basis of the assessment centre ratings. However, supervisors' ratings related poorly both with the assessment centre ratings and with the observed performance. Supervisors' ratings may be a poor criterion measure because they lack reliability (Thomson, 1970). It must be remembered that lack of reliability in either predictor or criterion measures lowers the upper limit of prediction statistically possible. While individual parts of the assessment centre procedure may have high reliability (Greenwood and McNamara, 1967; Jones, 1981), this is not enough.

More important than these technical difficulties, however, is the judgement as to whether these are suitable criteria to employ at all. As Klimoski and Strickland (1977) argue, such frequently used criteria as salary level and rate of promotion 'may have less to do with managerial effectiveness than managerial adaptation and survival' (p. 355). They suggest that assessment centre ratings may be reflecting the assessors' ideas of the sort of person who gets ahead in the organization, either because the assessors have a stereotype of the ideal company person, or because they know the sort of person who is promoted by those who have the authority to promote. The procedure, in a word, could be an exercise in self-perpetuation.

Some hints that this may be the case may be gleaned from the published research. In the account of the CSSB procedure (Anstey, 1971, 1977), for example, we learn that at the upper end of the criterion scale (rank attained) the interview rating was a better predictor than more objective measures, which predicted better at the lower end of the scale. In Hinrichs' (1978) research, he found that certain individual characteristics predicted better after 8 years; specifically, the correlation of rated aggressiveness predicted position attained 0.69, whereas the relationship was only 0.27 when the rating was originally made. Additionally, ascendancy, self-assurance, and economic and political values had increased in predictive power, whereas consideration, social and religious values, and responsibility had decreased. Despite the small number of subjects in this research, there is some suggestion that the qualities necessary for personal promotion, and those we might assume necessary for organizational relations, are incompatible.

Klimoski and Strickland (1977) suggest some alternative criterion measures, for example: the manager's assessed value to the organization; estimates of the costs of replacing him; measures of the extent to which the manager has achieved objectives; measures of contributions to the organization of whatever sort (sales contracts, inventions patented, contacts with other organizations effected, etc.); peer and subordinate as well as supervisor ratings. Moreover, there is a need to incorporate aspects of the organization as moderating variables—climate, employment practices, product technology. It is only when the benefits to the individual and to the organization are taken into account that meaningful criterion validity can be established.

7.4 HOW USEFUL ARE ASSESSMENT CENTRES?

It remains to ask whether the assessment centre method is so useful as to warrant the time and money it costs. Cascio and Sibley (1979) demonstrate that the costs of running assessment centres are minimal when compared with the benefits obtained from increased effectiveness. However, it is only when there is considerable variation in the effectiveness of managers as selected by other means that the introduction of an assessment centre procedure can have a pay-off. Once again, however, we have to return to the criterion problem; do the criterion measures which are typically used reflect effectiveness? If promotion is considered an adequate measure of effectiveness, then there are better ways of predicting promotion than by assessment centres. Hinrichs (1978), for example, obtained higher correlations using two managers' evaluations of long-term potential on the basis of evidence from personnel files than he did from OARs. As Hinrichs notes, (p. 600): 'It makes little sense to use a sledgehammer to swat a fly.' Moses (1973) even found that a short sledgehammer is little different from a long one in its effects.

On the other hand, there might be various serendipitous benefits to the organization and to the individual. Finkle (1976) notes that the managers who perform the assessments may improve their assessment skills as a result of the training received. They may also feel that they have a stake in a major feature of organizational policy, recruitment. Some senior managements consider that recruitment is such a major element in the organization's development and in their own power base that they are unwilling to surrender the responsibility. Indeed, some retain the right to approve or reject assessment centre recommendations. If this occurs, then the cynicism felt by the middle management assessors will probably negate other benefits of participation.

Another serendipitous outcome may be to the applicant's benefit. The assessment centre procedure, and especially the exercises, may act as a realistic job preview. Applicants may obtain a more realistic idea than they had before of the sort of task and the general values which the organization will be expecting of them. Indeed, the 'structural relations of assessors and assessees may simulate the relations between supervisors and subordinates in the organization at large. It may serve, therefore, as a 'realistic organizational preview' as well as a realistic job preview. Unfortunately, since they have got thus far in the selection process, and in the current economic climate, graduates may well accept any job offer made after their assessment centre performance. However, such acceptance does not necessarily imply long-term commitment. If the organization, either in its recruitment or its selection procedures, has not presented an accurate picture of its expectations of the individual, then disappointment of those expectations will perhaps result in turnover as soon as another opening presents itself (Wanous, 1978). Assessment centre exercises may come a little late in the social negotiation process to be of benefit in this respect. However, their potential as a source of information to the applicant is considerable. Cascio and Phillips (1979) found that annual turnover in a city corporation was reduced from 40% to 3% when work sample tests were used for selection purposes.

A final possible serendipitous benefit from the use of assessment centres is the well-established effect of severity of initiation (Aronson and Mills, 1959). If an individual has undergone a painful or difficult experience in order to become a member of a group he has to justify to himself the pain and the difficulty. They can only be justified if membership is considered really worthwhile. Since the initiation has already been undergone, the only way in which dissonance can be reduced is to evaluate membership highly. When the initiation takes the form of a selection procedure, beliefs as well as attitudes may be affected. For example, the accepted applicant may believe that the organization must be very selective indeed if it has to employ such a tough procedure. This boosts both the organization's value ('it must be good if so many apply') and the successful applicant's self-esteem ('I was successful—hundreds were not'). When a stringent selection procedure is followed by a severe initial training programme, as in the Royal Navy, identification with the organization may be very strong. However, it may be dangerous to place too much reliance upon this mechanism. It is the process of social exchange, conducted in many different types of episode, which determines the long-term relationship between individual and organization. The relationship is ultimately one of negotiation.

To conclude with Cascio and Sibley's (1979, p. 108) trenchant observation:

an optimal strategy for personnel selection may not be optimal for other personnel functions such as recruiting and training. Factors such as the loss resulting from selection error and the organisation's ability to evaluate success must also be considered. When attention is focussed solely on selection, to the exclusion of other related functions, serious sub-optimisation of the entire personnel system can result. In short, any selection procedure must be evaluated in terms of its total benefits to the organisation.

To which we could add: 'and to the individual and the community'.

7.5 GRADUATE RECRUITMENT: A SUMMARY

The main problem with graduate recruitment is that all the forms of assessment employed are tacitly assumed to be psychometric in nature. They are all based on the supposition that their primary purpose is to arrive at 'objective' assessments of applicants' characteristics, thereby predicting their future performance. As a consequence of these assumptions, conscientious efforts are sometimes made to rule out 'biases', subjective intrusions which distort objective accuracy. Such efforts are doomed to failure, since all the forms of assessment employed are social episodes. By implication, those modes of construing social reality which we habitually employ in social episodes will inevitably intrude. There is no point in trying to eradicate them; a far more sensible approach is to utilize them for all they are worth. Instead of evaluating every form of assessment in terms of the degree to which it matches up with the psychometric criteria of reliability and validity, we should seek to understand the psychological processes which underlie it. Theoretical understanding of each assessment method is infinitely preferable to thoughtless empiricism. Such understanding enables us to perceive the unique processes underlying each method, and hence its possible unique uses. Allied to our overall analysis of the selection procedure as a process of social exchange, understanding of each method permits general recommendations to be made regarding how selection might most appropriately be conducted.

First, however, it is worth recalling the evidence in Chapters 5–7 that social processes do continually intrude into graduate selection methods. We noted evidence that some recruiters preferred application forms which gave evidence of stability, others of variety; it is hard not to conclude that they were preferring applicants who were like themselves. In the interview applicants were judged on first impressions, judgements which interviewers subsequently confirmed by their questioning. Interviewers used non-verbal cues to make their judgements, but were unaware that they were doing so. They attributed characteristics to the applicant on the basis of unexpected behaviour, not on the basis of regular and predictable behaviour; and, as in many social episodes, there is doubt, in the minds of applicants at least, what the rules of the episode are, and whether their objectives are those of the interviewer. In the case of the final stage of selection, the assessment centre, we have seen that the exercises may well be serving the function of informing the applicant of some of the tasks he will have to perform. We have also discussed the possibility that overall assessment ratings may not be the result of a cool weighing-up of independent items of data, but of the exercise of assessors' implicit personality theories.

We have also considered alternative uses for these assessment methods, based upon (a) the nature of the psychological processes which are involved in their execution and (b) the overall conceptualization of selection as part of the process of social exchange. These uses may be summarized as follows.

The organization's *recruitment literature* and job advertisements should be construed as an effort to communicate its expectations, norms, values, and image to possible applicants. They should not be treated as an effort to attract the maximum number of applicants, thereby improving the selection ratio. They are the organization's first communication with the applicant in the overall process of social exchange which may conceivably last for the whole of his working life. The message, therefore, has got to be consistent with other messages sent during the selection procedure, and, if possible, with those sent during the first period of employment (Wanous, 1976, 1977, 1979). If this condition is not met, the applicant may commit himself further to the selection process, and then receive contradictory messages. Having made his commitment on the basis of his first view of the organization, and its congruence with his self-concept, he will feel betrayed. Unable or unwilling to withdraw from the final stages of the selection procedure to which he has already committed so much of himself, he will nevertheless not be committed to the organization. Hence he will probably use the training opportunities offered initially while looking for another job. The organization suffers the worst outcome for itself possible—spending resources upon an individual who bestows the benefits of that expenditure upon a rival organization. In a recent survey of UK organizations, Parsons and Hutt (1981) found data which bear out this analysis. These authors surveyed over 200 firms in industry and commerce, and discovered that half of their graduate recruits had left them after 5 years, but that most of these losses took place during the first 3. Of those who left, one in three considered that they had received misleading information during the recruitment and selection procedure.

The *application form* can be seen as a mode of self-presentation, in which the applicant is encouraged to review his past achievements and experiences in the light of his background and opportunity. He can also be allowed to present his view of himself, his strengths and weaknesses and the way he has responded to demands made upon him. He may be requested to indicate his intentions regarding his employment and subsequent career, what he expects to be asked to do, and how he imagines himself in 10 years' time. Such an application form permits self-assessment, and makes use of those psychological processes which are peculiarly involved. Only the individual has real access to his self-concept, his intentions, and his aspirations. He is likely to be able to provide a useful profile of his strengths and weaknesses and to give an account of his past response to role expectations. This type of application form can aid the process of social exchange considerably. It firstly enables the applicant to express and clarify his self-concept. Secondly, it provides an initial picture which both parties can use at interview as a basis for further discussion. Furthermore, the applicant's view of self in the future, and by implication his view of the organization's present and future expectations for him, will also be available, so that the interviewer can assess its accuracy and offer more correct information.

It should be remembered, however, that organizations often use the application form as their sole means of pre-selection. Therefore they are comparing the applicant's occupational self-concept with their own expectations of him; and, to the extent that his idea of his future expresses his current understanding of what the organization will expect of him, they can also assess the realism of this understanding. Furthermore, they can compare the applicant's past record with his expectations of the future and judge how realistically the two are related. Nevertheless, such a use of the application form for pre-selection is very much second-best; it permits no real communication between the parties. The organization cannot be sure that the applicant has expressed his view of himself clearly, nor the extent to which he understands what the organization will expect of him.

Application forms may be augmented by *references*. The advantage of these is that they permit assessments to be made which potentially are based upon a considerable amount of wide-ranging evidence. As was argued in Chapter 3, this behavioural evidence can only be accurately recalled if cues are given regarding typical situations in which it occurred. Referees could be requested for information regarding the applicant's response to new role demands made upon him in the past; and regarding performance of tasks similar to those which will be expected of him by the organization.

The *initial interview* is a crucial episode in the social exchange process. Confusion about rules and roles seems widespread among applicants, with the consequence that even the initial conditions for successful communication are not always met. Furthermore, while one of the applicant's objectives may be to discover more about the organization's expectations, the interviewer's is currently more likely to be to gain evidence upon which to base an assessment of the personal attributes of the applicant. This assessment may well be matched against a positive stereotype of the ideal employee and/or negative stereotype of the false positive choice—the type of person who has been selected in the past with dire consequences. Hence the interview does not at present permit the communication of the appropriate messages from either side. The interviewer is asking questions aimed at assessing the applicant; he is not trying to discover what the applicant thinks the organization will expect of him. The applicant is trying to present himself as his vision of the interviewer's ideal employee.

There are two functions of the interview from a social exchange standpoint. The first function is for the organization's expectations to be communicated in such a way that the applicant understands and accepts them. One means towards this end is for the interviewer to discover what the applicant's present level of understanding of those expectations is. A more realistic understanding may result from the correction of specific misapprehensions. However, if the interviewer can persuade the applicant to clear up any questions he has regarding the organization, this is surely a preferable method. Unfortunately, the applicant may feel unwilling to ask such questions, since he may fear that unwelcome inferences may be drawn from any display of ignorance on his part. He may well have heard of the inclination of many interviewers to treat the applicant's 'homework' on the organization as evidence of the strength of his motivation to join it. Alternatively, he may have little idea of the questions to ask, since he knows little of the nature of organizations.

The second function of the interview is to communicate the applicant's view of himself, past, present, and above all, future. While the interviewer may be interested in discovering how this self-concept tallies with the evidence of his record hitherto, this is not the prime objective. The prime objective is to discover how it tallies with the organization's present and likely future expectations; for it is the extent of this congruence which will predict the success of future social exchange.

Hence both parties have the same objective. They both wish to discover organizational expectations and self-concept in order to estimate the congruence between the two. They need especially to have notions of the estimated futures of these two elements; their future outlines and their degree of probable responsiveness to each other. Thus we would expect the interviewer to refer to the career development policy of the organization, and the applicant to his own long-term career hopes and plans. Above all, we would expect both the elements, self-concept and organizational expectations, to be covered in a broad way. The extent to which both parties anticipate a clear distinction between private and work lives and the repercussions work will have on lifestyle; the extent of initial responsibility, training, and the nature of supervisory help; the group loyalties typically inculcated in the organization and the norms and values which underpin them; the organization's present and likely future policy position on such issues as discrimination, the environment, participation and industrial relations, new technology, and conditions of employment. These are but a few of the elements required for a broad-ranging understanding by both parties. If the organization has realized the breadth of understanding of itself required by the applicant, it may have succeeded in designing its application form and recruitment literature in such a way as to save responsibility falling so heavily upon the interviewer. However, the interview is still a vitally necessary part of the procedure, since it is a communication episode offering instant feedback to both parties.

The *assessment centre* offers the opportunity for interviews and a great deal more. In particular, it offers the applicant the chance to sample some of the tasks he will shortly be expected to carry out; it serves as a realistic job preview (Wanous, 1979). It also offers the organization the opportunity to estimate, by means of exercises, the present competence and trainability of the applicant in tasks for which his university course is unlikely to have prepared him. Aside from the exercises, the assessment centre also often includes the administration of psychological tests. The results of these can provide additional information to the organization regarding the applicant's aptitudes in areas which his record has covered inadequately. If they are communicated to the applicant, together with a profile of the aptitudes appropriate for the initial job, the applicant himself can judge his suitability. Indeed, profiles are already presented to assessees when the purpose is to establish training needs rather than to select. Similarly, psychological tests of personality can provide useful information for both parties; they cover the sorts of behaviour to which neither applicant nor referee is likely to pay attention or remember. Such stable and enduring patterns of habitual behaviour are possibly relevant, to the extent that they might render certain sorts of organizational expectations uncongenial. On the other hand, a more direct way of discovering how the applicant is likely to react to certain sorts of demand is to ask him. The assessment centre method has proved successful in predicting long-term promotion for those who stay with the organization; middle and senior managers are good at choosing those like themselves. Whether they reject those who might have benefited the organization more, or lose such entrants after a year or two, is a matter for organizations to decide.

What is most important is to conclude all the three episodes of the selection procedure with a discussion regarding the decision taken or to be taken. After the decision is taken on the application form the applicant should be informed that the organization had decided that it was in neither party's best interests to continue the process further. However, this was not an evaluation of the applicant's personal worth, but a judgement regarding the probability of success of a long-term relationship. The interview, too, may conclude with a decision, this time taken by both parties in consultation. It may be more useful for both parties to take more time to consider the degree of congruence, however, and in this case a discussion of the decision to be taken by both parties can conclude the interview. Finally, the assessment centre is ideally suited to a final session in which both parties indicate what they now think they know about each other. The importance of such exchanges to the organization may be considerable. The drawing of attention to decision-making procedures and evidence is usually useful. The word gets around among students that the organization cares; and as far as the applicant is concerned, she may, even though rejected, not be put off from applying to other organizations of the same type; many are (Herriot et al., 1980).

Thus, in summary, the graduate recruitment procedure can be seen as a series of episodes of social exchange. After each episode the two parties have to take a decision on the basis of congruence of self-concept and organizational expectations. After the first episode information has been exchanged between the parties; however, the nature and format of this information may not have been designed with the communication of self-concept and expectations as the primary objective. After the second episode, the interview, a much more informed decision is in principle possible for both parties. However, such is the uncertainty over roles and objectives in current practice that this end is not often achieved. After the third episode, the assessment centre, certain sorts of information could have been fully exchanged. However, the applicant may still have had inadequate opportunity to elucidate his ideas of his future, and the organization its plans.

Of course, the notion of degree of congruence as the basis for both parties' decisions is not altogether a helpful one. It implies a degree of agreement both between the immediate expectations of both parties and also between their longer-term estimations of the future. What such congruence estimates cannot encompass is the degree of adaptability of the organization and of the individual when things do not turn out as expected. The best predictors of such adaptability will be evident from previous sections of this book. In the case of the organization, an examination of its structure and function relative to its technological, economic, and social environment will reveal its adaptability (see Chapters 1 and 4). In the case of the individual, his record in respect of new and perhaps unexpected role demands will be relevant. So will his previous efforts at negotiating new roles for himself. The danger of predicting behaviour from few such instances in special situations, however, will by now have become clear.

8

Careers and Decisions

8.1 CAREER AND SELF-CONCEPT

The emphasis hitherto has been upon the idea of assessment of the individual by the organization. Consequently, we have concentrated upon what the organization does with the applicant in order to assess the extent to which she is likely to fulfil its expectations. We have seen, however, that these events must be construed as a social exchange, a relationship rather than an assessment. In the light of this realization it must be evident that we have paid little attention to the graduate as one of the parties in this relationship. Moreover, we have implied an extraordinary request of recruiters: to consider the applicant's view of herself as the most important information to be obtained if the negotiation is to be successful. In order to justify such a request, we must present the evidence which indicates the central part played by the self-concept in the occupational behaviour of graduates. We will also have to explore not merely the *functions* which the self-concept plays, but also some of its *content*. That is, we shall have to examine what is known about such things as the values and expectations of graduates, whence they are derived, and how they change.

First, however, we must place the self-concept into its context: the context within which it is changing and developing. That context is best conceptualized as the individual's *career*. The broadest possible definition of a career is that given by Super (1980) where it is taken to be 'the combination and sequence of roles played by a person during the course of a lifetime' (p. 282). Van Maanen and Schein (1977) suggest that 'the concept is a shorthand notation for a particular set of activities with a natural unfolding history—involvement over time in a given role or across a series of roles' (p. 31). One feature which both these definitions have in common is the emphasis upon the concept of role. Super (1980, p. 285) goes on to make explicit the social exchange process which the use of the term implies.

97

The term 'role' needs to be understood and defined in terms of both expectations and performance. *Expectations* can be categorised as (1) the expectations of observers, and as (2) the conceptions of the player. *Performance* also has two definitions: (1) enactment of the roles as shown by satisfaction and satisfactoriness, and (2) shaping of the role, as both it and the expectations of others are redefined by the actor better to suit the developing conception of the role. It is in *role shaping*, as well as in the *choice* of positions and roles, that the individual acts as the synthesizer of personal and situational role determinants.

Thus, for Super, the individual is in dynamic relation with the expectations of others. Thus the recruitment of graduates is to be seen as one particular set of episodes of social exchange within a whole series.

The second feature which Super's and Van Maanen and Schein's definitions of career share is that neither insists that the roles concerned are all related to work. On the contrary:

> one recent by-product of this somewhat eclectic concern for the individual in the workplace has been the realisation that *change* must be central to any account of the person's relationship to a job. An understanding of this relationship at any particular time must be based on knowledge of the changes that typically occur in a person's life and psychology as a result of passage through the life cycle (Van Maanen and Schein, 1977, p. 33).

Super goes so far as to specify nine major roles played during the life-cycle and four principal theatres in which they are played. The roles are child, student, leisurite, citizen, worker, spouse, homemaker, parent, and pensioner. This order corresponds to the order in which the positions are typically first occupied. Not everyone occupies all positions during their career. The four theatres are the home, the community, the school and college, and the workplace. Roles are normally associated with one theatre, but many spill over into others (e.g. some people take work home). Clearly, individuals will be playing more than one role, in more than one theatre, at any one point in their careers. Super terms this simultaneous combination of roles the *lifestyle*. However, during the course of a career lifestyles change, since 'roles wax and wane in importance and in the quality of performance, theatres are entered and deserted' (Super, 1980, p. 288).

Super (1977) has devised a 'life–career rainbow' to illustrate the career pattern. This presents the nine roles set against the chronology of the life span. It indicates the approximate age in middle-class western industrial society at which the onset of the role occurs, and the relative emphasis upon each role at different periods in the life-cycle. The *caveat* regarding the cultural specificity of the life–career rainbow is necessary, as is demonstrated by its representation of the worker role as commencing after age 20. However, the value for our purposes of the rainbow is its visual impact in pointing out the number and intensity of roles which are commenced during the late teens and twenties. Citizen, worker, spouse, homemaker, and parent roles are quite frequently all undertaken for the first time within this limited time-span.

Also of value is Super's idea of changes of theatre. A change of position, or even of occupation, can occur without a change of theatre; but during the late teens and the twenties, the parental home is often left, and so is the college. The workplace and one's own home are new theatres. Using a more sociologically orientated conceptual framework, the young person is moving from one type of institution into another. The values and norms of different institutional types are likely to differ more than the values within different parts of the same type. Thus while the student may have noticed differences between high school and university, those differences are as nothing compared to those between the norms and values to be found in education and in industry. Thus a change of theatre implies a very radical change in the role expectations directed towards the new entrant; for she will be expected to take on the norms and values of the new theatre.

The process by which these roles are taken on has already been described within the framework of social exchange theory. To recapitulate, it was suggested that role expectations are sent by the organization and received and hopefully understood by the individual. She then examines the extent to which they are congruent with her self-concept. She might merely comply in fulfilling incongruent expectations, but such compliance would not result in any internalization of the role. Only if there is some perceived congruence will internalization occur and the self-concept adapt to the new role which she has accepted (perhaps in a modified form after negotiation). Such a dynamic change in the self-concept in interaction with the environment is a feature of several accounts of personal development, for example, that of Erikson (Munley, 1975).

It follows that during the period when the graduate leaves college she is undergoing a period of considerable change in her self-concept. This is because she is engaged in several different sorts of social exchange regarding new roles and new theatres simultaneously. Some of these new roles—e.g. wife, mother, and worker—may be in conflict, with the consequence that these may be conflicting elements in the self-concept (or a perceived need to reject one of the roles). Not only so; those role expectations which relate to work may come at several levels simultaneously. There may be the general expectation to leave the education theatre and enter the *workplace* (often coincidental with the expectation to leave the parental home). There may be more specific expectations regarding the taking on of an *occupational* role. Finally, there may be tasks, norms, and values expected of the incumbent of a particular position in a particular *organization*.

All of these role expectations are entirely relevant to the graduate's negotiation with a particular organization. At the level of *lifestyle and theatre*, the combination of roles the individual is prepared to take on is of great relevance. If she is unwilling to leave the parental home or the college, but wishes to push back the frontiers of theoretical physics, then the most basic expectations of a *worker* are likely to be disappointed. If she is unsure whether she is prepared to sell goods or services to customers or clients, then certain *occupational* role requirements are unlikely to be met. If she is unwilling to spend the first year of employment moving around several different plants in order to receive general management training, she will fail to play the required *organizational* role.

Organizations will incorporate all these three levels of expectations in their role-requirements of graduates. Hence the whole career, as broadly defined by Super, is the legitimate interest of the recruiter. By implication, the self-concept is also the legitimate interest of the recruiter, to the extent that it incorporates past and present roles and also predicts the extent to which work, occupational, and organizational roles will be considered congruent and incorporated. It follows that the traditional academic analysis of occupational choice, followed at a later period by organizational choice, is a misconception. Organizations choose graduates, and graduates choose organizations, because they have negotiated on the basis of career and self-concept.

8.2 SELF-CONCEPT AND ANTICIPATORY SOCIALIZATION

We can no longer avoid a more detailed consideration of the self-concept, given its centrality to the whole argument of this book. To sum up the main features of our treatment of the self-concept thus far, we may say, first, that the self-concept has been seen hitherto in process terms. It has been considered as the way by which the expectations of others have been perceived and evaluated, and our responses to those expectations monitored. Second, it has been seen as having a past, present, and future aspect; it incorporates the roles we have taken on in the past and perform now, but it also conceives of likely responses to future role expectations. This future orientation is of the utmost importance to the present argument. For it will be argued that it is only when the graduate has developed a strong future orientation as part of her self-concept that she is in a position to engage in the social exchange process with employers.

The social exchange process as we have characterized it in the graduate recruitment case is of the organization presenting to the graduate the values, norms, and task expectations that the organization will have of her if she joins. Yet many of the expectations that the organization will actually have remain uncommunicated. This is because the recruiter *assumes* that the graduate has already come to terms with the change of theatre from education to the world of work; and with the general lifestyle expectations of a particular occupation. It is with shock and surprise that the recruiter for a manufacturing organization reports after interview that applicants 'think making a profit is evil', or 'believe all engineering to be dirty and dangerous'. The reason for such self-presentation on the part of the applicant is that she has not developed the general worker nor the specific occupational elements of the future part of her self-concept, let alone the notion of herself as a potential employee of this particular organization. She does not possess a way of anticipating *any* of the expectations the organization will make of her, nor of imagining her own likely responses to them. Thus she comes to the interview in no position to negotiate at the same level of discourse as the recruiter.

How might such a future element of the self-concept be developed, granted that in the case of the graduate it cannot be inferred directly from past experience in the theatre of work, in the appropriate occupation, and in a similar organization? There are several answers to this question, and the evidence which suggests that they may each be true will be reviewed later. First, the graduate may have acquired information about work in general, about occupations, and about specific organizations. This may have been in the form of literature, second-hand reports from friends, or a presentation by an organization. Second, the individual may have actually experienced work at a realistic job preview, in vacation work, or as a sandwich student. Third, she may have engaged in various activities at different stages of her life which have incorporated elements of the roles of work, occupation, or organization (for example, positions of responsibility at school).

Regardless of whether these anticipatory roles are undertaken voluntarily or thrust upon her, they present the opportunity for an actual test of their congruence with the self-concept. They may result in the individual actually incorporating the roles into her self-concept long before the organization presents them as what is expected. Or, at the least, they will have offered the opportunity of rehearsing the social exchange so that she will be used to asking herself whether she could ever become what the organization wants. It is with justice that sociologists term this process 'anticipatory socialization'. From the point of view of self-concept theory, it permits the self-concept to incorporate or reject elements in advance of the 'real' role demands of employment. Hence it permits more informed estimates of the congruence of role with self; it also reduces the amount of change that the self-concept inevitably has to undertake when one theatre is left and another entered. Where the opportunities for such anticipatory activities exist, and where the individual avails herself of them, we may use the term *exploration*.

There are, however, other elements of the self-concept which have only been mentioned in passing hitherto. Super (1963) has analysed the self-concept in some detail, and distinguishes *dimensions* of the self-concept from *metadimensions*. Dimensions include such characteristics as intelligence, gregariousness, etc.; that is, dimensions indicate the individual's own estimation of the extent to which she 'possesses the qualities' typically assessed in selection procedures. Metadimensions include such features as self-esteem, stability of the self-concept, its clarity, abstraction, refinement, certainty, and realism. Some authors add the element of salience—how prominent is her self-concept in the mind of the individual? From Rogers (1959) comes the idea of the ideal self, but as we shall see, this is a very good predictor of occupational behaviour when it is defined as 'what one would like to become'. When Super analysed the nine metadimensions he postulated and related them to various features of career progression, he found that self-esteem and scope accounted for most of the variance. As the evidence will show, self-esteem and internal locus of control play a major part in predicting graduates' occupational choice. It is entirely to be expected that metadimensions such as self-esteem will be the main predictors in the case of graduates. This is because graduates' specific experiences and the specific characteristics inferred from them in their student lives are largely irrelevant or possibly even inimical to the world of work. It is such general features as their overall evaluation of themselves derived from the whole of their previous life and experience which predict occupational success.

8.3 STAGES AND TASKS

First, however, it is important to look in greater detail at the process of transition whereby the graduate moves from one theatre to another, relinquishing certain roles and taking on others. To the extent that the graduate has internalized the norms and values of the academic system into her self-concept the transition from an academic theatre to the world of work is likely to be difficult; for it involves actually losing aspects of the self which, if her self-esteem is high, are likely to be much valued by the graduate (Wooler and Humphreys, 1979). For example, she may have internalized a value system which places high priority on the importance of knowledge for its own sake and disinterested enquiry in the process of its acquisition (two of Merton's norms of science). Thus these are key losses to be faced, and the temptation to avoid them must be considerable.

However, Jordaan (1974) indicates how strong the pressure might be to make the transition, and how important it is to make it at the expected time in one's life:

> these expectations, based on what is thought to be typical of persons at a given stage and on what society would like to see happen at that stage, can be conceived of as developmental tasks. . . . Failure to deal with a developmental task at the appropriate time, or conspicuous lack of success in dealing with it, is believed to impede or delay the individual's development and to make it difficult for him to proceed to, or deal effectively with, the tasks of the next stage.

Thus these developmental tasks are to be seen as normative and age-graded (e.g. starting work), as opposed to normative history-graded events (for example, economic depression or the onset of information technology) and to non-normative events (for example, the suffering of an industrial accident or the inheritance of a large sum of money).

It is important to stop at this point, and reflect upon the use of the term 'stages' by Jordaan in the quotation above. Much recent theorizing in life-span developmental psychology has posited the existence of an invariant sequence of stages. Levinson *et al.* (1978), for example, on the basis of a sample of but 40 men from the eastern United States, 10 from each of four occupational groups, propose an extremely detailed and age-defined theory of life-span development. They distinguish four major eras (childhood and adolescence, early, middle, and late adulthood) and many stages within these eras. All of these stages and eras, and the transitions between them, are tied to various chronological age bands. One would have thought that the experience of cognitive developmental psychologists would have served as a warning against such age-specific formulations. The theories of Piaget have been repeatedly demonstrated to be false in respect of the age of transition postulated from one stage to the next (see e.g. Bryant, 1974; Meadows, 1983). This is because one can never say that because an individual does not demonstrate a particular cognitive process when faced with certain tasks, therefore she does not possess the capacity for that process. In other words, one should be very chary of inferring absence of competence from a specific poor performance.

For Levinson *et al.* developmental tasks are what define each period or stage:

> A period ends when its tasks lose their primacy and new tasks emerge to initiate a new period. The orderly progression of periods stems from the recurrent change in tasks. The most fundamental tasks of a stable period are to make firm choices, rebuild the life structure and enhance one's life within it. Those of a transitional period are to question and reappraise the existing structure, to search for new possibilities in self and world, and to modify the present structure enough so that a new one can be formed (Levinson *et al.*, 1978, p. 53).

In such an account as Levinson's, the stages sound as though they are an inevitable progression, a preordained series of adaptations by the individual of herself to the environment and of the environment to herself. While Levinson preserves the idea of a series of dynamic transactions between individual and environment, he endeavours to specify what form these transactions take, and at what age they occur. Instead of making the assumption of transition between invariant stages, it seems preferable to consider the transition or 'passage' (Sheehy, 1976) as being between theatres and between roles.

Interesting recent work by Owens (1982) further emphasizes the importance of role expectations in individual development. Owens and his colleagues (Neiner and Owens, 1982) administered biographical questionnaires to college students at three points in time: at entry to college, during final year, and around 7 years after graduation. Each questionnaire sampled different information, yet membership of a particular subset of students at one point in time predicted membership of the same subset later in many cases. These 'pathway followers' are discriminated from those students whose career pathway was not predictable. Pathway and non-pathway followers are differentiated by such features as religious activity, intellectualism, athletic interest, and academic achievement (male students) and by warmth of maternal relationship, social leadership, conformity to the female role, and popularity with the opposite sex (female students). It seems, then, that those who conform to typical role expectations (in this case the roles for male and female college students and graduates'in the southern United States), do follow a predictable pattern in their lives. However, there is clear evidence of the individual's capacity to negotiate several different pathways within the usual role expectations, or to reject so many of them that her career is entirely unpredictable. As Hopson and Scally (1980, p. 181) put it: 'For ourselves, the diversity of adult experience makes us reluctant to talk of stages, cycles, or seasons. There is an inevitability to all those terms which appears too restrictive.'

Nevertheless, we are concerned with those upon whom there is a strong social expectation at one point in their lives to make a transition from one theatre to another. The new roles awaiting them in their new theatre are largely novel to them, and may well threaten aspects of their present selves. How are they to react?

8.4 TRANSITIONS

Transitions, then, are likely to be difficult. The transition from college to the world of work is a change of theatre and roles, a change which is likely to affect core aspects of the self. Recent theorizing by clinical counselling psychologists (e.g. Adams et al., 1980) suggests that there are common models of response to a wide variety of transitions. The earliest observations related to reactions to personal loss (e.g. loss of one's spouse or one's job). However, the analysis was subsequently extended to other transitional situations in which one loses an aspect of one's self. Counselling psychologists refer to an initial stage of immobilization, when the individual does not know what to do because of the unfamiliarity of the new situation. The next response is to minimize the change, to represent it as less than it is. Thus the losses associated with it appear not too heavy. When reality is perceived, depression is a frequent reaction, but when it is accepted the individual can unhook from the past. She is now in a position to test out possible approaches to the new situation, and tries to put a meaning onto it. Having found a satisfactory meaning, she can internalize it so that the new role requirements become part of her self-concept.

The origins of this account in clinical psychology and in observed reactions to bereavement are obvious, and the consequent emphasis upon the inevitability of the loss is inappropriate in the present discussion. For example, some of us refused to accept the suggestion that we should come down from the ivory tower and leave the education system at all; we became eternal students and, in the end, professional academics. Others left the academic theatre, but refused to accept the commonly held expectation of them that they would enter the world of work. Thus, this major transition from theatre to theatre must be seen as another subject of social exchange and negotiation; not as an inevitable and pre-ordained event.

Nevertheless, the importance of the clinical analysis is that it points to the strain and loss involved in making transitions. It suggests that there are various ways of coping with such transitional strain. First, one can make a proactive response—anticipating the expectation to leave one theatre and enter another, and taking some sort of preparatory action. This may take the form of giving oneself more time to think about it and plan for it; for example, the student in her final year may allocate a priority position in her cognitive timetable to considering her future. She may even temporarily drop out of the furious academic cramming of the final year for a couple of weeks in order to do so. She may also establish various zones of stability in other areas of her life so as to buffer her against the transition—a serious personal relationship, for example, designed to last whatever else changes. Another proactive response is to associate with others facing the same transition, or else to solicit help from professional counsellors. The idea of anticipatory socialization offers various half-way houses—the possibility of adjusting gradually to the transition by trying out in advance how one might react to the new roles.

For the student, applying for a job is in itself a proactive response. It is a (very obvious) way of anticipating the fact that she will be expected to move into the world of work after finishing college. The transition is easier if a specific role in the new theatre is already reserved for her; but, as has been stressed repeatedly, the student's application may have other proactive functions as well as this. It may well be a form of anticipatory socialization, in which she uses the social episodes of the selection procedure. She is trying out in advance her future self against the likely future demands of work in general or of a particular occupation (as well as of a specific employer).

At least the graduate applicant is acting in a proactive manner, for which she deserves credit. The force of academic norms and values at university is such that performance in degree examinations is considered the correct preoccupation for final-year students. This signal of academic excellence is the culmination of all those other academic hurdles, the successful leaping of which has enabled the student to achieve status and reward in the academic theatre hitherto. Moreover, final examinations form a powerful ritual conclusion to role performance in this theatre and, together with graduation day, bring down the curtain with a finality which then permits the future to be considered. If this has been the response of the student to transitional strain, however, then the only possible action is reactive, after the event. Because the academic theatre has been left in the course of events rather than as a conscious decision, the reactive response is more likely to be withdrawal or disengagement from the task.

However, the making of a conscious decision is not necessarily in itself a solution to the problems of transition. It may relieve the anxiety associated with transitional strain, but be unconsidered. In terms of the present analysis, internal (mental) or external negotiation regarding the congruence of self and role demands would not have been undertaken in such unconsidered decision. Planned procrastination may be an entirely appropriate proactive response. For example, Herriot *et al.* (1980) found that engineering students in their final year often increased the number of alternative engineering specialities they were willing to consider; this adaptability resulted in the vast majority securing the type of job they wanted. The picture of the final-year student narrowing down the range of alternatives she is willing to consider before deciding on one, and then trying for it, is wide of the mark in this instance.

In sum, the proactive response mode, typical of the individual with an internal locus of control (Rotter, 1966), is clearly appropriate to the student in her final year. It is another example of the benefits of developing a future self-concept and rehearsing future social exchanges, which Super insists are crucial to occupational and career success.

8.5 DECISIONS

There is a more micro level of analysis than we have considered hitherto, however. It is that of individual decisions.

Decision points occur before and at the time of taking on a new role, of giving up an old role, and of making significant changes in the nature of an existing role. These are illustrated by . . . decisions to enter or not to enter the labor market, to apply for and accept or decline a particular job . . .' (Super, 1980, p. 291).

Such decisions, according to Super, involve the the individual

becoming aware of an impending decision (*growth*); he or she formulates the question, reviews premises, identifies facts needed to round out an understanding of the situation, seeks these data, evaluates and weighs the old and new data, identifies alternative lines of action, and considers their various possible outcomes and their respective probabilities (*exploration*); he or she then weighs the alternatives in terms of values or objectives, selects the preferred plan of action, stores the alternatives for possible future reference, and pursues the plan on either an exploratory basis or with a more definite but still tentative commitment (*establishment*) (Super, 1980, p. 293).

This account however, is a prescriptive rather than a descriptive one. It is 'rational, emergent career decision making such as might be the result of effective career education in a well-adjusted, well-situated individual' (Super, 1980, p. 293). Are decisions taken in this cool rational way in practice? Much of the evidence suggests, on the contrary, that the self-concept is involved in a much more powerful way. Graduates are much concerned with their self-esteem and with the approval of others; they look to their peers for information and advice, and are prey to considerable anxiety regarding these decisions. This is precisely what we would expect from our previous analyses; current aspects of the self and of self-esteem are at risk in a transition; new and unfamiliar roles will require adjustments which the graduate may not be willing to make.

The rational model of decision-making has had some success in predicting graduates' intentions and choices, however. The basic elements of decision theory are the individual's beliefs about the probability of each of several outcomes; and her evaluation of those outcomes. Each probability is multiplied by its evaluation, and those products are summed. Such a sum of products is obtained for each of the courses of action being considered, and that alternative which has the highest sum is chosen. The model is thus a linear additive one, with alternatives being compared by the decision-maker on the basis of their overall balance of benefits and costs (subjectively defined). Such a model has been used in a wide variety of research topics in organizational psychology (Mitchell and Beach, 1976; Mitchell, 1982). Investigations of graduate job choice indicate that it predicted with some success the choice of a business career (Mitchell and Knudson, 1973) and, indeed, of functional speciality within business (Wanous, 1972). Similar success was obtained in predicting preference for specializations in professional psychology (Holmstrom and Beach, 1973). Organizational choice is also predicted by the same model (Oldham, 1976; Herriot et al., 1980). One immediate caution must be added at this point, however. It is that the criterion variable in these studies was often a measure of preferences or intentions regarding which of the alternatives the students would choose, obtained at the same time as the predictor variables were measured. Hence the subjective probabilities and evaluations of outcomes might be *post hoc* rationalizations of a known preference. The predictive power of the model when the criterion is the occupation, function, or organization actually chosen or entered is much decreased.

There are, however, more serious objections to the use of the rational decision-making model as an account of graduates' behaviour during their final year. These objections may be summarized under two main headings. First, the linear additive model is more prescriptive than descriptive. It ignores the entire social and career context of behaviour. Second, it ignores the vast range of individual difference in modes of decision-making evidenced in the research literature. The title of Janis and Mann's (1977) superb review and analysis exemplifies the first of these objections; it is entitled *Decision-making—a psychological analysis of conflict, choice, and commitment*. After outlining the prescriptive model, Janis and Mann review other modes of decision-making which are more likely to be employed. Perhaps the most likely is the method known as 'satisficing'. That is, an alternative is accepted as soon as it comes along, provided that it meets some single pre-set criterion.

Often this criterion is 'Is it better than the present state of affairs?'. Hence, in the case of satisficing, there is no need to compare alternatives simultaneously. It is the probable strategy for an individual upon whom pressure to move from one theatre or role to another is being put. Alternatively, the criteria for acceptability of an alternative when it comes along may be relatively few in number and easy to apply. If several alternatives present themselves, they may be looked at in random order sequentially; the first one that meets the criteria may be chosen, leaving others untested. Clearly, the satisficing mode is often reactive in nature—the individual is reacting to pressure to decide, and also to the occurrence of alternatives as they present themselves.

There are other modes of decision-making as well. Mathematical decision theorists (e.g. Coombs *et al.*, 1970) have stressed the comparative model, as opposed to the independent linear additive model. By this they refer to the comparison of the alternative choices along one criterion dimension. Any alternative which fails to match up to the first criterion considered can be eliminated. Then the second criterion can be applied, and more eliminated until the preferred alternative emerges. This mode may be particularly likely to be employed when the graduate is faced with alternative job offers which she finds hard to distinguish between. There may be only one feature which clearly differentiates them for her, since they do not differ much on other criteria of which she is aware. Thus she may employ this single criterion because it enables her to make a decision, not because it is in itself an important factor.

According to Janis and Mann, the major reason for the use of a satisficing or a comparative mode is stress; the stress arising from the conflict involved in making a decision. Many theorists have also emphasized another sort of stress—the stress on the capacity of the human information-processing system. This latter form of stress is based upon research in experimental cognitive psychology which sets upper limits upon our capacity to deal with information simultaneously rather than sequentially (e.g. Atkinson and Shiffrin, 1968). This research, however, has dealt with situations where information is being presented to an individual at a fast rate without the possibility of her recording it except in memory. To apply it to career decision-making is to ignore the invention of writing.

According to Janis and Mann there is considerable personal stress involved in making career-related decisions. This arises for several reasons. First, there are the costs involved in taking any career-related action. Time is taken from final-year studies, and personal risks are taken in applying and taking on the possibility of rejection. More generally, steps such as application for a job imply the setting in train of the departure from the education theatre, with consequent loss of such elements of the self-concept as the values of being a scientist or a student. This feeling of the difficulty of reversing a decision once taken, with the consequent perception of its importance, is a second cause of stress. A third is the classic approach/avoidance conflict; both costs and benefits ensue from any decision once taken and acted upon. Hence Janis and Mann echo several of the points made by transition theorists reviewed earlier in this chapter.

On these assumptions, greater stress will result when there is a high degree of commitment to one's present role, and when there is the possibility of social disapproval or self-disapproval involved in a new role. Hence, the more academically motivated a student, the greater the stress of making the transition to the industrial or commercial theatre. Further, the more the student's friends or parents despise industry or commerce, or the more she herself believes its values alien to her own, the greater the strain. Perceived risks in all the alternative courses of action drive the student to seek support from her peer group, and look to them for appropriate decisions. She may continue to suffer high stress and panic, taking a hasty decision after considering one or few alternatives.

Thus, as noted on p. 106, the taking of a decision is not *per se* an appropriate action. A student might take a rapid decision in order to relieve stress. On the other hand, she might avoid a decision altogether, thereby at least avoiding possible risks and conflict with present priorities (e.g. studies); although, of course, such a strategy of inertia means that she will still face pressure from some others to take some sort of career decision. Careers counsellors have often remarked upon this avoidance strategy (e.g. Zytowski, 1975).

The evidence regarding graduates supports Janis and Mann's analysis. The more decided a student is, the less anxiety she demonstrates, both in general, and regarding career decisions (Walsh and Lewis, 1972; Hawkins *et al.*, 1977). Engineering students were shown to give considerable weight in their decisions as to which engineering function to take up to how they believed important others would feel about it (Herriot and Ecob, 1979). These perceptions of social approval were particularly weighty in their decisions not to engage in production or sales and marketing; it was social *dis*approval of such activities which turned them away (the British disease strikes again!).

The most frequent career-related event during engineering students' final year was a lengthy talk about careers with friends; this was a far more frequent event than consultation with academic staff or careers advisers (Herriot *et al.*, 1980). Moreover, the best predictor of change of intention was the number of times an individual was rejected, either before or after interview. Such rejection was related especially to a change in intention to work for a particular type of employer. Thus, for example, if a student had been rejected by a large private organization (e.g. Shell, IBM) she was likely to switch her allegiance to smaller private or public sector organizations. These findings clearly point to the part played by social factors and by self-esteem in the specific decisions of the student's final year.

Glueck (1974) looked at different modes of making decisions, comparing maximizers (those using a linear additive strategy), satisficers, or validators. He found that the number of job interviews undertaken by 30 male college students at a south-western university in the USA varied significantly with mode of decision-making. As Janis and Mann would predict, maximizers made more applications and attended more interviews than the others, being willing to search out more alternatives.

Both Janis and Mann, and Harren (1979) indicate that some level of stress is a necessary condition for a decision to be taken at all. Such stress is likely to be the consequence of the variety of social expectations held of the student to take steps towards making the major transition from education to the world of work. As we noted above (p. 106), the decisions made in response to these pressures may often be hasty and ill-judged, mere compliance. It is only when decisions are made as part of the social exchange process, with self-concept being compared with occupational and organizational role expectations, that satisfactory decision-making occurs. These different origins of decisions explain why the research literature on degree of decidedness is somewhat confused.

8.6 DECIDEDNESS

Having arrived at an occupational or organizational decision, then, is no guarantee of having made an appropriate decision. Conversely, those who are as yet undecided may be so for several reasons. They may be keeping their options open, and indeed, there is some evidence that students' choices often *decrease* in specificity during their undergraduate career. For example, Titley *et al.* (1976) found an interesting pattern in the choices of students at Colorado State University who changed their major subject during their course of study. In each successive year from first to fourth, students' occupational choices decreased in specificity! Students may also fail to make decisions, however, because they have an insufficiently developed or inadequate knowledge of occupational or organizational expectations. They may be prevented from making decisions by anxiety, or by conflicting expectations of them (for example, their family might hope that they will enter a particular profession, while they themselves may tend towards an entirely different occupation (Barak *et al.*, 1975)). Or else, they may find two or more alternative occupations equally desirable, and be caught in the classic 'approach–approach' conflict.

Where indecision is a consequence of these latter factors we would expect those with high self-esteem and inner locus of control to be more decided. Several measures of decidedness in college students have recently been developed whereby such hypotheses can be tested. For example, Osipow *et al.* (1976) have constructed a scale for undergraduate students, and Hartman *et al.* (1979) for postgraduate students. These measures include such items as 'I know I will have to go to work eventually, but none of the careers I know appeals to me'; and 'I can't make a career choice right now because I don't know what my abilities are'. Osipow *et al.* predicted 81.3% of the variance in whether or not a student presented herself at the careers guidance service for help regarding her indecisiveness. This predictive power was achieved by four factors only: anxiety and lack of structure and confidence; perception of some external barrier to choice; approach–approach conflict (see above); and conflict about how to make a decision. In line with these findings, level of decidedness is predicted by self-identity (Holland and Holland, 1977) and by self-esteem (Maier and Herman, 1974), even when personality, decision-making ability, and occupational interests are similar in all the students. On the other hand, level of decidedness is not predicted by academic achievement: Ashby *et al.* (1966) found that the least and the most decided students were higher in academic achievement than those in the middle, while Tilden (1978) found no increase at all in vocational maturity scores on the Career Development Inventory (Super) with increasing college grade level. An interesting finding in the Ashby *et al.* study was that the most undecided group was also the most dependent. Again, we are directed back to the self as the key predictor of decidedness. Gable *et al.* (1976) indicated that, for women students, those with an internal locus of control were likely to score more highly on the Career Maturity Inventory than those with an external locus of control.

At this point we must briefly discuss a matter of terminology. The terms 'maturity' and 'development' have been used to describe the criterion variable in some of the studies quoted above. This is because these words form part of the name of the questionnaires devised by Super and Crites. They carry the implication that one individual has progressed further along a developmental path than another if she has acquired the knowledge and attitudes which the questionnaire samples. It seems preferable to avoid this implication, for when we consider more closely the contents of these inventories, it becomes clear that they tend to sample attitudes and knowledge indicating the extent of the individual's *exploration* of occupations. Let us consider the Career Development Inventory (College and University form) of Super *et al.* (1981) by way of example. This instrument yields five basic scales:

(1) Career Planning, consisting of a self-report on current level of involvement in career planning activities and on how much the respondent knows about the kind of work she is currently considering as a career.
(2) Career Exploration, also a self-report scale, dealing with the student's attitude towards sources of help in career planning and with amount of help already obtained from these sources.
(3) Decision-making, using brief sketches of career development situations to measure the student's ability to apply knowledge and insight to career planning and decision-making.
(4) World of Work Information, assessing knowledge of the career development process (as exemplified by career development tasks) and knowledge of the occupational structure.
(5) Knowledge of Preferred Occupational Group, which tests knowledge of the job characteristics, psychological and training requirements, and

socioeconomic aspects of the occupational group selected by the student from among 20 groups covering most of the occupations in our economic system.

Clearly, such measures as these indicate much more than decidedness. They reflect the student's resources for making occupational decisions, both in terms of her own knowledge and of her use of outside help. If a student scores highly on such an inventory she is extremely unlikely to make a hasty decision because of mere compliance to social pressure, for she has acquired the means to enter into a worthwhile social exchange relationship with an employer. She has developed a picture of the occupational roles which will be expected of her, and she has gained the skills necessary to help her make appropriate decisions in the course of social exchanges with employers.

Recent work by Greenhaus and his colleagues has explicated the part played by some of the variables we have been discussing. Little of the variance in the degree of decidedness could be explained by the notion of career salience (Greenhaus and Simon, 1977). Career salience is the degree of importance placed upon work by the individual. Those undecided tended to place less importance upon work than those more decided, but the relationship was not particularly strong. However, when Greenhaus and Sklarew (1981) added further variables as predictors, a much clearer picture emerged. First of all, they found that the relationship between career salience and the degree of exploration of the world of work was moderated by the students' locus of control. For students with an internal locus of control, salience predicted exploration $r = 0.50$, whereas for those with an external locus of control, $r = 0.18$. Thus it is only those who see themselves as controlling their own careers whose degree of exploration of work reflects the importance they place on it. Again, the central position of the self-concept is evident. Greehaus and Sklarew (1981) also included a measure of anxiety in their predictors, and discovered that this too acted as a moderating variable. In this case, highly anxious students and non-anxious students differed with respect to the relationship between the amount of exploration they had done and their satisfaction with their occupational decision. For anxious students this relationship was negative: the more exploration they had done, the less satisfied they were with their occupational choice. For the non-anxious students, on the other hand, this relationship was positive. We may infer no particular direction of causality—exploration may have occurred after choice in order to justify it and to fill out the new self-conception it implies. Anxious students may fail to relate knowledge of self and occupations adequately to occupational choice; or they may fail to justify and incorporate their decision subsequently into their self-concept. Either way, the more that anxious students explore, the less they are satisfied.

To sum up the discussion of the last two sections, the picture of the student as a rational decision-maker is likely to be prescriptive rather than descriptive, if by 'rational' we imply a conscious weighing up of alternatives in terms of costs and benefits. Rather, the graduate is rational in another sense; that of relating her self-concept—past, present, *and future*—to the expectations being presented to her. To revert to our earlier analysis, decisions are not isolated personal events. They are, rather, modes of adaptation to social exchanges on the part of the individual. Early decisions in the student's final year (e.g. to read brochures, to start applying for jobs) are in response to pressures to engage in such activities. These may be merely compliant responses, or they may be taken after the student has compared expectations with her self-concept. In this latter case it is the future element of the self-concept that is crucial; decisions to apply are consistent with the student's views of herself as obtaining and entering a certain type of employment when she graduates.

The only research known to this author which actually compares self-concept and 'rational' decision-making models in students is that of Wheeler (1983). He found that students' perceptions of how well their abilities matched those required by particular occupations predicted their occupational preference significantly better than a decision theory model based on 15 outcomes. Both male and female students perceived male-dominated occupations as more desirable, and also as more difficult for success. However, this latter finding was significantly stronger for females than for males. Thus the self-concept of females, affected as it is by the absence of female role models in male-dominated occupations, prevents their opting for careers in such occupations (Hackett and Betz, 1981).

This chapter has dealt with a wealth of theory and a certain amount of evidence. Nothing in the ideas of career, developmental task, transition, or decision is incompatible with the basic conception of social exchange. Societal expectations regarding the transition from the educational theatre to that of the world of work; the expectations of significant others regarding the occupation the student will enter; the expectations of individual organizations regarding her future role; all these are different forms of social message. If the student has developed a future self-concept of herself as working, in an occupation, and in a certain sort of organization, she is in a position to test these messages for congruence with her self-concept. If she has failed to develop such a self-concept, or even to anticipate having to engage in these social exchanges, her career will be a series of involuntary roles into which she finds herself thrust.

We must conclude this chapter with a caveat, however. The emphasis of a chapter on career development and decisions must inevitably be upon the student as chooser rather than the organization. However, as we will see in the next chapter, the student's self-concept is part of a series of social exchanges. It is in dynamic interaction with the outside world, and it is only a matter of convenience and emphasis whether we construe the self as the initiator or the outcome of such exchanges.

9

Occupational Choice and the Self-concept

9.1 PERCEIVED CHARACTERISTICS OF THE SELF

Very unusual recommendations to graduate recruiters have already been implied in this book. It has been suggested that the best predictor of a satisfactory and lasting relationship between graduate and organization is the graduate's self-concept. To the extent that this is or becomes congruent with the organization's expectations of the individual, the parties will remain in a satisfactory relationship. The expectations of the organization will relate to general occupational and professional behaviour, as well as to the specific tasks of a job. Moreover, there are also organizational value priorities and norms of behaviour which are expected of employees. It may often be the case that the graduate is expected to project to the outside world the same image as the organization seeks to project. It follows that many different features of a graduate's self-concept are of concern to the organization if it is to conduct a fruitful negotiation with him.

Certainly, before being willing to give up the idea of assessing qualities of personality, organizations will wish to be made familiar with the evidence which relates elements of the self-concept to subsequent occupational behaviour. This evidence relates to three such elements: first, ratings of the self as presently conceived along various *dimensions of personality*; second, evaluations of the self, or *self-esteem*; third, ideas of the *future self*. Much of this evidence concerns the relationship of these elements of the self-concept with occupations rather than with organizations. If the analysis of Chapter 8 is correct, however, a wide variety of new role demands are being made of a graduate in his first job. He is not merely expected to be a satisfactory employee of organisation X, but also a satisfactory engineer (for example), and a satisfactory employee in general.

First, then, we will review the evidence which relates to the dimensions of the self-concept as presently conceived. The usual methodology of these investigations was to obtain self-descriptions and also descriptions of stereo-typic members of various occupations. The same personality dimensions were employed for each description. It was found that these two types of description were less discrepant for occupations in which the individual was more interested (Blocher and Schutz, 1961) or which he preferred (Oppenheimer, 1966; Ziegler, 1970). A typical experiment was that of Healy (1968). He found that accountancy and medical students could be discriminated by these 'incorporation scores', as they were termed. He also found that such scores predicted the results of professional doctors and accountants on the Strong Vocational Interest Blank. As in other studies, the differences between self and occupational stereotype on each of the large number of dimensions were weighted equally; although some might in reality have been more salient than others. In a very large-scale study of over 20,000 students, Baird (1970) related their self-ratings of traits, of life goals, and of competences, to their scores on the Vocational Preference Inventory. It was noteworthy that it was the non-academic predictors which accounted for most variance in the Inventory Scores. It is not merely occupational preferences such as these which are predicted by self and occupational congruence, however. It is also the student's actual choice of major subject of study. Students who made changes in their subjects had a greater discrepancy between their self-concept and occupational role expectations than those who did not (Warren, 1961).

A final study indicating the importance of self and occupational congruence is that of Ziegler (1973). He surveyed 428 male college students studying 39 different major subjects. He extracted 14 factors of occupational interest (e.g. agriculture, personnel, education). Hypothetical members of their most preferred occupational interest group were described by the students in relatively different terms from members of other, non-preferred occupations. Moreover, those descriptive adjectives shared by both self-descriptions and occupational member-descriptions were similar across subjects for each occu-pational preference. For example, students preferring science research as an occupation all tended to describe both themselves and also typical research scientists as clear-thinking, curious, imaginative and intelligent.

Research which dealt specifically with self and *organizational* congruence was conducted by Tom (1971). Using the Adjective Check List, Tom had 100 students describe themselves and also a range of employers who recruited on that campus (University of California). The congruence between self-image and organizational image was closer for those organizations which the student preferred. It is worth noting that this result was not obtained when the comparison was between students' own value priorities (as measured by the Study of Values) and the perceived values of the organization. However, the difficulties of using a standardized test for the purposes of comparison become starkly apparent when we consider closely the way particular test items are used. The Study of Values, for example, contains the following item:

Viewing Leonardo da Vinci's picture 'The Last Supper', would you tend to think of it
(a) as expressing the highest spiritual aspirations and emotions
(b) as one of the most priceless and irreplaceable pictures ever painted
(c) in relation to Leonardo's versatility and its place in history
(d) the quintessence of harmony and design.

This item, when applied to the organizations, was changed to read 'If the organization acquired Leonardo da Vinci's picture "The Last Supper" for display in the reception room, the probable motive is because it (a) (as before), (b), (c), (d).' Doubtless the reader can think of a few more plausible motives!

More seriously, the evidence reviewed indicates that the characteristics of the self and of occupations predict preferences and choice. Super's (1953) theory of occupational choice would suggest that this is because individuals seek to actualize, express, and enhance their self-concepts in their occupations. Of course, the relationship need not be unidirectional. The individual may change his self-concept to accord with his preferred occupation or intended employer. The extent to which an individual has decided upon and committed himself to an occupation or to an employer should predict the extent to which the self has adapted to a perceived role. Thus, all forms of anticipatory socialization would be expected to reduce the gap between self-concept and occupational stereotype; relevant vacation work or sandwich courses, for example, should both have this effect. The picture is not one of the individual actualizing his self, but of the social influence process in which self-cognitions adapt to experiences as well as selecting them.

However, it is not possible to tie this process down to the period of time of the student's study at the university. In the study by Healy (1968) already quoted, there was no difference in degree of self and occupational congruence between undergraduate and postgraduate students. Marks and Webb (1969) found no difference between freshmen, seniors, and postgraduates in the traits they attributed to an hypothetical electrical engineer and architect. Further, this occupational image, common to all three groups, was closely related to the self-concept of the freshmen taking each of these subjects. Thus we may well look earlier for signs of self-occupation congruence; Hollander and Parker (1972) found it in high-school students.

It may well be objected at this point that these experiments are all highly constrained by the experimenter's methodology. By administering the same questionnaire to tap both self and occupational or organizational concepts, the experimenter is assuming that the student naturally uses the same categories to describe both. Some evidence suggests that this assumption may be justified, however. The repertory grid technique usually permits respondents to produce their own constructs to describe the object of their attention. When Coxon (1971) asked students of social science to describe eight occupations, the following seven constructs were most frequently elicited: practical *v.* theoretical; masculine *v.* feminine; rational *v.* intuitive; altruistic *v.* egotistic; influential *v.* uninfluential; well-paid *v.* poorly-paid; honest *v.* dishonest. Clearly, these are potentially person descriptions as well as occupational ones. Similarly, Edwards and Whitney (1972) found that when individuals were describing their activities, their competences, their occupations, and themselves, the same six characteristics emerged after factor analysis for all four domains. In their seminal chapter, Starishevsky and Matlin (1968) suggest that 'occ talk' and 'psych talk' are translatable from one to the other.

These latter authors go on to make the important point that those who have more structured, clearer, and more certain self-concepts will be more able to make appropriate choices. Clearly, our discussion has moved on from the conception of the self as a set of characteristics or dimensions (see p. 101). We will first mention some evidence which indicates that individuals who have a cognitively complex mode of thinking *in general* are more likely to make appropriate occupational choices. Bodden (1970), and Bodden and Klein (1973) found that those high in cognitive complexity were more likely to enter the occupation they preferred. Moreover, the general nature of this metadimension and its effect is pointed to by the finding of Haase *et al.* (1979) that specific occupational information has no effect on cognitive complexity. The benefits of cognitive complexity are apparent in the individual's 'career maturity', as evidenced by the Career Maturity Inventory. More complex individuals demonstrate more 'mature' attitudes and competences.

It is the crystallization of the *vocational* self-concept in which we are more interested, however. This has been measured by Barrett and Tinsley (1977a) in their Vocational Rating Scale. As they put it:

> the degree of crystallisation of the vocational self-concept system can be defined as the degree to which the constellation of self-attributes which the individual considers to be vocationally relevant is well formulated. 'Well formulated' here refers to the degree to which the separate vocationally relevant self-concepts possess clarity and certainty for the individual, and the constellation of self-concepts as a whole possesses internal differentiation or structure (pp. 307–308).

Examples of the items in the Vocational Rating Scale are 'I know my own values well enough to make a career decision right now', and 'I just don't know if I have the traits that some lines of work require'. Higher crystallization scores were obtained for older *versus* younger female students, for graduates *versus* undergraduates, and for students with high self-esteem. This latter finding leads us on to a detailed consideration of self-esteem in relation to occupational choice.

9.2 SELF-ESTEEM

Self-esteem is the second component of the self-concept which has been extensively researched in relation to graduate occupational and organizational choice. Self-esteem is supposed to act as a moderating variable between self-occupation congruence and occupational choice. A moderating variable is a variable which predicts the degree of. relationship between two other variables. In this case the relationship is that between degree of self-occupation congruence and occupational preference and choice. It is a well-established finding that while this relationship is high for students of high self-esteem, it is much lower or non-existent for students of low self-esteem.

Typical of such research is the finding of Korman (1966). His subjects were students in the schools of business administration in two large state universities, who had made the choice of specializing either in sales or in accounting. The students of sales rated themselves as showing more initiative and possessing more job freedom than those of accounting; however, this difference was only found for students with high self-esteem, not for those with low self-esteem. On the assumption that the stereotype sales executive does indeed possess more initiative and job freedom than the accountant, this finding shows that self-occupational congruence predicts occupational choice only for those with high self-esteem. Korman (1967) went on to show that the same applied in the case of perceived ability requirements; students of high self-esteem were more likely to see themselves as meeting the ability requirements of their chosen occupation than students of low self-esteem. Actual occupants of the accountancy and sales professions saw themselves as having the needs and the abilities appropriate to their profession, and also as practising the appropriate professional ethics (Korman, 1969). But, again, this was more likely for high than for low self-esteem individuals. Students with high self-esteem are more likely to aspire to high-prestige occupations, are unwilling to settle for anything less prestigious, but will accept something less satisfying than their ideal (Bedeian, 1977). They are more likely to be decided in their occupational choice than students of low self-esteem (Resnick et al., 1970; Maier and Herman, 1974), and are less likely to be dogmatic (Maier and Herman, 1974).

There is some evidence for self-esteem also moderating the relationship between self-organization congruence and organizational choice (Behling and Tolliver, 1972). However, Mansfield (1973) failed to find a moderating effect, although the only aspect of the self-concept he explored was that of self-perceived abilities.

There is, however, considerable disagreement regarding the theoretical explanation for the moderating effect of self-esteem. One explanation would be that of Super: individuals choose occupations in order to enhance and express their self-concepts. Students with high self-esteem are likely to have better-developed and more crystallized self-concepts than those of low self-esteem (Barrett and Tinsley, 1977). Not only are their self-concepts more crystallized, but so are their ideas about occupations (Starishevsky and Matlin, 1968). As a consequence, more occupational choices which are consistent with their self-concept are made by those with high self-esteem; and they are more likely to be satisfied with such choices (Leonard *et al.*, 1973; Greenhaus and Sklarew, 1981). Moreover, students with high self-esteem are more likely to perceive themselves as inner-directed rather than outer-directed. Therefore, we would predict that they would pay less attention to their perceptions of others' occupational satisfaction when making their occupational choice than would students of low self-esteem. Greenhaus (1971) found that this indeed was the case; low self-esteem students of teaching, nursing, and education used their perceptions of others' satisfaction as cues, and their own satisfaction with their choice was consequently highly predicted by these perceptions.

However, there is another possible explanation for these findings. Students' motives may not be so much to enhance their self-concept as to reduce the cognitive dissonance which might be caused by a discrepancy between their self-concept and their behaviour. This is a specific example of the cognitive consistency theories which were prevalent in social psychology in the 1950s and 1960s. The idea underlying such theories is that inconsistency is painful, and is to be avoided if possible, or, if experienced, reduced. Korman (1966, 1970) suggests that this is the motivation for occupational choices being made which are consistent with the choosers' self-concept. The self-concept of a person of high self-esteem 'is defined by a sense of personal adequacy and a sense of having achieved need-satisfaction in the past.' Persons of low self-esteem, on the other hand, are 'characterised by a sense of personal inadequacy, and an inability to achieve need satisfaction in the past'. As a consequence, they 'are less likely to choose those occupations which they perceive to be most likely to fulfil their specific needs and to be in keeping with their self-perceived characteristics'. Such a choice of a 'non self-appropriate' role would be more in keeping with their cognition of themselves as non-need-satisfying individuals, and they would then be more likely to accept these influences, social or otherwise, which would maximize the probability of their entering an occupation which they would perceive as 'non-self-appropriate' (Korman, 1966, p. 480). In other words, students of low self-esteem will be predicted actively to choose occupations which will not satisfy their needs. They will search out advice which will lead them to avoid contradicting their view of themselves as people incapable of satisfying their own needs. They are not merely dependent on the advice of others; they are dependent on bad advice. They are not merely failing to search for satisfaction—they are actively searching for dissatisfaction; and all this in order to remain true to themselves.

This is a very strong prediction, in the sense that it is counter-intuitive (like many of the predictions of cognitive dissonance theorists). It also suffers the typical shortcoming of much of the cognitive dissonance research; a failure to rule out alternative explanations. The specific prediction which follows from Korman's position is, as Dipboye (1977) has pointed out, that of a negative correlation for students of low self-esteem between self-occupation congruence and chosen occupation. They should choose an occupation which is perceived as contrary to their needs. The evidence does not support this prediction, since the relationship is usually slightly positive or non-significant. Korman (1977) replies that he does not predict a negative relationship—there are strong social pressures for achievement and need satisfaction, regardless of the specific advice sought by the low self-esteem individual. These pressures confound the predicted relationship. In other words, other variables intrude upon the strong dissonance prediction.

However, Dipboye (1977) makes a nice, and logically conclusive, point. The need for consistency must be one of those needs which the person of low self-esteem strives to avoid satisfying! Why then should he seek to satisfy this particular need by avoiding the satisfaction of other needs? Only if self-consistency is the strongest of all his motives should this occur. Why should we assume that it is?

There are all sorts of reasons why those of low self-esteem should seek the advice of others to justify their choices. They may be outer-directed rather than inner-directed. They may fear failure, and therefore use advice as a means of hedging their bets; they can then attribute failure to the advice rather than themselves. The may take the advice of others in order to gain their approval and thereby directly boost their lagging self-esteem.

All in all, the evidence seems more consistent with Super's position than with Korman's. We may conclude that high self-esteem leads a person to choose an occupation and an organization appropriate to his self-concept because he wishes to express that self-concept. Expression of the person's concept of what he is like at present is itself rewarding, for it confirms the individual's view of himself as he is. However, we might also predict that yet more rewarding would be the realization of the self as the person would like to become; the fulfilment of aspirations, the actualization of the ideal self. The next section deals with the relationship between the future element of the self-concept and the occupational choice of students.

9.3 THE FUTURE SELF

One of the major ways in which an individual expresses his future self-concept is by his stated intentions. There is a very considerable amount of evidence that students' expressed choices for the future are better predictors of what they actually do than any other predictor. They predict actual choice of college major and first occupation entered better than does a measurement of interests (the Vocational Preference Inventory) (Gade and Solia, 1975). Borgen and Seling (1978) found the same to be true when the measure of interests was the Strong Vocational Interest Blank. However, it is advantageous for the measure of interests and the expressed intention to agree; when they do, students are less likely to change their major subjects, and more frequently enter jobs which are appropriate for their major subjects (Holcomb and Anderson, 1978). The superiority of stated intention over other measures extends to measures of aptitude, achievement, and personality (Richards, 1971; Elton and Rose, 1970). What is more, prediction based on stated intentions can predict a considerable time ahead—5 years in the research of Cooley and Lohnes (1968), and 14 years for McArthur and Stevens (1955).

The expression of an occupational intention may be taken to be an expression as much of the ideal self (the person the individual would like to become) as of the future self (the person the individual thinks he will become). Clearly, the more inner-directed an individual, and the higher his self-esteem, the more likely he believes himself to attain his ideal. Consequently, we may infer, the more likely he is to make efforts to attain it. Thus we would expect his ideal self to be a better predictor of his future for the high self-esteem, inner-directed student than for the low self-esteem, outer-directed one. In the case of the latter, his ideal self would not be considered within his practical reach, so it would be reflected in his fantasy rather than in his actions.

Some evidence that this may be the case is available in the already quoted study of Healy (1973). Healy calculated not only the degree of congruence between self and occupation, but also that between ideal self and occupation. He found that for this occupation (accountancy), degree of self-occupation congruence discriminated accountancy from non-accountancy students ($p <$ 0.05) while degree of ideal self-occupation congruence discriminated with p < 0.01. In accord with the present hypothesis, self-esteem was a moderator, in that the predictive power of ideal self and occupation for high self-esteem accountancy students was greater than for low self-esteem students. Commenting on this finding, Healy remarks that the accountancy students wished to actualize themselves through, rather than in, their occupation. That is, they hoped their occupation would change them so that they became more like their ideal. 'Their goal is not realised when they enter the occupation, but only when the occupation has changed them' (Healy, 1973, p. 49). Reverting to the discussion in Chapter 4, the negotiation between the organization and the individual is going to depend more on the extent to which the individual believes the organization will help him achieve his ideal self than on the extent to which the organization appears congruent with his view of himself as he is.

The idea that future aspirations are good predictors is supported by further research based on Holland's Self-Directed Search questionnaire. Although this evidence does not relate aspirations to self-esteem, it nevertheless points to their importance as predictors. Much of this research uses the 'daydreams' section of the Self-Directed Search, which asks individuals to identify the occupations which feature in their daydreams. Holland and Gottfredson (1975) find that such daydreams, provided they are consistent with earlier ones, predict the preferences, competences, activities, and self-ratings which are tapped by other parts of the Self-Directed Search. 'Taken together, the findings imply that a person's vocational aspirations have considerable psychological meaning; a pattern of related aspirations imply [sic] decision-making ability, psychological integration and predictability' (Holland and Gottfredson, 1975, p. 360). O'Neil and Magoon (1977) went one stage further by demonstrating that the daydreams section of the Self-Directed Search actually predicted various subsequent outcomes better than the other parts of the questionnaire. Specifically, the college major choices and the immediate and longer-term vocational plans of 171 freshmen of Holland's 'investigative' type (see pp. 147–8) were more successfully predicted by their daydream code than by their summary code. The same was found for 152 college women by Touchton and Magoon (1977). Of course, all this research makes the assumption that daydreams are evidence of aspirations. They could also be the reflection of expectations (which are beliefs about the occupation the individual thinks he will enter rather than the occupation he would like to enter). The daydreamer may be rehearsing to himself the roles he thinks he will be shortly playing—a sort of anticipatory self-socialization!

Nevertheless, assuming for the sake of this discussion that daydreams reflect aspirations, may we conclude that they predict occupational choice because the individual is motivated to achieve his aspirations? Apparently not; much recent evidence suggests that this is an incomplete account. Incomplete in two ways; first, the individual adjusts his aspirations to accord with his occupational experiences; and second, these aspirations are the result of earlier such adjustments in the course of his childhood and adolescence. In a word, the appropriate paradigm to describe what is going on is the social influence paradigm rather than the individualistic self-actualization one. Gottfredson and Becker (1981) express this point of view forcefully in the title of their article 'A challenge to vocational psychology: how important are aspirations in determining male career development'. Presenting longitudinal data on 1394 employed white males (admittedly not all graduates), they found that their subjects achieved congruence between their aspirations and their job more often by changing their aspirations to fit their jobs than by the reverse. Their present job field predicted their future job field 5 years later better than did their aspirations. A further very interesting finding was that middle-class men were no more likely to achieve their aspirations than working-class men. Gottfredson and Becker attribute this finding to the opportunity structure, 'which both conditions aspirations to narrow ranges early in life and affects the direction of early career development'. Thus it is anticipated opportunities as much as real opportunities which predict levels of aspiration. Social classes differ with respect both to occupations aspired to, and to occupations expected; they are similar only in respect of fantasies.

The evidence cautions us against the individualistic ideas of occupational choice proposed by many vocational psychologists. It emphasizes that the future element of the self-concept, like other elements, is not the determinant of occupational choice. Rather, it is an adaptive feature in a continuing process of socialization involving the individual and those with whom he negotiates social reality. At the graduate stage these negotiations primarily involve prospective employers; but the self-concept which the graduate brings to the recruitment negotiation is itself the product of long previous interchanges with other individuals, groups, and institutions. The following sections explore how the student's self-concept is a function of such social exchanges.

9.4 COLLEGE, SELF-ESTEEM, AND ASPIRATIONS

The central importance of self-esteem and of aspirations in occupational and organizational choice has been evidenced in previous sections. There is some evidence that these elements of the self-concept are affected by the college environment. In particular, the perceived academic standards of the college are one such factor, and the possibility of work experience is another.

First let us consider the case of the campus at a frog-pond, as the American researchers so charmingly put it (Davis, 1966). A simple hypothesis would be that most universities and colleges transmit values to the effect that study is worthwhile, and that graduate study is to be aimed for especially, since it is important both for entry into various professions and into the academic profession itself. It should be noted at this point that US and UK universities differ in this respect. In the UK many graduates enter a profession with a first degree only, and subsequently receive professional training on the job. They may or may not have to take further formal examinations, and if they do, these are unlikely to take the form of Masters degrees. Hence in UK universities postgraduate degrees do not have the same implications for occupational entry as they do in the USA. Taught Masters degrees are not uncommon, but the majority of postgraduate work is primarily research. Hence, in the UK, aspiration to do postgraduate work, if it has any occupational meaning, tends to reflect the student's desire to remain in academic life. In the USA, on the other hand, such aspirations reflect the desire to enter various lucrative and high-status professions. Hence academic and occupational aspirations are often synonymous.

In accordance with our simple hypothesis, there is evidence that educational aspirations rise in US universities from the first to the final year (Wallace, 1965; Thistlethwaite and Wheeler, 1966). Thus we would expect colleges to differ, to the extent that the more academic the college, the higher the student's aspirations. An alternative hypothesis, however, is that the student judges his own ability by comparing himself with others within his college. This appears to lead to opposite predictions, for example, for students in a highly selective college where the academic standards are high. According to the first hypothesis, more students should go for postgraduate study since the college values it highly. According to the second, less should do so, since self-comparison with others where others are highly able implies lower self-rating and therefore lower educational aspiration. The obvious difficulty with this argument, of course, is that the average student in a selective college is by definition more able than the average student in the less selective college. Hence he is no less able in comparison with his peers. Werts and Watley (1969) express the situation happily in the title of their paper—'A student's dilemma: big fish—little pond or little fish—big pond' (miraculously, frogs have been transmuted into fish!). They found that there were lower aspirations in the selective college, apparently supporting the idea that student's self-esteem and consequent aspirations are derived from comparisons of themselves with others within their own college. No attention, these authors conclude, is paid to the standards of their own college relative to others (about which they are ignorant—Davis, 1966). Drew and Astin (1972) provided further evidence in support of the view of the college as a frog-pond. In a large-scale national longitudinal study of college freshmen, they actually measured the self-evaluation of the students (omitted by Werts and Watley). They found that internal college grades correlated 0.26 with changes in self-evaluation, whereas the degree of college selectivity bore no relation to self-evaluation. Drew and Astin controlled for high-school achievement and scholastic aptitude, avoiding their confounding effect evident in earlier studies. The relationship of grades to occupational intentions (as opposed to self-evaluation) was established by Hind and Wirth (1969), who demonstrated that students who got low academic grades shifted their aspirations towards lower-status occupations.

In an effort to sort out the somewhat confused findings in the area, Bassis (1977) reanalysed the data of Drew and Astin. He first established the relationship between achievement at high-school and college selectivity ($r = 0.63$) and also between these high-school grades and self-evaluation on enrollment at college ($r = 0.66$). On the other hand, college selectivity was not related to self-evaluation on enrolment, whereas it was after the first year. College grades were more strongly related to self-evaluation after the first year, however, than was college selectivity. Hence, we may conclude that, during the course of their first year at college, there is some evidence for students adjusting their self-assessment based on their college grades in the light of their perception of the selectivity of their college. Since their previous self-evaluation had been based on the grounds for their admission to the college (high-school achievement) this is hardly surprising. The upshot of all this analysis is that both within-college comparisons, and, to some extent, between–college comparisons, affect self-esteem and aspirations.

As we might expect, the UK situation is somewhat different. UK evidence suggests (McPherson et al., 1972) that it is academic failure which prompts occupational concern in students. Academic successes are swept along within the education system, success in which has automatically promoted them to the next stage in their academic career in the past. In the USA, on the other hand, those who do less well academically in one college major area tend to change to other areas of study; in particular, to those where they more resemble the other students in social class membership. On the other hand, those who intended to follow their father's occupation were less likely to change than other students (Werts, 1967). This leads us on to the topic of the next section—the effect of home background upon the occupational aspirations of students.

First, however, we must discuss another aspect of university life; the opportunity to enjoy work experience during the course of study. Such work experience provides the student with the chance to try out a work role in order to discover whether it is in practice compatible with his self-concept. It can also help him to make adjustments to his self-concept which bring it closer to role expectations, and hence make a successful negotiation with an employer more likely subsequently. There is some evidence that this is the case; Yen and Healy (1977) found that paid employment increased scores on Crites' Career Maturity Inventory and Super's Career Development Inventory in the case of junior college students. Occupational stereotypes also changed as a consequence of work placement, at least for business students but not for engineers (Roe, 1974). On the other hand, in many vocationally-oriented courses work experience serves to reinforce one's self-concept of oneself as a member of one's chosen occupation. For example, Cotgrove and Fuller (1972) found that sandwich-based chemistry students were more likely to intend to work in industry than full-time students in their first year, as well as in their final year, at university.

Moreover, the congruent occupational stereotypes of freshmen did not change significantly during undergraduate or graduate training (Marks and Webb, 1969). Indeed, such diverse groups as male and female staff and students of college and high school shared similar stereotypes of 15 occupations, and underlying their perceptions were certain common metadimensions of occupations such as status (Beardslee and O'Dowd, 1962). Beliefs about occupations are likely to be as much about general aspects of lifestyle associated with the occupation as about the specific tasks and training involved (Hudson, 1968). Indeed, knowledge of lifestyle is generally inadequate (Kirton, 1976), and brochures have tended to stress such aspects as the work itself, training and prospects rather than lifestyle (Hayes, 1969).

The implications of all these findings may well be that work experience fills out the occupational stereotype by revealing the lifestyle of typical members of the organization or occupation to the student. Otherwise, however, work experience serves to confirm already existing occupational stereotypes. The effect of the experience may well be to change the self-concept more than the occupational stereotype. The mechanism of self-consistency could be adduced to account for such a change, since the student has voluntarily committed himself to work experience. Therefore cognitive dissonance would occur if the occupational role he took on during his work experience (and to which he is to some extent committed as an occupational choice) were inconsistent with his self-concept. Once he has already engaged in the work experience, only his self-concept can change to reduce such dissonance. The *post hoc* nature of such an inference is not appealing, however, and it is probably safer simply to conclude that there is little evidence of occupational stereotypes changing during college years, but more of 'career maturity' and commitment increasing as a function of experience.

9.5 SOCIAL LEARNING AND THE SELF-CONCEPT

According to Super (1953):

> The process of vocational development is essentially that of developing and implementing a self-concept; it is a compromise process in which the self-concept is a product of the interaction of inherited aptitudes, neural and endocrine make-up, opportunity to play various roles, and evaluations of the extent to which the results of role-playing meet with the approval of superiors and fellows. The process of compromise between individual and social factors, between self-concept and reality, is one of role-playing, whether the role is playing in fantasy, in the counselling interview, or in real-life activities such as school classes, clubs, part-time work and entry jobs.

Two basic emphases emerge from this, the first statement of Super's influential theory of vocational development. They are: first, that young people may be evaluated by others in terms of the extent to which they fulfil role expectations; and, second, that they may use their playing of roles to discover and work out appropriate self-concepts for themselves. Thus the idea of anticipatory socialization, the trying-out of roles related to the world of work in advance of entry to that world, is present in Super's theory. So too is the very important word 'opportunity'—it is opportunity to play various roles which is taken to affect the self-concept.

From a theoretical background different to that of Super, Krumboltz *et al.* (1976) have outlined a somewhat similar theory. Using social learning theory as the basis for their suggestions, they propose that there are four major determinants of occupational preferences. They are, first, social reinforcement; second, modelling; third, direct reinforcement; and fourth, words and images associated with careers. Career decision-making skills interact with these determinants to predict preferences. Unfortunately, little empirical evidence has yet been adduced in support of Krumboltz's theory (see e.g. Ware, 1980). The connections of the social learning approach with that of Super may best be pointed up by the typology of social influence of Aronson (1981) and Kelman (1961), described on p. 50–1. Thus the approval and disapproval of others, the direct rewards and punishments for role-playing adduced by both Super and Krumboltz, are instances of the level of social influence known as *compliance*. The next level, that of *identification*, is represented by Krumboltz's insistence on modelling as a determinant. The young person is taken to identify with a model (perhaps his father), and to internalize elements of the model into his own thinking. Clearly, some elements internalized in this way are likely to be occupational. However, *internalization*, the final level, is not dependent upon whether an admired model exists or not. The influence of others has become part of the self, and changes in rewards and punishments, or in the identity of models, will not have an immediate effect upon the self-concept. We may suppose that it is the use of role-playing to try out the compatibility of others' expectations with one's self-concept which is a major source of change. By actually performing the roles expected of him, the young person can discover whether such roles are in practice incompatible with his self-concept; or he can incorporate them into his existing self-concept, thereby changing it. This is one of Super's major emphases.

These two psychologically-based approaches are not in principle incompatible with the sociological theorizing of such authors as Roberts (1981). In the context of a general analysis of occupational entry in terms of the opportunity structure of UK society, Roberts refers to graduates in the following terms:

> whether they become physicians, engineers, biologists or lawyers depends not so much on their aspirations as on the educational routes into which they are channelled and the career opportunities available when they graduate. The scope for manoeuvre at the highest level at which any group of young people can enter the labour market is normally extremely limited. Occupations are not merely different but are stratified into a system of inequality. Is the language of 'choice' really appropriate in explaining why so few university graduates become bus conductors? (Roberts, 1981, p. 285).

Roberts' general point is well taken. It seems clear from recent authoritative research in the UK (Goldthorpe, 1980; Halsey *et al.*, 1980) and in the USA (Ginsberg, 1975; Sewell and Hauser, 1975) that educational level is still closely related to earnings and occupational status, and that in the UK at least, the relative proportions of different socioeconomic classes within the university population have remained relatively constant (although that population has itself increased overall). As far as the UK is concerned, it is still true that those who enter higher education come from a favoured section of society: predominantly white, middle-class, able-bodied boys. Young people from upper middle-class homes are five times more likely to go into university than working-class children. Women form 37% of the undergraduate and 28% of the postgraduate population. While 5% of all school-leavers go on to university, only 1% of those with West Indian origins and 3% of those of Asian origins do so (Warren-Piper, 1981). (American readers will recall that there is a system of grant aid applicable to students at all UK universities.)

What is of more interest in the context of the present argument, however, is not the clear connection between social class and educational (and hence occupational) opportunity. It is rather any evidence which can demonstrate that social class has an effect upon occupational choice even after entry to university. Such evidence is indeed available. When college freshmen in the USA were asked their intended occupation, five out of the eight best predictors related to parents' occupation (Grandy and Stahman, 1974). The children of working-class parents tend to opt for occupations which are not too distant in terms of status from that of their father. Hence American freshmen are more apt to intend careers in engineering or teaching if they are from working-class origins (Werts, 1966; Katz et al., 1968). Engineering is the choice of working-class and of upper middle-class students in the UK, whereas pure science subjects were preferred by those of lower middle-class origins (Kelsall, 1972). This study also found that one-third of those undergraduates with fathers in professional careers wanted professional careers themselves, whereas only 13% of lower working-class students were aiming for the professions (note that these studies used the Registrar General's Classification of socioeconomic class into five categories, the top category including the professions (narrowly defined). DeWinne et al. (1978) found that there was a fairly strong relationship between immediate graduates' occupational choice and the occupation of their fathers. Specifically, graduates were likely to choose occupations of the same type as their fathers, where 'type' is defined in terms of Holland's six categories of occupational interest (e.g. intellectual, artistic, etc.) (see pp. 147ff.). Given the finding of Werts (1966) above, and Werts' (1967) further finding that students preferring the same occupation as their fathers are less likely to change preferences during their course than are other students, we may conclude that parental occupation continues to exercise a powerful influence throughout college career.

There are several possible explanations as to why this should be the case. Before speculating, it is worth examining the very interesting evidence produced by Cherry (1975). She asked 310 final-year students to indicate how important each of 12 attributes of jobs would be when making an occupational decision. After factor analysis, four factors emerged: educational considerations; personal success versus social value; interesting content versus meeting people; security versus variety and adventure. Working-class students scored higher on educational considerations and on security than did middle-class students. Moreover, there was an interesting interaction between social class and sex. Middle-class male students were more likely than other males to be interested in personal success and interesting content, whereas middle-class women were least likely of all groups to have these preferences. On the other hand, with respect to educational considerations and security, middle-class males and middle-class females did not differ.

These results tend to lead to several possible post hoc explanations, all of which relate to elements in the theories of Super, Krumboltz, and Roberts described earlier. First, working-class students place high priority on educational considerations, probably because they recognize that it is through the educational system that they have achieved their present position. They aim for security because this is the feature of employment which their parents lacked. Middle-class families are more likely to have the father-at-work mother-at-home pattern of employment which would explain the sex × social class interactions which Cherry found.

If we assume that children use their father as an occupational model, working-class students are unlikely to have a prominent model for a single one of the middle-class occupations to which their college education has opened the door. Perhaps this is why teaching is a favoured occupation for working-class students; it is an occupation for which they all have role models, since they have all attended school and college. There are other reasons, however, why a working-class student might tend to choose occupations such as teaching and engineering. It is related to the class structure and class consciousness, of UK society in particular. Occupations such as teacher and engineer are lower in status than most other occupations to which graduates aspire. It is conceivable that many working-class students choose occupations which will not distance them excessively from their family origins. Moreover, it is not merely the father's specific occupation which may provide a role model for that occupation (e.g. doctor, lawyer, diplomat). It is also the general features of a middle-class occupation which act as cues. For example, many middle-class people see their work as part of an occupational career, in which future development may be anticipated and planned for. They consider that professional membership requires qualifications and imposes obligations and standards. They see a connection between academic progress and occupational opportunity. They expect work to provide intrinsic as well as extrinsic satisfactions; and so on. In sum, the middle-class child has a role model not merely of specific occupations of higher status, but of a whole occupational style and way of life.

There are other aspects of families which do not have such overt class-related characteristics, but which have been demonstrated to affect students' occupational choice. These relate to the atmosphere of the family, and derive from the theory of Roe (1956). In her psychoanalytically-based theory, Roe suggested that preference for jobs was person-oriented or non-person-oriented, and that this orientation depended in particular on whether the child's dominant parent was accepting, avoiding, or concentrating upon the child. Wittmer *et al.* (1974) demonstrated that engineers reported colder relations with their parents than did counsellors, while Medvene and his colleagues explored the relationships within occupational groups. Medvene (1969) discovered that students intending different varieties of work as professional psychologists differed in reported interactions with their parents. Medvene and Schueman (1978) found that engineering students intending careers in sales or technical services (person-oriented) functions were more likely to describe their dominant parent as accepting than those wishing to enter basic research, applied R&D, or product and process engineering. Family atmosphere is also one of the most important predictors in Owens' work (see p. 103). Another feature of family life is the nature of the role models given to boys and girls, but this topic has a chapter to itself later in the book.

Perhaps the major feature of Super's and of Roberts' theories is opportunity; the opportunity to play various roles. In the case of Super's theory, the emphasis is on the way in which such role-playing aids the development of the occupational self-concept. In the case of Roberts, the emphasis is on the opportunity the individual has in engaging in roles which are necessary for occupational entry. Both of these emphases emerge clearly from the large-scale longitudinal studies of occupational development carried out in the USA by Super and his colleagues (The Career Pattern Study) and by Gribbons and Lohnes (The Career Development Study).

In a 21-year longitudinal study (Super *et al.*, 1967; Jordaan, 1974; Super, 1981), Super and his colleagues followed through about 300 school students from age 15 onwards. These were not all college students; indeed, by age 25 only 20% of them were degreed. However, what is of importance is the power of certain predictors in predicting various criteria. The criteria included four elements. First, *career satisfaction*; how satisfied is the individual with the direction his career is taking at age 25? To what extent is he using his abilities or does he expect to use them in his present occupation? How strongly does he wish to continue in his present occupation? Second, *early establishment*: how far has he got in achieving the goal he set for himself at age 18 for age 25? How many times has he changed his job since high school? Third, *occupational satisfaction*: how much opportunity has he had for self-expression? Finally, *career progress*: have his benefits and pay increased? Has he utilized his training and experience? Have his job changes been for realistic reasons? Has his job become better aligned to his interests and abilities?

The best predictors of these criteria are most enlightening. *Career satisfaction* is best predicted (in order of predictive power) by the following variables: parent's socioeconomic class; participation in school activities; after-school employment (i.e. part-time jobs); high-school grades; the degree of stability in occupational preference from 9th to 12th grade; the information acquired by the student about the preparation required for various occupations, supply and demand of jobs and hours of work; and finally, the amount of agreement between measured abilities and occupational preferences. *Early establishment* is best predicted by parental class and job information. Parental class is again the best predictor of *occupational satisfaction*, followed by participation in school activities, part-time work, hobbies, job information, ability–preference agreement, and acceptance of responsibility for implementing career decisions. Finally, *career progress* is best predicted by high-school grades, followed by job information and extent of hobbies.

A similar pattern emerges from the work of Gribbons and Lohnes (1968), although they concentrated more upon vocational activity during the school years as a predictor. They found vast differences in the vocational maturity of 8th, 10th, and 12th grade school students. The notion of 'maturity' (implying unidirectional advance) was not supported, since 17% of their sample of 111 school students remained in a state of 'constant immaturity'. They had a persistent fixation on fantastic, unrealistic goals. Twenty-eight per cent of their sample actually 'degenerated', with a progressive deterioration of aspirations and achievements, frustration, and loss of status. Thirty-nine per cent demonstrated 'emerging maturity', during which time they became more realistic in their aspirations and developed more detailed self-concepts. Finally, the remaining 16% enjoyed 'constant maturity', the persistent realistic pursuit of their stated occupational goal. At age 20, 50% were doing something out of line with what they hoped to be doing, while at age 25 this was still true of 40%. The degree of 'maturity' exhibited at school was a predictor of this subsequent degree of 'vocational adjustment'. Note, however, that only 25% of Gribbons and Lohnes' sample were in or had finished college at age 22. The main criterion used in this study was the individual's position on the Career Development Tree, a complex measure based upon division of progress into college *versus* non-college and, within college, science *versus* sociocultural and business studies. Degree of vocational adjustment as defined above forms part of the overall criterion measure. The best predictors at ages 16 and 18 were sex and readiness for career planning. At age 20, parental social class was the best predictor; at age 22 and 24 parental class, intelligence, sex, and readiness for career planning.

Both Super's and Gribbons and Lohnes' research indicate how important early background variables are in predicting subsequent career success (where attendance at college is considered to be part of that career). In particular we must note the prominence of socioeconomic class as a predictor; in Super's research, it is the best predictor of three of the four criteria, and in Gribbons and Lohnes' work it carries particular weight when the individual is starting on working life. While the measures relating especially to vocational knowledge and to vocational planning do serve to predict, there are other predictors which are as potent. These include intelligence and academic achievement, and also non-academic activities such as part-time jobs, hobbies, and school activities. Even these predictors are likely to be affected by social class to some extent, particularly academic achievement. Certainly in the UK, many private ('public') schools and schools in middle-class areas are more likely to achieve examination successes than schools in working-class areas.

We must conclude that the development of the occupational self-concept is a function of the social relations enjoyed throughout childhood and adolescence. There is more evidence for the influence of these pre-college factors than there is for change at college. The self-concept which the student brings with him to the graduate recruitment procedure, in particular his self-esteem, his aspirations, and his ideas of career progression, can only be seen in the context of his entire social experience.

10

Sex-Roles, Selection, and Choice

10.1 THE EXISTENCE OF STEREOTYPES

The previous chapter concluded with the judgement that students from homes of lower socioeconomic status might be at a disadvantage. This disadvantage was primarily concerned with their relative lack of opportunity to model their selves upon incumbents of middle-class occupational roles. Hence their self concept was likely to be less crystallized than that of middle-class students. In particular they might not yet have acquired those general assumptions and aspirations relating, for example, to long-term careers within an organization or within a profession. We must remember, however, that those working-class students who have achieved university entrance are unusual people; perhaps one of the reasons they are there is that they found different role models from those of their contemporaries.

In the case of working-class students there is little evidence to suggest that the employers of graduates discriminate against them. It may be the case that entrance to certain professions is still facilitated by the eminence of one's parents in that profession, but in general, socioeconomic class as such does not seem to be a major factor in graduate recruitment. There is another factor, however, which affects the self-concept of the student and the role perceived for her in the organization: it is that of sex. It will be argued in this chapter that many women students' occupational self-concepts and the stereotypes held of them by employers coincide. Hence the social exchange and negotiation process is facilitated, because both parties share the same views of what the student wants to become. Consequently, women continue to be appointed to positions consistent with female stereotypes.

There is little evidence of major psychological difference between men and women (Maccoby and Jacklin, 1974). The one achievement-related characteristic which consistently differentiates the sexes is self-confidence and esteem. Since the self-concept is at least partly derived from the social exchanges one has experienced, this feature is unlikely to represent an inherent rather than a culturally derived characteristic. While there is relatively little evidence that men and women differ, however, there is a vast amount of evidence to indicate that men and women are *perceived* to differ. The term sex-role stereotyping 'refers to the belief that a set of traits and abilities is more likely to be found among one sex than the other' (Schein, 1978, p. 259). In the terminology of Chapters 2 and 3, sex-role stereotypes are part of a very widely held implicit personality theory. Just as the concept 'extraversion–introversion' subsumes a large number of subordinate traits, so the overarching construct 'male–female' embraces an even broader range of characteristics. The sequence of inferences from sex-role stereotypes is fairly clear, and runs like this: women have characteristics x, y, z, men have characteristics a, b, c; occupations X, Y, Z require characteristics x, y, z, and women are therefore more suited to them; occupations A, B, C require characteristics a, b, c, and men are therefore more suited to them. Moreover, managers are essential in a large number of occupations and in all organizations; management requires characteristics a, b, c, and therefore men are better managers in general than are women. Note well that beliefs about occupations are involved in this logic, as well as beliefs about men and women.

Such beliefs are to be found in children as young as first grades (Looft, 1971), and children are firmly convinced of a woman's place (Schlossberg and Goodman, 1972). The stereotypes held are depressingly similar across a wide range of individuals. In work, men are held to be more competent, independent, objective, dominant, active, competitive, ambitious, and self-confident (Broverman *et al.*, 1972). As mentioned above, we should not be surprised if some of these expectations are acted upon by men and women, so that the holding of stereotypes is a self-fulfilling prophecy. Male and female students agree (with the remarkably high correlation of 0.97) in their ratings of the masculinity, femininity, and neutrality of 129 occupations (Shinar, 1975), although the women perceived occupations in general as less masculine than did the men.

The way in which these stereotypes may be used by those in positions of power can be seen in the research of Schein (1973). Her subjects were 300 male middle managers, who were asked to rate men in general, women in general, and successful middle managers on 92 descriptive terms. The successful middle managers were credited with those traits more commonly ascribed to men in general than with those more commonly ascribed to women in general. They were considered likely to be stable, aggressive, self-reliant, certain, vigorous, to desire responsibility, and to possess leadership ability. Schein concludes 'The results suggest that, all else being equal, the perceived similarity between the characteristics of successful middle managers and men in general increases the likelihood of a male rather than a female being selected for or promoted to a managerial position' (p. 99). One slight caveat to these conclusions is that ratings by female middle managers were not obtained, so we can only agree with Schein's conclusions when the selectors/assessors are male middle managers. There is a glimmer of hope in Schein's findings, however; she discovered some requisite characteristics for successful middle management which were neither male nor female. Intelligence, competence, and creativity were not sexually stereotyped, and these are more ability than personality factors.

Students believe that interviewers select on the basis of their beliefs about the sexes. Cecil *et al.* (1973) asked undergraduate and graduate students of business management how much importance they thought interviewers would place on 50 variables commonly used to evaluate job applicants. The interviews were for a white-collar job, and the applicant was male or female. Four of the 50 variables were judged significantly more important for the male than the female applicant; they were ability to change one's mind on an issue, being persuasive, having exceptional motivation, and being aggressive. Four, again, were judged significantly more important for the female. They were: possession of clerical skills, having finished high school, having excellent computational skills, and being immaculate in dress and person. Clearly men are expected to need to get ahead, women to be nice and efficient.

It is not only at the stage of selection that students expect supposed sex differences to be at work. When asked to rate the likely happiness of male and female occupants of male and female-dominated occupations, Feather's (1975) student subjects thought that occupants of occupations dominated by their own sex would be happier. When Feather content-analysed the reasons given why this should be so, he found that the number of reasons of given categories differed according to the sex of the student respondent and whether the outcome was happy or unhappy. Particular reasons given included the ideas of male provider, dominant male, female caretaker, the overcoming of traditional sex roles, the occupational benefits, and the occupational qualifications.

A final group of experiments suggests that students have actually taken over for themselves these beliefs about what are appropriate and inappropriate characteristics and values for men and women to have. Sampling men and women students in business administration, liberal arts, and education, Miner (1974) found that in the first two areas of study, men had greater 'motivation to manage' than women. This was manifested particularly in desire for power, assertiveness, and desire to compete. Among the students of education, however, no significant difference was found between the sexes. This points to the questions tackled in subsequent sections of this chapter: to what extent can we generalize across subject areas of study when some of them are traditionally male-dominated and others female-dominated? and to what extent can we make generalizations about the sexes, when male and female persons differ among themselves in the extent to which they consider themselves masculine and feminine? Indeed, sex itself does not account for much of the variance in the motivation to manage (Bartol *et al.*, 1981).

Wheeler (1981) demonstrated that the outcomes from their work desired by male and female business students did not differ significantly, whereas there were significant differences between the female business students and female education students.

A final, most interesting, piece of research suggests that nature of occupation and self-concept are not the only additional factors which need to be taken into account when examining sex effects: social class is also involved. Cherry (1975) asked 310 students in their final year of undergraduate study to indicate how important various attributes of jobs would be to them when deciding on their occupation. After factor analysis, Cherry isolated four factors: educational considerations, personal success or social value, interesting content or meeting people, and security or variety and adventure. Women rated social value and meeting people higher than did men. There was, moreover, an interesting sex × social class interaction: middle-class men were *more* likely than working-class men to rate highly personal success and interesting content; middle-class women were *less* likely than working-class women to have these priorities. In her longitudinal study, Cherry went on to show that these job values successfully predicted the type of occupation in which the students were subsequently engaged at age 26. (See p. 128).

10.2 STEREOTYPES IN SELECTION

Given the existence of sex stereotypes in the area of work evidenced in the previous section, we can now go on to examine those studies which show that they are operating when students are selected for organizations. This literature is not easy to interpret, as is evident from the reviews by Arvey (1979) on the employment interview and Reilly and Chao (1982) on selection procedures in general. The problem is not helped by the frequent use of students as 'selectors' instead of real graduate recruiters. This regrettable practice leaves much of the research open to criticisms regarding its degree of generalizability. Furthermore, when students are subjects and their teachers are the researchers, the tendency to reply in a socially desirable way is likely to be increased. Social desirability is a very complex confounding factor in the case of sex stereotype research. Is the student wanting to be accepted by 'society in general', in which case she will demonstrate the sex-role stereotypes she believes society in general to hold? Or does she wish to be accepted by enlightened liberal opinion? Or does she wish to help the teacher/experimenter by providing the evidence for stereotypes which she thinks the experimenter is looking for?

An influential study which did not use students as 'selectors' was carried out by Cohen and Bunker (1975). Their subjects were 150 recruiters at two university placement centres. These recruiters were given job descriptions, completed application forms, interview transcripts, performance evaluations, adjective rating scales and biodata forms, all describing hypothetical applicants for two positions: editorial assistant and personnel technician. These two positions were considered to be female sex-typed and male sex-typed respectively. More female applicants were recommended for the former job, more males for the latter. In a similarly realistic study, Zikmund *et al.* (1978) sent application forms to 100 personnel directors for accountancy jobs. The sex of the 'applicant', and the level of their scholastic performance (high *versus* medium), were varied. The number of replies received and the number of positive responses were both related to the sex of the applicant, with male applicants being more favoured. The number of positive responses was also related to scholastic performance.

It may not only be the sex-typing of the job which interacts with the sex of the applicant in selection decisions. Rosen and Jerdee (1974) varied the nature of the demands made by a job. The jobs for which their business student 'recruiters' were selecting required aggressive interpersonal behaviour and decisive managerial action; or else they required clerical accuracy and dependable performance. Rosen and Jerdee found a sex × job demands interaction, with men being much more likely than women to be selected for the demanding job, and little more likely to be selected for the undemanding one. It is interesting in passing to see how difficult it is to manipulate sex as a factor alone; Rosen and Jerdee thought they were doing so by designating the applicants Mr Lewis or Mrs Lewis!

Another feature which might be taken into account by selectors is attractiveness, with the more physically attractive applicants standing a better chance. Dipboye *et al.* (1975) had 30 student 'recruiters' and 30 professional interviewers rate bogus applicants on the basis of application forms for a managerial position. The students rated the applicants higher overall than did the professionals. Both groups rated male applicants higher than females, attractive ones higher than unattractive ones, and those with high scholastic standing higher than those with low standing. This latter factor accounted for most of the various in the ratings. Dipboye *et al.* (1977) went on to demonstrate that these results held true regardless of the sex and physical attractiveness of the student 'recruiter'. Why should physical attractiveness have an effect on selection decisions? Heilman and Saruwatari (1979) suggest an interesting answer. They found that attractiveness was always an asset for male applicants, but only for females when the position being applied for was non-managerial. Their explanation was that attractiveness increases the probability that sex-related attributes will be perceived by the selector. Therefore unattractive women and attractive men will be perceived as more motivated, unemotional, and decisive, and indeed they were rated as such by the subjects. We must remember, though, that in this experiment the subjects were students, being asked to make a direct male *versus* female comparison by two female staff experimenters. Heilman (1980) adds further evidence to support this explanation for the attractiveness effect. One hundred male and female MBA students evaluated a woman applicant for a managerial position. When this applicant was one of only 12½ or 25% females in an otherwise male applicant pool, she received less favourable ratings. Furthermore, she was likely to be considered less ambitious, unemotional, decisive, and tough than if she had been one of a more sizeable proportion of females. Again, the inference is that the more noticeable the woman's gender was, the more likely are sex-related characteristics to be attributed to her, and hence the less likely she is to be selected for a 'masculine' position.

The complexities of the situation are evident from further work by Muchinsky and Harris (1977). For a job in a child day-care centre, female applicants were rated more suitable than male ones by student 'selectors'. However, in mechanical engineering, a typically masculine occupation, there were no sex differences, although there was a male advantage in the less sex-typed job of copy editor. Perhaps attributional processes are at work here—the women mechanical engineering applicants must be good to have got into that area in the first place! This study demonstrates that we need to know a lot more about the stereotypes that are held about occupations, as well as those that are held about men and women, before we can understand the processes of sex-stereotyped selection. It would help if the investigators in this area used the same descriptive categories for the male and female applicants and for typical job incumbents (as did Schein, 1973).

Further support for the idea that selectors are biased because they hold sex stereotypes is provided by Simas and McCarrey (1979). These investigators reasoned that the more authoritarian an individual, the more likely she is to hold simple stereotypes. Their sample of 144 personnel officers rated applicants on the basis of videotaped interviews for suitability for entry-level managerial administrative trainee posts. The highly authoritarian officers had a greater preference for male applicants than did their less authoritarian colleagues. This preference was due to a higher valuation of males on their rating scales rather than a devaluation of females (relative to their colleagues). Rosen and Jerdee (1975) go further, suggesting some of the functions which sex-role stereotypes may serve for the person who holds them. One of these functions is ego defence, which is one of the explanations proposed for high authoritarianism.

Stereotypes are strongly resistant to contrary evidence. The success of women in managerial roles or in masculine occupations might be expected to decrease the bias in selection or in promotion procedures. However, the rationalization of such successes is very easy, given the opportunity to make attributions regarding their cause. Social psychologists have shown that women's successes in general are likely to be attributed to the ease of the task or to effort (Feldman-Summers and Kiesler, 1974) or to luck (Deaux and Emswiller, 1974). Carrying this over into the employment field, Cash *et al.* (1977) had 72 personnel consultants explain the subsequent success or failure of men and women applicants in masculine, neutral or feminine jobs. Women's success in feminine jobs was attributed more to ability than their success on neutral or masculine jobs. Women's success on masculine jobs, on the other hand, was attributed less to ability than was men's success on these masculine jobs. Furthermore, such success on the part of women was attributed more to luck than men's success. Moreover, when women succeeding in masculine occupations were compared with women succeeding in neutral or feminine occupations, they were again credited with more luck. Overall, failure in out-of-role occupations was attributed to inability, failure in in-role occupations to bad luck. Success in neutral or feminine occupations on the part of both sexes was attributed to the ease of the tasks involved. These findings demonstrate how it is possible to marshal a veritable armoury of rationalizations for women's success which prevent such success feeding back into the selection procedure.

The important thing to note here is that it is attributions which affect decisions, not so much the sex of the individual concerned. Heilman and Guzzo (1978) provided MBA students with different causal explanations for the equal success of men and women employees. These were luck, effort, task difficulty, and ability. They also allocated rewards to these hypothetical employees which differed according to the cause of success. Successful employees whose success was attributed to their ability were allocated higher rewards than others. The subjects' task was to rate the suitability of these rewards for each employee. There were differences in rated appropriateness according to the reason for success, but no differences based on the sex of the employee. Thus it seems likely that discrimination in selection is based on sex-role stereotypes and reinforced by causal attributions regarding the subsequent performance of men and women.

Now we must consider whether the same stereotypes are part of the self-concept of graduate applicants as well as existing in the minds of recruiters. Before we do so, however, it is worth stressing that these findings about sex discrimination in selection do not merely imply certain beliefs about men and women. They also imply beliefs about occupations. It is only because occupational stereotypes exist that occupational sex-stereotyping can occur. Specifically, it is only because, for example, managers are typically thought to be, and to need to be, aggressive, ambitious and self-confident, that women, held not to have these qualities, can be discriminated against. It follows that changes in employment practices may be effected by changes in beliefs about occupations as well as by changes in beliefs about women. McGregor's (1960) distinction between Theory X and Theory Y managers seeks to bring about such a change in occupational stereotypes.

10.3 PIONEERING WOMEN AND THEIR MODELS

Now we turn from selection to choice. What sort of a woman is it who chooses an occupation which is male-dominated? According to Wolkon (1972) they are more interested in mastery, in independence, and in economic factors than women who enter female-dominated careers. When compared with women who are oriented towards home-making rather than a career of any sort, they value mastery, independence, dominance, and economic and social factors. Such women do not enter male-dominated occupations because they are social isolates or because they are in conflict with their families; there was no evidence in the research of Almquist (1974) that 'pioneer' and 'traditional' women differed in these respects. As Wolkon had also found, they were more committed to a career than traditional women. They were more keen to use their special abilities and to achieve a high income. Those intending entering a female-dominated occupation felt people were more important than things, and were more inclined to help others and to suit their parents than were the pioneers. In her longitudinal study, Almquist noted that there was much change in intended occupation during the 4 years at college.

> Such flexibility in outlook meant that the students were receptive to influences operating in the academic environment. The woman who eventually selects a male field partakes differently of this milieu than the woman who settles on a traditional field. She is more likely to immerse herself in departmental and professionally related clubs which offer a fair bit of occupational socialisation. She enjoys a more intimate relationship with faculty in her major, usually through student-originated independent study projects or by working as an assistant to him/her. Such contact reinforces her interest and raises her self-concept (Almquist, 1974, p. 20).

There is little doubt, however, that the foundations of occupational orientation have been laid long before. Almquist's pioneers were more likely to have college-educated mothers than traditional women, and their mothers were more likely to have occupied a job. They were also more likely to report having used someone as a role model. When mothers were divided into four groups—highly educated working, highly educated non-working, lower educated working, and lower educated non-working—it was found that the lower educated non-working mothers differed from the other groups in having more daughters in traditional occupations. Highly educated working mothers were more likely than the other groups to have pioneer daughters (Tangri, 1972). Not only did pioneer students have better-educated mothers; they also had more role models in general (O'Donnell and Andersen, 1978). They had less feminine role perceptions in general than traditional women, including, for example, attitudes about marital relationships and obligations (Crawford, 1978). They were also more likely to have brothers as their adjacent siblings (in birth order).

Although female students in general are more influenced by female role-models (Basow and Howe, 1979), career-oriented students were more highly father-identified than home-oriented students, and perceived their fathers as less accepting (Oliver, 1975). Moreover, not only fathers are additional role models to mothers. Joesting and Joesting (1972) had men and women students rate the value of being a woman. As many as 26% thought that there was nothing good about being a woman when their instructor was male, and only 5% when she was female. The authors conclude that qualified female role models may enhance the self-image of women students. Again, however, we need to beware of the demand characteristics of the investigation. Moreover, it must be stressed that women do not need female role models. Weishaar *et al*. (1981) found that most said they had been influenced by no-one in their choice of occupation! Of those who admitted influence, more said they had been influenced by males than by females. Traditional women said they had been more often influenced by females than males; pioneers the reverse. Strongest influence and greater certainty of occupational choice was attributed to an influencer who worked in a field which was closely related to the students' own field of choice. This was a much more important factor than the influencer's sex. There are probably different *outcomes* when career-oriented women identify with their fathers than when they identify with their mothers. The former believe more strongly than the latter that career women are positively accepted by their male colleagues at work. The latter have more favourable attitudes towards their own advancements than do the former (Ridgeway, 1978). This latter finding ties in with that of Oliver (1975) quoted above. She found that fathers were perceived as less accepting by career-oriented women.

In summary, the literature gives much evidence of differences between pioneer women (those who choose male-dominated occupations) and traditional women (those who choose female-dominated ones). However, these differences do not relate to the sex of the role-models used purely and simply. Nor should we limit influence to those with whom the woman student has identified. Furthermore, attention has primarily been directed at those influences which promote pioneer choice. There are many more influences maintaining the current occupational imbalance, including even the careers information available at college (Astin, 1977). Indeed, Yanico (1978) showed how sexist language in written information can affect students' perception of how appropriate particular occupations are for men or for women. When the pronoun 'he' and the noun 'men' were used for male-dominated occupations, and the pronoun 'she' and the noun 'women' for female-dominated ones, existing biases were increased as measured by changes in ratings made before and after reading. This finding was true for male-dominated occupations. When the language used was neutral ('he/she' or 'they'), there was some decrease in bias, but this was less for men in their ratings of female-dominated occupations than for women in their rating of male-dominated occupations. Unfortunately, there was no control group included in the design of this experiment, but its potential importance is clear—it indicates that there are all sorts of subtle ways in which existing stereotypes may be reinforced.

10.4 SEX-ROLE STEREOTYPES AND OCCUPATIONAL CHOICE

The distinction between those women students who choose male-dominated occupations and those who choose female-dominated ones may lead to a mistaken inference: that there are only two forms of sex-roles. These are one in which a woman considers herself to possess masculine traits to a high degree and feminine ones to a low degree—and the reverse, predominantly feminine. Constantinople (1973) and Bem (1974) have argued that there are two more categories: those who consider themselves to possess both masculine and feminine traits to a high degree, and those who consider themselves to possess neither. The first group Bem terms androgynous, and the second indeterminate. The findings of Spence *et al.* (1975) confirm that individuals do not always construct their self-concepts in terms of straight masculine or feminine self-concepts. These investigators had more than 400 male and female students make ratings of typical male and typical female students. They then rated themselves on the same sex-role questionnaire. The sets of ratings bore little relation to each other, indicating that crude stereotypes do not carry over into the self-concept.

When researchers started looking at these more sophisticated ideas about internalized sex-roles, they found that they predicted better than sex itself, and than the various background variables such as family which had been used as predictors hitherto. For example, Moreland *et al.* (1979) tried to predict choice of occupation in male and female students in all years of their courses. They found that androgynous women's career progression was greater than that of undifferentiated women, although there was no significant difference between androgynous women and feminine or masculine women. In the case of men, masculine men were more advanced in terms of college and major choice than feminine and undifferentiated men. For men, masculine qualities predicted progress whereas feminine qualities were either not related or were negatively related to progress. Moreland *et al.* (1979) conclude:

> In summary, to understand women's tasks, it appears particularly important to help them acquire and/or maintain self views that include both feminine and masculine qualities. In contrast men's progress in career decision making is predicted almost entirely by their endorsement of masculine qualities (p. 336).

The next question to ask is how, exactly, sex-role stereotypes are involved in the decision-making process. Harren *et al.* (1978) investigated in more detail how the choice of college major is made. The criterion variables in their study were choice of college major and degree of satisfaction with that choice. Using the technique of path analysis they were able to show that it was progress in the decision-making process which predicted choice and satisfaction directly ($r = 0.55$). Individuals' cognitive styles and their sex-role attitudes each affected decision-making progress rather than final choice, while the sex of the student, in its turn, was a fairly strong predictor of sex-role attitudes ($r = 0.47$). Thus we have sex affecting sex-role attitudes, one of two factors predicting decision-making progress, which is the proximal factor affecting choice.

This distinction between sex and sex-role as predictors is a most important one; the greater the superiority of sex-role as a predictor over sex, the more confident we can be that the situation is far more complex than simply male people accepting male stereotypes for themselves and female people accepting female stereotypes. Stockton *et al.* (1980) found in their study of nearly 700 male and female students of elementary education and business studies that sex role accounted for more of the variance in choice of major than did sex itself. However, in this research, sex-role does not predict strongly for men. They tended to choose male-dominated majors regardless of sex-role orientation. It was women for whom sex-role predicted most strongly, with masculine women more likely to choose male-dominated majors, while androgynous women were equally likely to be found in male- or female-dominated majors. Wertheim *et al.* (1978) echo this finding; they discovered no significant differences between the sexes in assertiveness, locus of control, Machiavellianism, and other traits. There were, however, differences between students studying law, management, education, and social work; and students' membership of these study groups was predicted by their sex-role orientation. Note that it is personal sex-role orientation, not students' attitudes to women, which is the predictor (see Harren *et al.*, 1979).

The cognitive complexity predictor is also an interesting one. Both Harren *et al.* (1979) and Lawlis and Crawford (1975) found that cognitive complexity predicted women's choice of a male-dominated major. Lawlis and Crawford had subjects rate themselves in terms both of roles and of the relationships involved in those roles. So, for example, the roles of sweetheart/spouse, parent, boss, friend, enemy were rated on a grid of which the other axis was such relationships as respect, dependence, identity, sexual relationship, and acceptance of feelings. The finding that pioneer women were more differentiated in terms of their positions on this grid suggests that they are capable of a wider perception of roles in general, and therefore have a less restrictive choice of specifically vocational goals. They are also more likely to have congruent career preferences than women who choose female-dominated occupations (Wolfe and Betz, 1981); by 'congruent' is meant the fact that the students' patterns of interest are similar to those of individuals already in the occupation to which the students aspire.

Perhaps these studies on sex-role stereotypes may best be summed up by considering the work of Yanico *et al.* (1978). They looked at women students in home economics, women in engineering, and men in engineering. There were more masculine women in engineering, more feminine ones in home economics, and an equal number of androgynous women in home economics and engineering. The picture of sex stereotypes predicting occupational choice which has dominated the research reviewed above is thus confirmed in the work of Yanico and her colleagues. However, they also found that feminine women in engineering were less satisfied with and certain of their choice than androgynous or masculine women in engineering. This finding echoes the theme of this book: that it is aspects of the self-concept which predict occupational adjustment.

10.5 SEX ROLES AND THE NEED TO ACHIEVE

We saw in Chapter 9 that the aspects of the self-concept which seemed most related to subsequent occupational choice, adjustment, and success were self-esteem and aspirations. We would expect the need to achieve to be related to these aspects of the self-concept; those with a high need to achieve should have fairly high aspirations. We might predict that self-esteem would, as usual, act as a moderating variable; for students of high self-esteem the relation between need for achievement and aspirations should hold strongly, since they believe themselves capable of success in high-level jobs. When we carry these speculations over into the field of the employment of graduate women, their implications become clear. We would expect women with a high need to achieve to be engaged in male-dominated occupations. This would be firstly because those are the occupations with higher rewards and greater status; and second, because achievement orientation is part of the masculine sex stereotype. We have already seen that masculine women are more likely to be found in male-dominated jobs, so it follows that such women should have a high need to achieve.

When career-oriented and home-making-oriented women were compared, the former had a higher need to achieve and lower affiliation needs than the latter (Oliver, 1974). The connection between need to achieve and sex-role orientation was established by Alper (1973). He found that when the thematic content of women students' responses to the Thematic Apperception Test were analysed, masculine and feminine women differed. The masculine women told stories of women's success in critical tasks, while the feminine ones described women as being successful assistants to men.

Next, to consider the connection between need to achieve, sex-role stereo-types, and aspirations. This connection was clearly established by Ory and Helfrich (1978). They found that more men than women students aspired to professional careers, and that these would-be professionals had higher need to achieve than the other students. The highest need to achieve of all was demonstrated by women would-be professionals, and it was these same women who had the least traditional sex-role attitudes.

Perhaps there are distinctions which should be made between types of career orientation. Marshall and Wijting (1980) distinguished between women who are highly *centred* on an occupational career—they consider it more important than other areas of their lives; and women who are highly *committed* to an occupational career. These latter women intend to work throughout the various stages of their lives, but might place child-raising higher on their list of priorities. It is the career-centred women who have a more masculine sex-role stereotype and a higher need to achieve. Unfortu-nately, this useful distinction was not apparently made in the only piece of research known to this writer which relates self-esteem to women's career orientation. Stake (1979) used as her subjects 80 female business students and 111 former business students. She asked them questions about their home-making or occupational career choices and administered tests of self-esteem and sex-role stereotypes. Women with a strong career orientation had higher self-esteem. More interestingly, self-esteem moderated the relationship between career orientation and sex-role stereotypes in the following way: non-traditional sex role attitudes were very highly related to career orientation for women of high self-esteem. For women of low self-esteem, however, the relationship was far less strong. This finding supports our earlier analysis; that is, only women who believe themselves capable are willing to take the risk of actualizing their masculinity in the male-dominated world of work. On the other hand women who have low occupational aspirations are likely to have traditional feminine stereotypes and a high motivation to avoid success (Esposito, 1977).

We should beware of assuming that it is at college that sex-role stereotypes have their most important effects. Earlier social conditioning may have resulted in women failing to attain the necessary conditions for entry to vocationally oriented education. For example, in the UK almost all university degree courses in engineering require mathematics and physics Advanced Level. Subjects for Advanced Level (normally three only are taken) are chosen at the age of 16. A far greater number of boys than girls take these subjects, whereas this is not true for arts subjects such as English, History and Languages. Interesting differences are reported between single-sex and coeducational schools in this respect, with pupils at girls' schools more likely to take scientific subjects than girls at coeducational schools. There is a possibility that girls and women may perceive negative social consequences as likely if they choose male-dominated subjects of study and occupations. This would tie in with the finding of lower need for affiliation in career-oriented women (Oliver, 1974).

Taking this argument further, it is possible that in some cases what appears to be sex discrimination in selection procedures is not directly discriminatory. Terborg (1977), for example, argues that women may either not be qualified for certain occupations, or be less qualified than male applicants. The example quoted above of engineering in the UK would be typical of the first category; there will actually be fewer female than male engineering graduates, and therefore fewer women will be appointed. The situation will be compounded when there are a disproportionate number of applicants from certain degree subjects. Let us consider the example of a large UK private sector manufacturing organization which had many more engineering than personnel posts to offer graduates. However, there were many more applicants per post for the personnel jobs than for the engineering ones. The applicants for the engineering posts were, almost invariably, taking engineering degrees. Now comes the final and obvious link in the chain—by far the majority of the engineering students were men, while the majority of the arts and social science students were women. Sex was the best single predictor of whether an applicant's application form would be accepted or rejected, yet we would be extremely unfair to the organization to accuse it of sex discrimination.

In the USA, research has pinpointed the area of scholastic aptitude which is involved: readers will not be surprised to learn that it is mathematics. Goldman and Hewitt (1976) found that the mathematical sub-test of the Scholastic Aptitude Test Battery predicted choice of major field of undergraduate study very successfully. Further, most sex differences in choice of major may be attributed to women being worse at mathematics. Goldman and Hewitt's title for their paper implicitly cautions us to beware facile explanations however; it is 'The scholastic aptitude test "explains" why college men major in science more often than college women'. A sexual imbalance in college and occupation is not to be explained by a similar imbalance in a test of aptitude. We need to ask why it is that these differences in mathematical aptitude and in the choice of scientific subjects at high school exist.

The case of women graduates has been explored in depth in this chapter. Race, handicap, and other possible sources of stereotypes have not been covered. The interested reader is referred to Reilly and Chao (1982), Boehm (1977), and Hunter et al. (1979) for the often highly technical question of whether certain selection devices are more valid for whites than blacks. The major point which has been made in the present chapter is that sex is a specific instance of a more general thesis. That thesis is that occupational and organizational outcomes depend upon the negotiation of an agreement. The agreement is between the organization and the individual, to the effect that the individual is willing to accept and act upon the organization's expectations of her. This willingness will be contingent upon (a) her own self-concept, (b) the degree of congruence between this and the organization's expectations which she is willing to tolerate and (c) the organization's willingness to adapt its expectations.

In the case of women graduates, the sex-related elements of their self-concept have been shown to play a powerful part in their choice of occupations and their aspirations to management status. In a similar vein, the sex stereotypes held by recruiters have been clearly demonstrated to predict their selection preferences. If it were true that recruiters' sex stereotypes were as sophisticated as those of graduates, then we might expect fruitful negotiations to occur; for the expectations of organizations would take account of masculine, feminine, androgynous, or undifferentiated sex-roles of applicants. It would be sex-role not sex, self-concept not surface attributes, to which recruiters would pay attention. Unfortunately, there is little evidence that many recruiters make these distinctions clearly, either in their view of women graduates or of jobs. As a consequence, female, not feminine or androgynous persons are likely to be appointed to 'feminine' jobs; and male, not masculine or androgynous persons appointed to 'masculine' jobs. Underlying the whole question of bias is the idea that organizational expectations may be defined in terms of the personal qualities supposed necessary for success; for it is personal qualities which form the primary subject-matter of sex stereotypes. It is only when an interactive developmental perspective is taken—when the individual's aspirations, the organization's future plans, and the likely social exchanges between the two parties are the key elements in the recruitment process—that sex bias will be reduced.

11

The Content of Congruence

11.1 A TYPOLOGY

The main focus of this book is upon process, not structure: the process of social negotiation whereby organizations and individuals adjust their expectations of each other so as to achieve a workable degree of congruence between the two. It has been argued throughout that it is the individual's and the organization's views of themselves which determine the extent of this congruence. The individual's self-concept has evaluative as well as descriptive components, and future as well as present dimensions. The organization sees itself (or should do so) not merely as an aggregate of jobs, but as having norms, values, and an image. Negotiation implies repeated communication between the parties, and mutual adjustment.

Little attention has been paid thus far to structure: the structure, or content, of the individual's self, and the nature of the environment in which he operates. One theory of structure dominates the literature, that of Holland (1973). Holland's theory is essentially a description of the person and of the environment in terms of six types, which apply both to persons and to environments. They are the following: realistic, investigative, artistic, social, enterprising, and conventional. Holland describes each type as follows (Holland, 1973, p. 14):

Realistic . . . a preference for activities that entail the explicit ordered or systematic manipulation of objects, tools, machines, animals; and an aversion to educational or therapeutic activities.

Investigative . . . a preference for activities that entail the observational symbolic, systematic, and creative investigation of physical, biological, and cultural phenomena in order to understand and control such phenomena; and an aversion to persuasive, social, and repetitive activities.

Artistic . . . a preference for ambiguous, free, unsystematized activities that entail the manipulation of physical, verbal, or human materials to

147

create art forms or products; and an aversion to explicit, systematic, and ordered activities.

Social . . . a preference for activities that entail the manipulation of others to inform, train, develop, cure, or enlighten; and an aversion to explicit, ordered, systematic activities involving materials, tools, or machines.

Enterprising . . . a preference for activities that entail the manipulation of others to attain organizational goals or economic gain; and an aversion to observational, symbolic, and systematic activities.

Conventional . . . a preference for activities that entail the explicit ordered systematic manipulation of data, such as keeping records (etc.); and an aversion to ambiguous, free, exploratory, or unsystematised activities.

It will be noted immediately that these types are couched in terms of interests and aversions; positive and negative feelings towards certain sorts of activities. This terminology reflects the origins of the six types. They are derived from the factor analysis of several different interest inventories, including Holland's own Vocational Preference Inventory. Although these inventories are different in form and content, factor analysis has revealed similar factor structures for all of them. However, Holland's theory is not just a theory of the structure of interests; it is rather a theory of the structure of the person, of environments, and of the relation between the two.

First, we must examine Holland's claim that the six types describe the person as a whole rather than merely the person's interests. This claim is elaborated in Holland's excellent review article (1976a). To quote: '. . . vocational interests, vocational choices, and characteristics of people in related occupations are manifestations of a common personal disposition or construct' (p. 522). 'A common set of dimensions or categories can be obtained not only from these highly correlated methods—vocational interests, choices, and occupational membership—but also many of their correlates—aptitudes, competencies, self-ratings—which are domains normally assumed to be divergent, (p. 528). It is not our purpose here to review the evidence for the commonality of this factor structure across domains; the most sophisticated and thorough investigations are those of Cole and Hanson (1971), Edwards and Whitney (1972), and Ward et al. (1976). Suffice it to say that self-ratings are one of the domains in which the six-type factor structure emerges; and also to note that in his 1973 book, Holland maintains that certain types of environment affect the individual's self-concepts. For example, an investigative environment encourages people to see themselves as scholarly, as having mathematical and scientific ability, and as lacking in leadership ability. Hence, although Holland's theory explicitly describes the person rather than the self-concept, we may not be taking too many liberties if we assume that the structure of the self-concept is considered to be similar to that of the person. This is particularly reasonable if we remember that many of the measures require the individual to give an explicit account of the domain in question, implying that he is aware of his own personality. For example, interest inventories ask straightforward questions about preference for various activities. We must also note, however, that a six-type description of the self-concept omits some of its most important characteristics (especially, for example, self-esteem). Hence, we would not expect descriptions of the self based on Holland's typology to account for a high proportion of the variance in occupational choice; for we know already that self-esteem is a powerful predictor of these outcomes.

Holland (1973, 1976a) has introduced several refinements to the theory. Persons and environments may be characterized not merely by one of the six types; they may be categorized by a two-type code, or even a three-type code, representing the two or three types on which the individual scores highest. Hence, someone categorized as (conventional, realistic, investigative) would have scored highest on the conventional, second on the realistic, and third on the investigative factor. Such an individual would be termed highly consistent. This is because certain relationships obtain between the six types. Given the order realistic, investigative, artistic, social, enterprising, and conventional, imagine that they are arranged in a circular manner, with each type being allocated a segment of the circle. Realistic will occupy the first segment, investigative the next, and so on round the circle until conventional occupies the next segment to realistic. Holland maintains that adjacent types are more closely related than those with a segment intervening, whereas types with two segments intervening are likely to be opposed to each other. The reader will recall that in the verbal description of types (above) the aversions of one type are the preferences of another. Thus the artistic type has a preference for ambiguous, free, unsystematized activities while the conventional type has an aversion to them. Artistic and conventional types are separated by two other types. To return to our example above, the individual who is coded conventional, realistic, and investigative is considered *consistent* because these three types are adjacent. If he scored much higher on the conventional type than on the other two (and also, therefore, than on the remaining three types), he would also be highly *differentiated*; he would in other words, be 'all of one type'.

Holland's description of environments is based on the assumption that 'a major portion of the force of the environment is transmitted through other people' (Holland, 1973, p. 6). Hence, 'by calculating the distribution of (personality) types in an environment, you will know the environment'. However, Holland immediately qualifies this statement by saying that a simple 'census' of personality types as the source of information for environment types is insufficient. Environments are seldom homogeneous in terms of types, and sub-units of the environment may have disproportionate influence; indeed it is not clear which particular environment has greater influence over the individual at any point in time. Moreover, some individuals within an environment will have more influence than others, and therefore their types should have differential weightings in the definition of the environment.

As far as the relationship of the individual and the environment is concerned, *congruence* is predicted. That is, individuals of a particular type will tend to choose occupations of the same type; they will be less likely to choose an occupation of an adjacent type, and least likely of all to choose one of a more distant type. Further, consistency and differentiation in the individual are predicted to be related to satisfaction with, and stability of, vocational choice and achievement.

These relationships are predicted not only with occupational choice, but also with choice of major field of study at college. In this series of predictions based upon the theory, Holland is treating an occupation as an environment. However, it is worth remembering that the criterion variable is normally occupational choice, defined as the student's stated *preference* for an occupation at any point in time during his undergraduate or postgraduate study. Hence it is not congruence between the type of person and the type of occupation which is predicted; rather, it is between the type of person and his conception of an occupation at that point in time at which he is asked to state his preference. Super (1981) criticizes Holland's theory for this reliance upon expressed preference as the criterion variable.

The congruent relationship is taken to be dynamic in nature; each type of environment attracts its own personality type, and at the same time reinforces its own characteristic achievements, activities, competences, and predispositions. Hence, individuals self-select for environments and are reinforced in that selection. Environments provide opportunities, demands, and encouragement.

The implications of these theoretical propositions for graduate occupational choice and recruitment are clear. We would expect students of certain types to prefer occupations of the same type. We would also predict that they would self-select into colleges and into major subjects of study congruent with their type. As a result of the reinforcing effect of the college environment, congruence should become greater during the student's period of study. Any changes in major area of study or in occupational preference should be towards majors or occupations which are more congruent with the person.

Given, however, the greater difficulty of changing college in comparison to the difficulty of changing major or occupational preference, then we might predict cases in which the causal direction was primarily in the opposite direction. That is, the college environment, or important parts of it, might be incongruent with the student's choice of major, occupational preference, and personality. This environment, consequently, with its powerful and present social pressures, might lead the student to change his major or occupational preference, perhaps in a direction less congruent with his personality than it was originally. Then the environment may itself cause change in the personality type of the student. According to Holland, the individual moves from activities to interests, then to competences, then to values and changes in the self-concept. Thus, by way of example, a student might enter a primarily arts-based college but select to study physical sciences, a course congruent with his investigative personality type. However, most of his friends at college are, because of the nature of the college, studying arts subjects. The student conforms to social pressure and changes his major to arts. Consequently he engages in activities and acquires interests and competences in the study of arts which change his value priorities and self-concept. Thus, the sequence is from behavioural conformity to internalization.

An alternative sequence of events would run as follows. The students' attitudes, values, and preferences change as a consequence of his relation with his reference group of peers. As a consequence of this change of personality types, he searches out an environment more congruent with his changed personality, and changes major and occupational preference. Thus the sequence is one from identification and internalization to behaviour. A close reading of Holland (1973) suggests that he prefers the first of these two causal sequences as an explanation of change. However, because of the lack of specificity in his account of the relationship between the person and the environment and of the process of social influence and negotiation, Holland finds it difficult to predict whether individual and environment will grow closer together or whether the individual will change environments. Part of the problem is caused by the difficulty in specifying what an environment is, and in determining which of several environments is predicted to have most influence. It is only when we analyse in terms of social process that we can clearly delimit a sequence of social episodes and their outcomes.

Nevertheless, it is clear that Holland's postulate of congruence embodies much of the social process theory proposed in this book; for it stresses the degree of similarity between individual and environment as being the basis for the relationship between them. Now we must examine the strength of the evidence in support of Holland's theory in relation to graduates; but whilst examining it we must bear continually in mind that the *occupational* context is only one element of the organizational environment for which the graduate is self-selecting and being selected. He is also entering, at a more general level, the world of work; and, at a more specific level, a particular organization.

11.2 TYPES IN EVIDENCE

Initial research by Abe and Holland (1965) demonstrated a clear relationship between types and the vocational choice of large numbers of college freshmen, and also between types and choice of subject major. In a large-scale longitudinal study, Holland (1968) related types (defined in terms of a three-type code) to 22 dependent variables, including competences, life-goals, self-ratings, and occupational preferences. Differences were found between individuals of different codes; differences were smaller for three-type codes than for two-type codes, and for two-type than for single-type codes. For male students, Holland found that the more differentiated the student, the greater was the stability over time of his occupational preference. A slight relationship was also found between consistency and stability. There was also some slight evidence for students being more likely to maintain their occupational preference over time when the college contained many students who had preferences of the same type. Holland *et al.* (1975) confirmed more powerfully the relationships of differentiation and consistency with other variables, in this case with decision-making ability as indicated by the Self-Directed Search instrument (Holland, 1971, 1972).

The prediction that the relationship between personality and field of study will grow closer over time was supported in the work of Walsh and Lacey (1969, 1970), although it is worth noting that this was true only for three of the six types in the case of male students, and for four in the case of females. Walsh *et al.* (1972) found that college seniors report more change consistent with field of study than do freshmen.

The benefits of congruence for the individual are indicated by Walsh and Lewis's (1972) discovery of greater stability of choice, and less alienation, emotional disturbance, and anxiety among those male students whose single-type code was congruent with their field of study. In the case of women students, those whose personality code was congruent with their occupational preference were of greater vocational maturity (Walsh and Hanle, 1975). This was indexed by the Career Maturity Inventory, and in particular, by its attitude scale. From this finding, we may conclude that 'congruent students tend to be more involved in the career choice process, more oriented toward work, and more independent in decision-making when compared to the incongruent and undirected students' (Walsh and Hanle, 1975, pp. 94–95). Congruent female undergraduate students are also more certain in their choice of major than incongruent ones (Spokane and Derby, 1979). In terms of more general characteristics of personality, congruent students tend to be more dominant than incongruent ones, have a higher capacity for status and responsibility, a greater sense of well-being, and be more self-controlled, tolerant, and intellectually efficient, and more oriented towards conventional achievement (Walsh, 1974). The benefits of congruence are also demonstrated in the case of highly specific subjects of study, for example, theoretical engineering (Bruch and Krieshok, 1981). These authors found that students of the investigative type showed greater persistence and attained higher grades in these theoretical subjects than students of the realistic type, even though they were matched for general and mathematical aptitude. Overall, degree of congruence of personality type with choice of major and with occupational preference appears to be related to many other variables which are in their turn related to occupational choice and adjustment. Indeed, when congruence, differentiation, and consistency were all regressed onto the stability of occupational preference of students, consistency and differentiation did not increase significantly the amount of variance accounted for by congruence alone (Villwock *et al.*, 1976).

Thus there is a considerable literature relating degree of congruence to other aspects of students, using concurrent research designs. Research seeking to test the basic congruence hypothesis has developed in two further directions. First, there is a limited amount of longer-term predictive validation; and second, congruence between person types and highly specific areas of professional study has been explored. As an example of the first research direction, O'Neil *et al.* (1978) found quite successful prediction for investigative-type freshmen whose type was ascertained in 1970. Seven years later, a questionnaire revealed that their graduate major, ideal and projected career plans, and job entered were congruent with their type. It is important that more such evidence is acquired, since it reduces the dependence of Holland's theory upon expressed preferences and upon major choice (sometimes affected by immediate environmental pressures). Walsh *et al.* (1977) have looked at the degree of congruence between type and job for graduates now in work, but such research is not common. There is, nevertheless, clear evidence that the degree of congruence of a first job predicts the category of job held 5 and 10 years later (Holland *et al.*, 1973).

The second type of evidence regarding congruence comes from studies in which specific areas of study are predicted successfully by personality type. For example, Utz and Hartman (1978) showed that the Self-Directed Search questionnaire distinguished between different specialities chosen by students majoring in business; the group specializing in accounting were clearly differentiated from those in marketing and behavioural studies. Other studies demonstrate differentiation along personality characteristics closely related to Holland's types. For example, Scott and Sedlacek (1975) found that physical scientists scored higher than engineers on introspection and intellectual dimensions, lower on social and conventional ones.

These findings lead us on to consider evidence which relates other dimensions of personality than Holland's types to students studying different subjects. Of course, this evidence does not indicate the extent to which students choose subjects because they are a certain sort of person, and to which they are a certain sort of person because they are studying a particular subject. This latter question is explored in greater depth in the next section. The evidence relating characteristics of persons to courses of study is somewhat diffuse, having no real theoretical framework to direct it. Direnzo (1974) found that degree of dogmatism (as measured by the Rokeach Dogmatism Scale) differentiated behavioural science, liberal arts, business administration, and physical and natural science students. Authoritarianism, a related characteristic, discriminates in the same direction, with higher authoritarian Israeli freshmen entering to study biology and chemistry, lower authoritarians to study psychology and philosophy (Weller and Nadler, 1975). In American and Israeli colleges, freshman choice of subject can be attributed more to the individual's self-selection for that subject, since he is unlikely to have specialized during his school career. In the UK, however, many university subjects are unavailable to students since they have not studied the appropriate Advanced Level subjects at school between ages 16 and 18.

11.3 VALUE PRIORITIES

Most of the research, however, has compared students studying different subjects in terms of the values they hold. The concept of value is somewhat ambiguously used in occupational and vocational psychology. Social psychologists such as Rokeach (1973) give values a central position in their accounts of the person. For Rokeach there is a limited number of values, which are identical for all persons, but held in different orders of priority. To quote:

> A *value* is an enduring belief that a specific mode of conduct or end-state of existence is personally or socially preferable to an opposite or converse mode of conduct or end-state of existence. A *value-system* is an enduring organisation of beliefs concerning preferable modes of conduct or end states of existence along a continuum of relative importance (Rokeach, 1973, p. 5).

The distinction between instrumental and terminal values (modes of conduct *versus* end-states of existence) leads to distinguishing values such as capable, ambitious, and polite from values such as freedom, salvation, and a world of peace.

Super (1973) holds a similar view in some respects. He believes that 'Values are objectives that one seeks to attain to satisfy a need. Interests are the specific activities and objects through which values can be attained and needs met (p. 190). Thus one values what one needs, according to Super (which involves us in some tricky negotiations about the definition of need). According to Lofquist and Dawis (1978), on the other hand, values are more basic dimensions of needs when needs are grouped according to underlying commonalities. Values are held to bear the same relationship to needs as abilities to skills. Regardless of their treatment of the specific relationship of needs to values, both Super's, and Lofquist and Dawis's, accounts treat values as central underlying dimensions of the person, in line with the social psychological tradition exemplified by Rokeach.

While some of the research reported in the literature continues to define values in this way, and operationalizes the concept in terms of values questionnaires such as the Allport–Vernon–Lindsay Study of Values, other research does not. Rather, we frequently find values defined in terms of the outcomes of occupations for the individual. As we saw in Chapter 9, the classical decision theory model of occupational choice maintains that individuals make subjective estimates of the probability of various outcomes and also evaluate them. It is the outcomes which are often termed 'values' in the research literature, and the 'strength' of these 'values' is indicated by subjects' rank orderings or ratings. The distinction between this latter operational definition of values and the definition of interests is thus one of part and whole; interests are positive feelings towards certain activities, but activities are only one among several types of outcome. Thus salary level would be a value, but not an interest, while travel abroad would be both a value and an interest.

Perhaps it is the choice of instrument to measure values which determines the definition favoured by researchers, rather than the reverse (a somewhat cynical suggestion). Researchers defining values as outcomes will tend to use such instruments as Super's Work Values Inventory, while those investigating values as basic features of the person will favour the Allport–Vernon–Lindsay instrument. When the Work Values Inventory was factor analysed by O'Connor and Kinnane (1961), using data obtained from nearly 200 college subjects, the following six factors were found: security, economic, and material; social, artistic; work conditions and associates; heuristic, creative; achievement, prestige; and independence, variety. These factors encompass most of those values which appear consistently in the literature.

The pioneering research in this area was conducted by Rosenberg (1957). He found that engineers and scientists among Cornell University undergraduates were least likely to consider helping others as an important value, while scientists in particular paid little attention to the extrinsic rewards of a job, such as pay and status. The work values Rosenberg investigated were security; prestige; money; working with people not things; leadership; freedom from supervision; being helpful to others; creativity; using special abilities; and adventure. Similar differences between arts and science students were found in a UK sample by Entwistle and Wilson (1977). Using a UK version of the Allport–Vernon–Lindsay Study of Values, they found that science students scored lower than arts students on radicalism and social values, but higher on economic and theoretical ones. Duff and Cotgrove (1982) showed how such differences in values predicted preference for careers within or outside industry in the UK. Fretz (1972) differentiated US law, medical, engineering, business, and education postgraduate students on the basis of values. Those values which were most powerful in distinguishing these groups from each other were the more extrinsic ones of pay, advancement, working conditions, fringe benefits, and prestige. Work values can even succeed in differentiating between students studying specializations within a subject, as Izraeli et al. (1979) found when they discovered different value priorities in industrial engineers from other engineering students. Sex differences may also be present, with males placing a higher value on profit and esteem, females on service to others (Wagman, 1965). Note here too the work of Cherry (1975) described on p. 135.

Of particular interest, particularly in Britain, are differences in values among science and engineering students related to working in industrial organizations. Cotgrove and Box (1970) investigated these values in final-year and postgraduate chemistry students in three UK universities. They distinguished 'public', 'private' and 'organizational' scientists on the basis of questions derived from the Mertonian norms of science. Public scientists scored highly on all four of these norms—communality, or the sharing of scientific information by publication; disinterestedness in the pursuit of scientific knowledge; organized scepticism regarding the grounds for accepting or rejecting scientific theories; and universalism, the belief that scientific knowledge is equally valid however it is obtained, provided scientific method is used. These 'public scientists' among the students expected to get higher degrees than did the other students, and admired those members of faculty who themselves were prolific publishers in the scientific journals. 'Private scientists' scored highly only on disinterestedness and organized scepticism, while 'organizational scientists' scored highly only on organized scepticism. Public scientists tend to wish to enter an academic career, private scientists the Research and Development Division of an organization, while organizational scientists were willing to work in a variety of divisions. Taylor (1979) finds a similar distinction between engineers at one prestigious engineering college in the UK. Some students have primarily managerial goals—they are interested in pay, promotion, and policy-making. Others have primarily technical goals, wanting to be involved in new technological developments and interesting work now. The former are more likely to come from higher socioeconomic class families; the latter to have attended non-selective state schools (comprehensive schools).

It is tempting but dangerous to infer from these last two pieces of research that universities exercise a malign influence upon the student, perpetuating the 'British disease' of unwillingness to be involved in 'getting one's hands dirty' actually manufacturing and selling. At first sight the picture could be painted of middle-class young persons retaining any entrepreneurial and achievement orientation inculcated by their families, while working-class students, with no such models, latch on to the value systems they see exemplified in the university faculty. Since these are largely inimical to industry's needs, the university has been seen as corrupting the youth (*pace* Socrates!). Before any such conclusion can be drawn, however, a causal relationship between university course and students' value change must be demonstrated; not an easy task, as will be described in the next section.

We have described the ways in which values differentiate students in different subjects, and also industrial and academic values within the university. Finally, let us consider research which bears upon choice of job and organization. Singer (1974) found that for US students, jobs in which they could learn, accomplish something worthwhile, and work with congenial people were valued especially. The extent to which an organization demonstrated broad social concern was not a major criterion. Williamson and Whitehead (1980) in the UK found that intellectual challenge was the most frequently desired outcome, with a high starting salary a long way behind. When the values of a particular type of student are examined, however, the picture is somewhat different. In their analysis of job factors and organizational factors in job choice by 62 graduate management students, Feldman and Arnold (1978) found the following order of importance; pay, fringe benefits, use of skills and abilities, responsibility, leadership, autonomy, independence, flexibility of hours, and types of service provided by the organization. Individual differences, such as the individual's growth need strength, were related to this order of importance, however, with the more intrinsic outcomes such as autonomy being valued more by those with high growth need strength. Indeed, features of organizations are considered by students to be associated with the relative balance of intrinsic and extrinsic factors: Extrinsic outcomes are believed more probable in large organizations, intrinsic ones in smaller organisations (Greenhaus *et al.*, 1978). When students were choosing between three UK manufacturing organizations, a social relations orientation was the best predictor of choice (Rammage, 1975).

Whatever the origins of students' value priorities, it seems clear that they are likely to have different values from recruiters. In a small sample of students and recruiters from one university, Vecchiotti and Korn (1980) found evidence of considerable differences. Using Rokeach's value survey they discovered that students placed a higher priority than recruiters on those terminal values relating to social and aesthetic areas: mature love, inner harmony, true friendship, a world of peace, and a world of beauty. Recruiters placed a higher priority than students on self-respect, a sense of accomplishment, an exciting life, social recognition, a comfortable life, and salvation. In terms of instrumental values, students were higher on honest, loving, helpful, courageous, cheerful, forgiving, and obedient; recruiters on responsible, capable, ambitious, self-controlled, logical, polite, and clean. Given these considerable differences, we need to know whether recruiters' personal values are those they look for in applicants, and also whether they are those of the world of work in general and the recruiters' organizations in particular. Vechiotti and Korn faced their recruiters with a profile of an imaginary applicant, and did indeed find that, regardless of the sex of this 'applicant', they chose their own predominantly masculine values as more important for the job.

Overall, it is difficult to make many generalizations about values, except to say that students of different subjects have different value priorities, even at the beginning of their college careers.

11.4 EFFECTS OF COLLEGE

It would be very interesting to be able to discover whether universities and colleges were responsible for changes in the values and aspirations of students. Unfortunately there are grave methodological difficulties in arriving at such an inference of causality. These difficulties are well described by Schaie (1973) and Hampson (1982, chapter 8) with reference to developmental research in general, and by Whiteley *et al.* (1975) regarding effects of college. To illustrate them, let us consider the testing of the hypothesis that universities give students value priorities contrary to those of industry.

It would not be satisfactory to test this hypothesis by comparing first-year with final-year students at one moment in time. If a difference were found, it might be due to the college experience; or it could be due to the fact that the final-year students were older; or that they had had different experiences from the younger students during the different years in which they were brought up (for example, the older students might have been brought up for some years during a war which the younger ones were too young to understand). Thus this cross-sectional research design leads to inconclusive outcomes.

The same is true of a longitudinal design, where a sample of students is tested when they are in their first year and again when they are in their final year of study. Here, the difficulty is that we do not know whether they might have changed in the same way even if they had not been students. Perhaps people as they get older tend to change their values in particular ways and develop more differentiated values (Pryor, 1980); perhaps there were general cultural changes in the nation or the world which resulted in changes in values for people of particular age groups. A control group of young people who did not go to college would be beneficial; but college students are a self-selected group, who might have chosen to attempt to enter college precisely because they held different value priorities from others in the first place. Thus the longitudinal design for research also has its problems.

Finally, it will also be the case that the results of cross-sectional or longitudinal research are specific to the period of time in which they are collected. The prevailing cultural climate at the time might result in different outcomes. We would imagine that the different social, cultural, and economic climates of the 1960s and the late 1970s and 1980s would foster different value priorities in the young, and research supports this assumption. In their immense longitudinal study of over 100,000 US students in 600 colleges and universities, Astin and Panos (1969) and Astin (1982) found differences in the proportion of students taking particular major subjects; arts, social sciences, education, humanities, and, recently, natural sciences have decreased in popularity, and business, engineering, and computer science increased. When rating life-goals, students in 1981 were more likely to place a higher value on being well off financially, and a lower value on developing a meaningful philosophy of life than students in 1971. They were more materialistic, more interested in power and status, less altruistic, and less likely to be concerned about social issues.

It is clear, then, that there are very considerable difficulties in drawing inferences from research upon the effects of college. One strategy of research is to demonstrate that students studying subjects which encourage opposite or contradictory values to each other become more similar to their subjects. Thus, for example, Weller (1979) used a cross-sectional design to compare first- and third-year students. First-year students of psychology, social work, and sociology were less authoritarian than students of economics, geography, biology, chemistry, and physics (although at $p < 0.10$, this difference failed to reach statistical significance). The third-year students, however, were more different; the social science students were less authoritarian than their first-year colleagues, while the others were more authoritarian. Since it is unlikely that there were general cultural factors which both encouraged and discouraged authoritarian values and attitudes, we may have more confidence that these changes were due in the main to the college experience; and not to the college experience *per se*, but to the study of particular subjects.

Another piece of research which avoids some of the pitfalls of the typical research design is the longitudinal research of Barton *et al.* (1973). They administered the 16 PF test to a large group of young people in 1965, and then in 1970 discovered what had been the major environmental events in their lives; in particular, whether they had gone to college or entered work. They found that for both groups, radicalism and intelligence had increased over time, and suspicion decreased. Thus age, plus changes in the cultural climate, rather than the college experience itself seem more likely explanations for the changes in personality. However, the college group increased significantly more than the work group in tendermindedness and imagination, the work group more than the college group in self-sentiment.

Both of these pieces of research suggest the explanation of *progressive conformity*: students become more like the subjects they initially selected. In those cases where a student enters a subject which is a minority interest in the college and/or among his peers, we could expect him to be more likely to change subjects than students in more popular subjects. His change should be to a more popular subject, but also to one similar in value priorities to the subject he originally selected.

The study by Astin and Panos (1969) supports these hypotheses. Changes in career plans and choice of major subject were towards choices that were popular among other students, but were normally fields related to those in which students had commenced their studies. There did seem to be some general trends, however, regardless of the nature and subject emphasis of particular colleges; engineering, physical sciences, and medical sciences became less popular, and college professor, business, and law more so. These changes in subject choice are parallelled in the contemporaneous research of Feldman and Newcomb (1969). They too found a general drift away from engineering, and towards education, business, and law. In their analysis of changes in values, Feldman and Newcomb found an overall increase in aesthetic values, and a decrease in religious and economic values. So too did Bayer *et al.* (1973). The same pattern was found in UK universities. Entwistle and Wilson (1977) showed that social, theoretical, and aesthetic values increased over the 3-year degree course of both arts and science students, whereas religious and economic values decreased. Making a lot of money was the only value which changed (decreased) in Jones's (1973) UK sample. At least in the late 1960s and early 1970s, students' values changed over the period of their course. But we cannot attribute these changes to college—they could have been due to getting older, and to the current cultural environment.

Moreover, we cannot be clear whether value changes cause or are consequent upon vocational preferences, choice of major, and occupational entry. The research evidence points both ways. In his pioneering study, Rosenberg (1957) distinguished between those choices of occupation which required specialized training and those which did not. In the case of the former, value change tended to follow on after occupational choice; in the case of the latter, it preceded. An explanation in terms of cognitive dissonance reduction immediately presents itself: if one has committed oneself to a costly course of study from which it is difficult to change, and which leads to a specific occupation, then by definition one has chosen an occupation. Therefore values and other beliefs have to be made consonant with this choice. Study of a non-vocational subject does not imply choice; occupational preferences expressed at one point in time may be changed without great personal or financial cost. Thus there is no real psychological reason for changing values.

There is other evidence that students' values change after a change of subject of study rather than before it. Elton (1971) found that engineering students who changed to arts or science subjects became subsequently more realistic, non-judgemental, intellectually liberal, and sceptical of orthodox religious beliefs than students who stayed in engineering. In terms of interests rather than values, students who left engineering lost their physical science interest, and gained social services, business management, or sales interests according to the Strong Vocational Interest Blank (Taylor and Hanson, 1972). The same is true after students have left college and entered an occupation, although again, there is a difference between occupations. The values of graduates in business, natural science, engineering, and medicine change to fit their occupations. In the case of individuals in education, law, and the humanities, occupational choice changed to fit values (Underhill, 1966). Contrary to the idea that values express needs, those with higher incomes value money more, those with higher work autonomy value work content more, and those in more socially oriented jobs value social contact more as they progress in their professions (Mortimer and Lorence, 1979).

If students enter college to study subjects which reflect their existing value priorities, and if the study of a subject results in the enhancement of these priorities, then we have to look elsewhere for reasons for change. Holland (1973) and others would suggest that the college environment is the main causal factor. Specifically, it suggested that the relative proportions of the number of courses in each of his six types, the number of faculty, and the number of students in each are indices of college environment (Richards *et al.*, 1970). The preponderance of one type would result in social pressure to change to that type. Indeed, Holland and Nichols (1964) found that the greater number of occupational preference changes occurred in the more heterogeneous college environments. Sometimes, the effect of the college environment can be so strong that it results in changes in choice of major subject which are less congruent than were students' original choices (Spokane *et al.*, 1978).

In summary, it is not clear how much of the changes in values and in major subjects and occupational choice which occur during college can be attributed to college. It does seem that what changes there are in major and occupational choice are often the result of conformity; and that value priorities can subsequently change to accord with the new 'choice'. While Holland has gone a long way towards delineating some of the structure of persons and occupations, the generally fairly low correlations he obtains reflect the selective nature of his theory. If the thesis of this book is correct, it is self-concept which predicts occupation, not personality. Self-concept includes several elements, such as self-esteem and sex stereotype which do not appear in Holland's theory. Hence, although it is reasonable to assume that Holland's personality types may be represented in the self-concept, they are certainly not sufficient to describe it.

However, the value of the interest inventories and, in particular of the Self-Directed Search, (Holland, 1971, 1972), is considerable. It permits students to establish the degree of congruence of certain aspects of themselves with various occupations, a necessary and important preliminary towards meaningful application to particular organizations. Moreover, in principle the analysis of the environment can be applied to specific organizations, just as it has been applied to colleges. The degree of consistency and of differentiation present in the organization, as well as its congruence with the graduate entrant's type, will have consequences for job satisfaction and stability.

12

Careers Services

12.1 COUNSELLING PSYCHOLOGY

One party to the graduate recruitment process has not yet been mentioned—the careers service. Long gone are the days when counselling psychology and recruiting officers shared the same underlying theoretical assumptions. In the days of Rodger's Seven Point Plan (Rodger and Cavanagh, 1968) vocational guidance and personnel selection both used the matching model; that is, both thought that their task was to match individuals to occupations or jobs by assessing the individuals in terms of the traits they possessed. They were then either recommended to, or selected for, jobs which were supposed to require those particular traits to a marked degree. As Wallis (1978) observed, this approach led to the idea of occupational choice as a one-off decision, with the counsellor needed at crisis point. The counsellor was seen as an expert in occupations, exercising a benevolent influence upon the client.

As shown in Chapter 1, many selectors have retained their underlying matching model, despite the difficulties of forming judgements about personality traits described in Chapters 2 and 3. Counselling psychology, on the other hand, has taken on board a wide variety of theoretical viewpoints (some of them already described in this book). However, common to all these viewpoints is the almost exclusive focus upon the individual, the person. Just as selectors have failed to consider the individual as part of a continuously changing social environment, so too counselling psychology has concentrated upon the client to the exclusion of her relationship with organizations. Indeed, the only social process in which counsellors seem interested is that of the counselling session itself, investigated *ad nauseam* in the *Journal of Counselling Psychology*.

This concentration upon the individual is explicable in several different ways. The first explanation relates to the urge of counselling psychology to achieve a professional identity. In America, there is even a Division of Counselling Psychology in the American Psychological Association. One of the features of being a professional is the strong emphasis on fulfilling one's obligations to one's clients. As a consequence, counselling psychology considers students' interests to be its paramount concern. On occasion, it has almost seemed as if counselling psychologists were self-appointed defenders of students against employers.

Another feature of would-be professionals is their technique of attaching themselves to another better-established professional group. In this case, many counselling psychologists in the USA and the UK see themselves as related to clinical psychologists and psychotherapists (who in their turn have a strongly medical historical allegiance). As a consequence, the individual is emphasized as the focus of the counsellor's concern, just as the patient is the doctor's. Furthermore, the counsellor's client is seen as someone with a problem, which has to be 'diagnosed', an aetiology found, and a remedial course of action prescribed. This medical model is pervasive in the USA and the UK. Taking the UK first, Nelson-Jones (1982) writes: 'Attempts to differentiate between counselling and psychotherapy are never wholly successful' (p. 3) and again: 'Counselling psychology is an applied area of psychology which has the objective of helping people to live more effective and fulfilled lives. Its clientele tend to be *not very seriously disturbed people* [my italics] in non-medical settings' (p. 5).

There is no better instance of the medical model at work, this time in a specifically career counselling context, than Crites' (1976b) attempt to synthesize several different accounts of counselling theory. He maintains that there are:

> three principal chronological stages of any career counselling encounter, regardless of temporal span: the beginning, during which a *diagnosis* of the client's problem is typically made; the middle, in which the *process* of intervention with the client is implemented; and the end, during whch the *outcomes* of the experience are enumerated and evaluated by the client and counsellor (Crites, 1976b, p. 2).

Diagnosis involves discovering what the client's problem is, and why she has that problem. Crites gives the example of a client who may be undecided about her occupational choice, either because of her specific immaturity in career terms, or because she is in general an indecisive person. Is the diagnosis to be indecision or indecisiveness? Exploration of the client's previous history of anxiety regarding the taking of decisions has to be explored before a diagnosis can be reached.

There follows the process stage, when the client, having been allocated to her 'nosological category' (Crites' words), and the counsellor engage in interview. This is 'a higher-order relational experience in which client and counsellor share responsibility for problem solution' (Crites, 1976b, p. 5). At the final outcomes stage the objective is to acquire those career-mature behaviours which are problem-solving. But probably more important, the counsellor encourages the generalization of these behaviours to the solution of other life problems. If the career counselling is efficacious, the client learns an approach to problem solving and decision making which can be used not only in future career adjustments but also in personal, marital, and social adjustments. Furthermore, the client gains confidence in his/her competence to solve problems and make decisions independently of others. The client becomes a responsible individual, personally as well as vocationally (Crites, 1976b, p. 5).

At this point one is tempted to query why counsellors are not available at every supermarket, so obviously beneficial are their ministrations. However, it was not my purpose in quoting Crites' account to ridicule his grandiose claims for counselling. Rather, it was to demonstrate the concern with the *individual case* and the adherence to the *medical model* typical of many counsellors. At the end of his theoretical account, Crites quotes a case study of Karen. This person was suffering from indecision, and received seven hour-long sessions of counselling! The sheer impracticality of his whole approach was pointed out forcefully to Crites by Holland (1976b), who believes that such vocational counselling should be the treatment of last resort. Individual counselling sessions of this nature, even if considered desirable, would not be feasible, particularly in UK universities where the careers service has been decimated by recent government cuts in university budgets.

Even the most humanistic of counselling approaches, that of Rogers and Maslow, implies that there is something wrong with the client. Rogers believes that 'individuals appear to have two motivational systems, their organismic actualizing tendency and their conscious self. As the self-concept develops, the actualizing tendency is expressed in the actualizing of the self-concept, which may or may not be synonymous with the actualizing of the organism' (Nelson-Jones, 1982, p. 19). Defining the organism as the self, we have a distinction here between the self and the self-concept.

> The self may be viewed as the real, underlying, organismic self expressed in popular sayings such as 'To thine own self be true' and 'To be that self which one truly is'. The self-concept is a person's perception of himself, which does not always correspond with his own experience or organismic self. Thus, ideally the actualizing tendency refers to self-actualizing where aspects of self and of self-concept are synonymous or congruent. However, where self and self-concept are incongruent, the desire to actualize the self-concept may work at cross purposes with the deeper need to actualize the organismic self (Nelson-Jones, 1982, p. 21).

One of the basic causes of such incongruence are conditions of worth, other people's evaluations of the individual which she has internalized into her self-concept. It is but a small step to conclude that counsellors should be concerned with remedying this incongruence, persuading individuals to accept their real selves and reject their conditions of worth. Some examples of conditions of worth relevant to occupational choice are 'I am not the sort of person who can handle life without being dependent on other people', 'High-status occupations are always better than low-status occupations' (Nelson-Jones, 1982, p. 421). As Crites (1976) notes, humanistic theories too involve the diagnosis of causes of problems—the difference from other theories is merely that the cause is always the same. Moreover, the so-called problem appears to lie in the difference between the client's and the counsellor's value priorities, with the counsellor disguising his attempt to impose his own priorities in the language of therapy.

Other theories of personal development and of counselling psychology could have been quoted, with the same objective: to demonstrate their concentration upon the individual client and upon the remediation of a supposed problem. The field of counselling psychology embraces several different theories and modes of treatment. They are reviewed with special reference to the USA by Harkness (1976), Healy (1975), Tolbert (1980), Corey (1977), and Weinrach (1979); and in the UK by Blackham (1978) and Nelson-Jones (1982). Each theoretical account infers modes of treatment from its theory, implying that successful outcomes of treatment offer support for the theory. Yet, as Claiborn's (1982) review clearly demonstrates, none of the particular theoretical constructions has been shown to be superior. 'Interpretations differing greatly in content seem to have a comparable impact on clients. No one interpretive framework has proven superior to any other in promoting therapeutic processes, such as client exploration, or in leading to positive outcome, however that is assessed' (Claiborn, 1982, p. 450). Indeed research has not even enabled us to decide what it is about counselling which produces any effect it does have. We do not know whether content is irrelevant, and any change is due to the counsellor's conveyed attitudes; whether any change is due to the provision of *any* conceptual framework whereby the client can construe her experience; or whether the higher-order content variables of the interpretation are important after all.

Given the emphasis upon problem-remediation, it is hardly surprising that students who had not attended the counselling service perceived the clients as suffering significantly more from psychological and interpersonal problems than they themselves were (Dreman and Dolev, 1976). In a large US state university, 64% of the students knew little or nothing about the facilities offered (Carney *et al.*, 1979). In both the USA and the UK major efforts have been made to change the image of careers counselling so as to remove any idea of remediation. For example, in their *Specialty guidelines for the delivery of services* (1981, p. 16) the American Psychological Association states

Counselling psychological services refers to services provided by counsel-ling psychologists that apply principles, methods, and procedures for facilitating effective functioning during the life-span developmental process. In providing such services, counselling psychologists approach practices with a significant emphasis on positive aspects of growth and adjustment and with a developmental orientation.

Super's career developmental theory is clearly to the fore in this account. Super himself says 'clinical psychologists tend to look for what is wrong and how to treat it, while counselling psychologists tend to look for what is right and how to help use it' (Super, 1977, p. 14). When spelling out the implications of developmental theory for careers counselling in Britain, Watts (1981) suggests:

1. that emphasis should shift from discrete decisions made at particular points in time to the underlying and continuous process of career development through which individuals decided who they were and the kind of lives they wished to and might lead;
2. that the matching process should be concerned not just with individuals' abilities and aptitudes, but also with their needs, values and interests: in other words, that it should cover not only what they could offer to their work, but also what their work could offer to them in terms of their total personality and life-style;
3. that guidance should be concerned not only with matching of existing attributes, but also with self-development and growth;
4. that guidance should be concerned not only with choice of occupational roles, but also with the interaction between such choices and the individual's evolving constellation of leisure, family and community roles;
5. that the aim of guidance should not be to deploy expertise to make decisions for people, but rather to use it to help people make decisions for themselves.

Despite these efforts by Super and others, the idea that students have problems which they need help in solving is still pervasive. In particular, the notion is still widespread that failure to be able to state a preference for an occupation is a problem, to be termed 'indecision'. As we have seen from Crites' article cited earlier in this chapter, much careers counselling relates to diagnosing this 'problem'. It only a problem, however, if we subscribe to the view that individuals have to decide on the occupation they wish to enter before they can take steps to enter the world of work. This appears a very prescriptive view of a process which may be far less logical. Selection of an occupation implies individual decision, whereas the more appropriate analysis is likely to be in terms of social exchange. As Ginzberg (1972) notes, in many large organisations the role of the graduate may not be defined in specific occupational terms until after she has joined the organization, and it may change several times after subsequent retraining. Moreover, the intuitive and inherently unsystematic nature of students' occupational behaviour suggests that theories of career choice that describe the choice task as a systematic process may be misleading. Such theories may impose order on a world of career uncertainty, where little order exists. If this is true, rather than counselling students to follow some systematic approach, such as adopting specific goals and rational plans to achieve them, counsellors should instead help students cope with a dynamic and uncertain choice task. A desirable outcome of career counselling might then be students' recognition of the unsystematic nature of career decisions; that is, that there is no purely rational way of preparing for a career (Baumgardner, 1976, p. 45).

A second, more technical, reason for rejecting the conceptualization of indecision as a problem, indicative of career immaturity, is the poor psychometric properties of measures of career maturity. Holland states: 'We don't have the tools to implement an approach with a heavy reliance on a diagnostic base' (Holland, 1976b, p. 13), while Kidd opines 'From a psychometric point of view, because of the lack of adequate concurrent and predictive validity data and the confusing findings relating to construct validity, the labelling of measures aiming to assess career attitudes, competencies, and skills as vocational maturity instruments would seem to be premature' (Kidd, 1981, pp. 362–363). For example, Crites' Career Maturity Inventory, although widely sued to diagnose 'immaturity' in career decision-making, has relatively poor validity (Holland et al., 1975).

Counselling psychology, then, remains primarily an individually-oriented field of endeavour. 'A single client is more manageable and understandable than the complexity surrounding her or his development' (Ivey, 1980, p. 13). A few counselling psychologists are realizing that their concern should be with the transactions of the client with her environment; in the case of the graduate these transactions are primarily those between the student and the organization. Concentration upon the student and her problems has rendered counselling psychology largely irrelevant to her practical needs because of its basically flawed conceptualization of the situation. Perhaps counselling psychology has been suffering from a surfeit of romantic individualism! (Warnath, 1975). Certainly, many counsellors working in the careers counselling services in universities would strongly disassociate themselves from many of the points described in this section under the rubric of counselling psychology. Instead they would see much of their task as one of careers education.

12.2 CAREERS EDUCATION

The idea of careers education frees the counsellor from the twin millstones of counselling psychology: the supposed need for face-to-face individual treatment, and the idea of a problem to be diagnosed. In his account of careers education in higher education, Watts (1977) suggests that its purpose should be to facilitate four outcomes: opportunity awareness, self-awareness, decision learning, and transition learning. Watts regards these outcomes as related in the following way: opportunity awareness and self-awareness lead to decision learning, which in its turn leads on to transition learning.

> By *opportunity awareness* is meant the help given to students to experience and gain some understanding of the general structure of the working world they are going to enter, the range of opportunities that exist within it, the demand different parts of it may make upon them, and the rewards and satisfaction that those different parts can offer (Watts, 1977, p. 169).

Opportunity awareness would also required knowledge of the entry paths into the different parts of the world of work. Watts' definition is noteworthy for several reasons. First, it stresses understanding of the world of work as a necessary condition for subsequent successful careers education. This is a welcome departure from the counselling tradition, which tends to regard occupational information as 'facts and figures' (Crites, 1976). It is downgraded because it cannot be construed in terms of the dynamics of personality, the language in which the 'client's problem' is usually couched. However, from the point of view of careers *education*, occupational information is potentially of the utmost value. This is because certain sorts of career information, presented in appropriate ways, can help the student understand what it is like to be at work; it can provide, in other words, the opportunity for anticipatory socialisation into the world of work (see p. 100). Appropriate career information will therefore be couched in terms of career in Super's sense (see p. 97). It will provide information not merely about the nature of the work involved in a particular occupation or the education, training and qualifications required (Hoppock, 1976). It will also involve 'less tangible, yet still important, aspects of occupational information relating to where the satisfactions are in differing kinds of occupations and to the social and psychological characteristics of specific work environments' (Nelson-Jones, 1982, p. 407). In the light of Super's developmental career model, it will inform of the way in which work roles and other roles taken on during the course of one's life might be related. It will also instruct regarding the nature of organizations in general, the frustrations of bureaucracies, and the individual's relationship with the organization. Students have had little opportunity to come to an understanding of organizations, their structure, and systems of power and influence. This is because the educational organizations in which they have grown up have seldom opened themselves up to the inspection and involvement of their student members.

There is general agreement that information is best obtained by the client rather than provided by the counsellor. Students can be encouraged and rewarded for seeking information (Borman, 1972). They can learn from a videotaped model how to set about doing so, and as a consequence engage in more frequent searches for information (Fisher *et al.*, 1976). It is worth asking, however, whether they wish to obtain more information on certain specific alternatives, in which case they may perceive their range of options to be reduced; or whether they wish to have their range of options extended.

As Mencke and Cochran (1974) found, some counselling interventions may have the former rather than the latter effect (see also Hayes and Hopson, 1971).

There are many different modes by which information may be obtained (Isaacson, 1971). Two modes with clear advantages are realistic job previews and computer-aided instruction. The benefits of appropriate sandwich placement or vacation work in aiding occupational socialization have already been described. Turning to computer-based systems, these potentially offer huge benefits. Super (1978) offers a comprehensive account of how they might best be utilized. Computers may simply be used as information storage and retrieval systems. Such systems 'are, from the point of view of the user, static, impersonal non-responsive in their inability to accept user replies other than requests for more data, and in the irrelevance of most of the stored data to any one user' (Super, 1978, pp. 19–20). All more advanced systems do not deal solely with occupational information. Rather, they try to match aspects of the person with aspects of occupations; or else they permit interactive exploration and choice. These functions will be dealt with later under another category of Watts' scheme for careers education.

The second of Watts' (1977) purposes for careers education in higher education is to facilitate *self-awareness*. It will be recalled that increased opportunity awareness and self-awareness are both considered necessary inputs to decision learning. There are many aspects of their self-concepts of which students could be more aware. Their interests and values may benefit from clarification and there are perfectly acceptable educational procedures for helping such clarification to occur. For example, interest inventories may be administered and self-scored. Workshops can be held in order to clarify values, and one such is reported by Ohlde and Vinitsky (1976). They held a workshop of 7 hours' duration for 600 students in a large state university who were undecided as to their choice of major field of study. Students were more aware of their value priorities than were a control group who had not undertaken the workshop, and this was true both for students of high and low self-esteem.

Other aspects of the self-concept which have been demonstrated to be influential in occupational behaviour can also be explored: in particular, the future self and aspirations. Hinkle and Thomas (1972), for example, employed 'life-line' sheets. Students were asked to mark points on these lines representing previous enjoyable and satisfying events in their lives. They were also asked to project the line into the future, years ahead, and then to stand at this future point and 'look back' on similar 'events'. The importance of such a future orientation is also indicated by the work of Kratzing and Nystul (1979). They persuaded students to engage in fantasies of the future, and found that this, together with three other dimensions affecting decision-making, led to increased career maturity as evidenced by the Crites Career Maturity Inventory. This increase was greater than that demonstrated by individual career counselling, vocational exploration, placebo, and no-treatment groups.

Not only may individuals be helped to express their aspirations; they may also be led to ask more profound questions about themselves in relation to their work. For example, they may need to explore how much of themselves they want to define in occupational terms (Daws, 1970). In terms of Super's (1980) career rainbow, to what extent are they willing to permit their work role to crowd out other roles at different stages of their lives? What needs and values do they wish or expect working life to satisfy, and which are they prepared to satisfy in other areas of their lives? Which demands of an occupation are they likely to find compatible with their own value priorities?

The final aspects of self around which careers education might centre are those relating to the perception of the self as actor. The individual with an internal locus of control is likely to have high self-esteem and sense of responsibility (Tyler, 1978). In addition, we might expect such persons to have a sense of strong personal efficacy (Bandura, 1977); that is, they believe themselves capable of engaging successfully in activities (in this case, those related to occupations). It is worth noting here that efficacy refers to belief in one's capacity to do things, not belief that one will achieve various outcomes from those actions. As far as careers education is concerned, this group of aspects of the self-concept presents some problems. If we continue, with Watts, to define the objective as self-*awareness*, then much of the research and practice is not aimed at that objective. It has been aimed, rather, at self-*enhancement*; at *increasing* self-esteem and sense of personal efficacy rather than making students more aware of these features.

One argument in support of such a practice is based on two assumptions: first, that these features of the self-concept normally facilitate careers-related behaviour when they are positive; and second, that certain groups of people are on average lower than others on these desirable features. There are some grounds for believing that this is true of women students (see Chapter 10). If we look specifically at self-efficacy, there is clear evidence that for certain occupations women have lower perceptions of their capability of completing the educational requirements and job duties. Betz and Hackett (1981) found that women believed themselves less capable than men at ten typically male occupations. The degree of strength of their feelings of self-efficacy was positively related to their willingness to consider these occupations for themselves, and their expressed interest in them. Hackett and Betz (1981) try to explain why it is that women should lack strong expectations of self-efficacy by suggesting that men and women differ in their access to four sources of information regarding self-efficacy. These are, first, the opportunity to achieve success themselves, and consequently to be aware of such achievement and to attribute it to their own efforts; second, the availability of successful role models; third, their degree of anxiety regarding their performance, both causing and resulting from low self-efficacy beliefs; and fourth, the encouragement and reward of others. Whatever the causes of women's decreased perceptions of self-efficacy, it is clear that their sense of identity can be positively affected by workshops and support groups. One example among many is the research of Loeffler and Fiedler (1979), who report increases in self-esteem, confidence, autonomy, and self-identification as opposed to other-identification. These were consequent upon a wide-ranging programme which included elements such as assertiveness training and power simulations.

Such programmes designed to help individuals from a group known to be disadvantaged in this respect to change their self-conceptions in a direction demonstrably favourable to their career seems entirely justifiable. However, the dangers of such basic forms of change are worth keeping in mind. To give two examples: Little and Roach (1974) gave women videotapes of models engaging in non-traditional occupations. However, if some of these women had feminine self-concepts, with which they were happy, such models would have been inappropriate. Forsyth and Forsyth (1982) had their subjects receive bogus evaluation forms (itself an ethically dubious procedure). The explanation given for these unfavourable evaluations by the experimenters were either internal to the subjects or external; they also implied that the subject had control over these reasons for the evaluations, or else did not have such control. An explanation in terms of internal controllable reasons for the evaluations rendered them far less harsh in the eyes of the subjects and led them to believe more in their own competence. However, this was true only for those subjects who already possessed a stronger internal locus of control. This use of so-called attribution therapy in the context of careers education would certainly appear unwarranted.

On the other hand, consciousness-raising activities such as those by Loeffler and Fielder (1979) described above, or more behavioural training as outlined by Thoresen and Ewart (1976), might with justification be included in careers education programmes aimed at self-awareness. Thoresen and Ewart describe procedures whereby individuals can learn to develop and sustain their own motivation; to observe their own behaviour more carefully than before; to organize their environments (for example, join self-help groups) so as to become more effective; and to evaluate the consequences of their behaviour in the light of their objectives. All these are necessary conditions for increasing and perceiving one's own effectiveness, and behavioural methods have proved useful in bringing them about (Krumboltz and Baker, 1973).

The third objective of careers education in Watts' (1977) scheme is to facilitate *decision learning*. Much early work in the teaching of decision-making assumed that the rational consideration of outcomes of alternatives was the appropriate objective. We have already seen, however (see Chapter 8) that this normative account does not actually describe what students do. Hence, such programmes as those of Katz (1966) and Gelatt (1962) were in fact trying to help students adopt a procedure which was different in kind from that which they appeared to be using. There is, perhaps, a case to be made for saying that some students, sometimes, are taking decisions partly on the basis of subjective probability estimates of outcomes and evaluations of those outcomes; and for such students, a process such as Mann's (1972) balance-sheet procedure may be of use.

Rather than describe a rational style which may be alien to the student, however, an alternative procedure is to listen to students' requests. Holland (1976) is convinced that 'consumers of vocational counselling want most of all to arrive at or confirm one or more vocational alternatives they can feel good about. Other outcomes—decision-making skills and enhanced general adjustment—are desired more by professionals than consumers' (p. 13). Such a search for an occupational preference may be a response to perceived social pressure; it may also be a form of anticipatory socialization, whereby the student starts relating her self-concept to occupational roles in the knowledge that she does not have to act immediately. Holland and Gottfredson (1976) maintain that the student can achieve her objective of being able to specify a set of occupational preferences by engaging in the Self-Directed Search. For example, the future possibilities task of the SDS requests students to 'list all the jobs or occupations you could do and would like, if you had enough money to get the necessary training, and if you could get the job when you finished your training or education'. Holland and Gottfredson suggest that high scores in response to this task actually require the student to demonstrate career choice competencies. It is unnecessary, they argue, for students to be asked questions 'about knowledge of problem-solving, planning, occupational information, self-appraisal, and goal selection' (Holland and Gottfredson, 1976, p. 23). These questions are typical of career maturity questionnaires such as those of Crites and Super. Holland maintains that the Self-Directed Search both encourages and demonstrates the student's ability to relate self and occupational concepts, and that such questions about her mode of decision-taking are unnecessary. It is like asking her questions about how to ride a bicycle instead of observing her doing so.

There is certainly considerable evidence to indicate that the Self-Directed Search (SDS) is as effective as traditional counselling. Krivatsy and Magoon (1976) found that, for a variety of outcome measures, the SDS alone was as effective as SDS plus individual assistance and as traditional counselling. On the other hand, this may only be true of the SDS, where type of person and occupational type are explicitly matched. When we look at a more orthodox interest inventory, the Strong–Campbell Interest Inventory, the same is not true. When a constant level of information was provided for all three groups, a group of students receiving counsellor help with their interest profile differed from groups which had an audio tape with their profile, or had their profile alone. They were more likely to request occupational information and to achieve their personal goals for the counselling session (Hoffman *et al.*, 1981).

Holland and Holland (1977) found that undecided students differed in terms of their sense of identity and vocational maturity, but McGowan (1977) demonstrated that 50% of previously undecided students were able to express a career choice after having undertaken the SDS. This finding was regardless of the students' level of anxiety as measured by Taylor's Manifest Anxiety Scale, although anxiety-management training may help; Mendonca and Siess (1976) succeeded in increasing exploratory behaviour and problem-solving ability, and reducing anxiety and difficulty in making decisions. They gave one group anxiety-management training, another problem-solving training, another both of these, and a final group neither. Problem-solving and anxiety-management training were more effective than anxiety training alone, which in its turn was more effective than problem training.

Group work may be just as effective as individual counselling or as the SDS in producing these effects. Hazel (1976) gives an account of a typical group programme while Graff *et al.* (1972) demonstrate general comparability of individual, group, and programmed counselling. Kivlighan *et al.* (1981) caution that group methods may suit person-oriented students more, while individual problem-solving methods such as the SDS may be more effective for primarily task-oriented students.

Not only group work, but also computerized advice systems, should have advantages where personal and occupational features are being related in a dynamic way. Super (1978) describes five different types of computerized guidance systems. The first type simply provides job and occupational information; the second offers facilities for matching personal with occupational characteristics, but these are static in nature. The third type permits interactive matching systems, whereby the student is offered information about occupations indicated as appropriate by her test scores; or else information about the degree of congruence between various occupations and the individual's profile. The fourth type of programme offers interactive exploration and choice facilities. The system asks questions of the student regarding what she wishes to know. These questions have multiple-choice responses provided, and the student is given information dependent on her choice. She may periodically ask questions at given points in the programme, and summaries of her positions and decisions are provided with any inconsistencies pointed out. In sum:

the computer asks the pupil what he or she would like to know about the occupation he has chosen to explore. The user's reaction to this bit of information is used as a springboard for further questions and answers about this or other occupations. Information is thus acquired as desired by the pupil, step by step, rather than being presented in what may be unassimilable blocks. . . . But genuine browsing is thus possible, with the user in control of where, how widely, and at what depth he explores. At the same time, the pupil is helped to find focus by being given information on how congruent his tentative preference is with his abilities, interest, values, stated educational plans, and earlier reactions to aspects of the occupation being explored (Super, 1978, p. 20).

The fifth and final type of computerized system concerns career development rather than occupations. Such systems help the student assess her readiness for future decisions by enabling her to observe her own modes of decision-making and her progress along a career decision-making tree. In the future, Super envisages programmes which help the student analyse the course of change in her life, and to plot alternative career pathways. Clearly the interactive potential of the computer is only beginning to be utilized, but such evaluative studies as have emerged are positive (e.g. Cochran *et al.*, 1977).

In effect, we have been considering all interventions which aid the student in relating personal and occupational features as facilitating decision-making, which is Watts' (1977) third objective for careers education. In the meantime, we move on to Watts' fourth and final objective: the facilitation of transition learning.

> By *transition learning* is meant helping students to gain the awareness and skills they need to cope with the transitions consequent upon their leaving undergraduate status. . . . Transition learning is, therefore, the facilitation of a realistic appreciation of the environment into which the student is moving. . . . In general, transition learning would seem to be an important element in careers education, anchoring the tasks of opportunity awareness, self-awareness and decision learning to future realities, and helping students to prepare not only for *formulating* decisions but also for *implementing* them (Watts, 1977, p. 171).

This final objective of transition learning is based largely upon the analysis of transition proposed by Adams *et al.* (1980). These authors emphasize the importance of preparing for transitions in advance of their occurrence. They stress the different styles of response to oncoming transitions in life. Some people act proactively, engaging in anticipatory socialization; others are reactive, and make unconsidered choices or do nothing. It will be argued in the next section that all careers education is aimed at facilitating transition learning in Watts' sense, and that so-called decision-learning is in fact a form of anticipatory socialization.

12.3 PREPARATION FOR RECRUITMENT

The analysis favoured throughout this book has been that of the student and the organization engaging in a social exchange. The episodes of reading brochures, application, first interviews, and final selection stage are all part of this social exchange, which may be terminated by either party after each of these episodes. We label these episodes together as the recruitment process, but we have argued that it is entirely arbitrary to treat recruitment as separate from the subsequent relationship of the student and the organization. Placement and initial training, commitment to the organization or to a profession, are all subsequent to and dependent on recruitment episodes.

For example, it has been argued forcefully that realistic self-presentation by the organization has effects upon subsequent employee commitment and trust. Given this analysis, we have a paradox which has been little noted hitherto. It is that there is no clear transition into the world of work. Students do not descend from the ivory tower with a sudden violent bump. On the contrary, they are expected to start a long-term relationship with an organization while still part of the university. Their final year at college is not a time for more anticipatory socialization—*it is for real*. Transition starts as soon as the student starts looking through organisations' brochures, often in the first term of the final year.

It follows that, if the main purpose of careers education is to help the student make the transition to the world of work, then it should be largely focused upon the immediate point of transition. That point is the recruitment process, so we are suggesting that careers education should be primarily aimed at the recruitment process, the initial exchanges between the student and the organization. This is probably the major focus of most careers work in higher education in the UK. In the USA the choice of major subject during the first degree, and the choice of graduate course, carry such profound occupational implications that they may justifiably attract much of the counsellor's attention.

When we return to the social exchange model of the recruitment process proposed in Chapter 7, it is clear that Watts' (1977) objectives for careers education are highly appropriate. It will be recalled that the social exchange is conceived, firstly as exchange of information, secondly as a bargaining situation. While information exchange is not interactive at the first stage (brochures and application form), it is at the second (interview). Hence the student's tasks in the first stage of recruitment are

(1) to understand the organization's messages about itself and its expectations, and to select that information which is relevant;
(2) to be aware of the nature of her self-concept, and to be capable of communicating it in the application forms, if necessary;
(3) to decide whether to proceed further with the exchange on the basis of the degree of compatibility of organization and self-concept.

At the second, interview, stage, the student's tasks are interactive. She has to discover features of the organization and its expectations which she wishes to know, while at the same time expressing her self-concept in response to enquiry. Moreover, the student may begin negotiating at the interview as well. Negotiating is a highly complex task, in which an understanding of the rules of the game and an appreciation of the dispositions of power between the parties is vital; so is the capacity to adjust one's position constantly.

At the final stage the student has to be at home in an organizational setting; possibly at the organization itself, or possibly a minuscule version of the organization in the form of an assessment centre run by managers but in a different location. She has to present herself in relation to the organization, but at the same time she has to be skilled at perceiving the nature of the organization from the way it works in practise.

Clearly, Watts' (1977) objectives for careers education are highly appropriate for these purposes. The facilitation of opportunity awareness will assist the students in understanding the nature of the organization when reading organizations' brochures, and later too. This aspect of careers education should stress, in addition to the nature of occupations, the nature of careers in organizations; the probable transfer of the student employee across functions during her working life, and the frequent training and development expected of her. Teaching in self-awareness will enable the student to understand her view of her self, particularly with respect to her short- and long-term aspirations. Decision learning involves practice in matching self-concepts with occupational and organizational perceptions, while transitional learning requires anticipation of, and anticipatory adjustment to, some of the major immediate new features of the world of work.

However, Watts' objectives seem to omit (or at least place little emphasis on) the recruitment process itself. Any social exchange requires social skills. These include the capacity to understand what organizations and their representatives are trying to say; the ability to express adequately in speech and writing the sort of person one thinks one is; and skill at bargaining and negotiation. In addition students will need to know the unspoken social rules involved in each of the episodes of the recruitment process. Students have to possess understanding and knowledge in order to undertake the recruitment process successfully; but they also have to communicate with, and relate to, an older person in a varied range of social situations, each with its own rules.

The teaching of these skills is not impossible, and various forms of training programme are available. Hollandsworth *et al.* (1977), for example give an account of how to help students to improve their interview skills while Prior-Wandesforde (1978) outlines a teaching programme aimed at helping unemployed graduates with each of the stages of the recruitment process.

By assisting students to acquire the necessary skill for the social exchange process, careers counsellors would not be engaging in 'unfair coaching'. Their purpose is to facilitate the social exchange process, to the benefit of both parties. They are not trying to help the student to present herself in a particularly favourable light. That is, they are not coaching in self-presentation (Goffman, 1959), defined as trying to appear to another person the sort of individual you think he wants you to be. Obviously, this is a considerable temptation for job applicants, particularly in times of recession. However, it depends upon the assumption (a) that one knows what the recruiter is looking for, and (b) that recruiters are drawing inferences from the *manner* of the student's communications with them rather than from their *content*. If all students come to the recruitment process with adequate communicative skills, recruiters will be forced to pay more attention to content in order to discriminate between applicants.

Given that it is a social exchange for which careers counsellors are helping students to prepare, we must remember again the context of this exchange. This context is overwhelmingly academic. The social norms and values of the university are likely to be contrary to many of those of other organizations (see the research of Cotgrove and Box described on p. 155). The counsellor will therefore have to help the student clarify her own values *vis-à-vis* their present institutional context, and *vis-à-vis* the values underlying the social exchange with the organization. It is all the harder for the student when we realize that this is the period when her allegiance to her academic values is supposed to be at its strongest. She is supposed to be concentrating her energies (in the UK) upon her final examinations at the end of her third year. The class of her degree will largely depend on these examinations, which are thus potentially the indication of her own and her teachers' view of her academic prowess. From an anthropological point of view, finals and the subsequent degree day are respectively the tough and the symbolic parts of a *rite de passage*. The pressures to complete her academic role before moving on to the world of work must be very strong. Hence the transition with which the counsellor has to help involves potential conflict. The counselling programme MAUD, by Wooler and Humphreys (1979) addresses itself partly to this problem; it helps students to appreciate the losses (for example, of valued activities and rewards) which inevitably accompany any transition.

There are other occasions during the student's final year when careers advisers may be of help. These occasions are typically where there are difficulties in the social exchange relationship between student and organization. In particular, rejection by an organization may lead the student to avoid contact with other organizations of the same type (Herriot *et al.*, 1980); she may have over-generalized from a sample of one, or else she may have drawn unwarranted conclusions about herself. Overall, however, it seems appropriate in summary to stress the two basic points of this chapter. First, counsellors are basically about education, not remediation. Second, education is for the transition to the world of work. It will therefore have as its major concern the preparation of the student for the recruitment process, the beginning of the student's part in the world of work. Consequently, the counsellor may begin to see her objective as to facilitate the social exchange of the recruitment process as well as serve the client's interests. Hence, the counsellor may see the organizations and their recruiting officers as part of her clientele.

13

Implications for Recruitment

13.1 THE ORGANIZATIONAL CONTEXT

We cannot consider the implications of our analysis of graduate recruitment without taking the wider context into account. Organizations as open systems have to adapt to their constantly changing environment. Perhaps that aspect of the environment which has the most immediate effect upon graduate recruitment is the economic climate. For example, recession can affect organizations in different ways, depending upon their recruitment policy. Some organizations, including many large ones, recruit graduates directly for specific positions within the organization. Thus the selection procedure serves both a selection and a placement function, and training is undertaken while on the job. Other organizations recruit a graduate intake for general training, subsequently placing them in specific positions. Others, again, select an intake of graduates, put them through an induction and placement programme, and then offer them training for the position in which they have been placed.

It seems evident that organizations who select for positions are more likely to be immediately affected by recession or by upturn in the economy. The positions open and available to graduate entrants will vary directly with manpower reductions or office or plant closures. Organizations which place graduate entrants later in their employment are able to cushion these effects to some extent. Training can be extended or adapted, or positions can be created in other areas of the organization. Moreover, long-term manpower policies can continue to be implemented without drastic interruption. One large UK organization is reputed to have had to headhunt for a whole generation of senior management, having done no graduate recruitment during a recessionary period.

Another advantage of the recruitment of graduates *en masse* is the opportunity to ensure from the start that the graduate entrant perceives the possibilities of an organizational career as well as those of a professional career. Many graduates have learned at university to perceive themselves as an engineer, psychologist, chemist, etc. These labels are actually applied more to identify them as students of a particular subject than as future professionals. However, they easily transfer to occupational and professional meanings on entry to the world of work. Consequently, professional identity and the achievement of professional qualifications and status are major objectives of many graduate entrants. Some use their first employers solely as a means to this end, and fully expect to move on after training and professional status are achieved. Thus, if an organization wishes to retain such graduates for longer than their professional training, it has to persuade them from the very beginning of their relationship that they can have a career within the organization. Frequent negotiation and planning of intra-organizational careers may perhaps produce more 'locals' and less 'cosmopolitans' (see p. 43). When graduates are immediately appointed to positions, they are likely to depend on their supervisor both for immediate advice about tasks and also for longer-term career advice. Superiors may be more or less capable of acting as mentor in both these areas, but individual differences are likely to affect the outcome a great deal. Supervisors may or may not have been trained in these areas, but in any event they are as likely to present a professional as an organizational career model to the new entrant.

Given the environmental uncertainty it is paradoxically true that organizations need clear overall recruitment objectives, while remaining flexible in how they achieve them. The old-fashioned treatment of selection as an isolated function, the success of which is gauged by its validity in predicting job performance, is entirely inappropriate. As Cascio and Sibley (1979) stress, the overall *utility* of a selection procedure (in conjunction with induction, placement, and training) is what has to be considered. One calculation which organizations need to make is the cut-off point at which the selection and training costs incurred for a graduate start to reap benefits. Clearly, this point will differ from organization to organization, and between functions within organizations. However, it does appear to be one of the basic criteria by which selection and training should be evaluated. Another popular criterion for a selection procedure is success at training. This may be an appropriate criterion for organizations such as the armed services, whose training procedures are specialized and not easily transferable to other organizations. However, for most graduate recruiters the loss of a trained person is a far greater cost than the loss of an individual early in training. The relative costs to the individual are hard to estimate; early withdrawal from training may represent wise self-selection out; severance after training may indicate pursuit of more favourable outcomes than those the individual perceives probable within the organization.

Another element of the criteria for graduate recruitment relates to the longer-term intra-organizational careers of graduates. Considerable attention has been given recently to the idea that those with particular expertise should be permitted to remain within that area without jeopardizing their advancement within the organization. Some organizations in manufacturing industry have upgraded the positions of those managing Research and Development units, for example. This is considered a way of avoiding the loss of those at the 'sharp end' of the organization who have ambitions to rise to top management levels. The traditional progression to the top through various managerial levels less and less related to the graduate's initial function is thereby avoided. However, organizations are likely to be interested in other models besides these two. Their modal graduate employee will probably remain in middle management, and her worth to the organization is likely to be expressed in the variety of jobs she is willing and able to be retrained for. Only flexible graduate employees who perceive the acquisition and development of new skills as worthwhile in themselves (rather than as a means of further advancement) will enable an organization to adapt to a changing technological and economic environment. Hence the number and value of new skills acquired by a graduate employee over a longer period of employment may also be a criterion of initial selection and training success. Such a criterion would imply the use of the applicant's expectations of future self-development as a predictor.

It is only when organizations have decided upon the criteria they wish to employ to determine the effectiveness of a selection and training programme that rational decisions can be made about their graduate recruitment procedures. The selection criteria, of course, force organizations into a consideration of what they want graduates for. These deliberations may well reveal that there are several different reasons for wanting graduates; their up-to-date technological expertise for certain functions, trainability and flexibility for others, and so on. It follows that different selection predictors, and even different methods of selection, may be necessary for different types of graduate entry.

Given that policy decisions about the way the organization will employ its graduate recruits, and about the criteria for ascertaining the effectiveness of their selection and employment, have been taken, what implications follow for the actual recruitment process? The first and immediate implication is that organizations can now make hypotheses about what will predict such outcomes. If a major outcome to be predicted is a longer-term career in the organization which more than repays initial training costs, then it is more likely than ever that aspects of the self-concept, especially aspirations, will be important predictors.

13.2 A REVISED RECRUITMENT PROCEDURE

Let us now consider the traditional graduate recruitment process in the light of the contextual considerations that we have just described, and also in the light of our analysis of it as a social exchange. The recruitment brochure should be telling the graduate what she wishes to know in order to decide whether or not to apply. This may not be what the organization thinks she needs to know, nor what it wishes her to believe about itself. The graduate is likely to want to know what tasks and responsibilities she will face in the first position she occupies, and what help, supervision, and training she will receive. She will also be concerned with the implications for her lifestyle of working for the organization. These aspects impinge directly upon the transition to the world of work which she knows she will have to make. The values of the organization and its image may be less her immediate concern; further, she may only wish to know about career progression in so far as it relates to professional qualification.

The organization will be wishing to discover information regarding the applicant, in particular, if our analysis is correct, the applicant's self-concept. Consequently it will request information about long-term career aspirations, particularly regarding career within the organization; does the individual perceive herself as having, primarily, an organizational or a professional career, for example. The bulk of the application form will, as at present, refer to past and present background, achievements, and interests. However, the major purpose of this information will be to enable the organization to judge whether there is continuity between past performance, present self-description and education, and future aspirations. This judgement will be based on an analysis of the graduate's past achievements in the light of her background and opportunities. Another reason why the applicant's account of her self on the application form should actually be a fairly accurate reflection of her self-concept is the absence of clues as to the sort of self-concept the organization will regard with favour. It would clearly be in the candidate's short-term interest to present the sort of view of herself which the organization expected. However, the major source of clues about this, the brochure, is unlikely to contain them. This is because, as we have seen, it will be concerned more with the immediate future than with the longer term.

Consequently, the organization will have biographical data to check upon the degree of realism involved in the applicant's self-concept; and it may feel reasonably secure that by this stage of the procedure it has not given too many clues as to the sort of self-perceptions it is looking for as selection criteria. In addition, it would be extremely beneficial to the organization to have available *at this stage* the results of, for example, the Self-Directed Search, a values questionnaire and, if appropriate, specific aptitude tests. Given these safeguards, the recruitment officer will endeavour to relate the applicant's self-concept, in particular her aspirations for the future, to the criterion variables. If the major criterion is, for example, staying with the organization for at least a certain period of time, and successfully undertaking initial and subsequent varied training, then it will not be hard to match the applicant's aspirations to these criteria and discover how congruent they are. If the criterion is successful performance in a specific highly technical position within the organization within 9 months of joining, then, again, aspects of the self-concept may be good predictors. In this case, short-term aspirations, self-evaluations of technical competence, and perceptions of efficacy will be the key evidence, supported by biographical and test data demonstrating technical interest and prowess. They can indicate those areas of activity in which the applicant has chosen to engage (given opportunities for doing so); and second, her proficiency in them. Hence they give an indication of the veracity of the areas of activity to which she claims to aspire, and possibly of her likely proficiency in those areas. It should be stressed, however, that it is the self-concept which is taken to be a basic predictor, adding considerably to the predictive power obtained from the biographical data alone.

At this particular juncture in the early 1980s, the pre-selection stage of the graduate recruitment process is attracting considerable attention. This is because the state of the graduate job market is such that there are many, many more applications than vacancies; in some large private sector organizations in the UK there are ratios of up to 20 to 1 at present. Hence the pre-selection stage has come under greater scrutiny since discriminations are having to be made between applicants who, on paper, have little to differentiate each other. At present, few organizations have empirical data which relate biographical data as predictors to whatever criteria they consider important. Given the absence of such research data, organizations may resort to any one of several strategies. They may increase the level of achievement required on those predictors which they have always used (they may, for example, now pass on for interview only those applicants expected to obtain first-class degrees from prestigious universities); or they may require more stringent evidence before they accept the applicant as fulfilling their stereotype of the ideal graduate employee, and permit the slightest non-stereotypic sign to exclude her. Alternatively, they may pay more attention to the style of the application rather than its content, allowing themselves to draw inferences from the applicant's form-filling behaviour about her personality.

A more fruitful approach is to devise application forms which tap information relating to the self-concept. Historical details, present self-descriptions and self-evaluations, and future aspirations are all parts of the application form, with the questions regarding the future asked in considerable detail. The questions asked, of course, depend upon what the organization has hypothesized are good predictors; these predictors are of specific criteria, so it is obvious that in order to draw up an appropriate application form the organization needs to have done a lot of thinking about its objectives for its graduate intake. Further, it needs to know a lot about itself (for example, its norms and values) in order to ascertain its degree of congruence with the applicant's own expectations and values. Thus effective pre-selection is not merely an initial sift; it requires policy decisions regarding the use of graduate employees; the devising of measures of the degree of attainment of these objectives; the hypothesis of predictors of these measures; and the operationalizing of these predictors on the application form. Above all, it requires research to evaluate effectiveness of whatever pre-selection procedure is used. Many organizations assume that certain biographical details are good predictors, for example degree class- or grade-point average. How do they know?

Up to this point, then, the social exchange between graduate and organization has proceeded in orderly fashion. The organization has opened the exchange by communicating to potential applicants what it has found by market research that they want to know. The graduate has continued the exchange by applying, providing the organization with the information it wants to know by means of the application form, and perhaps other means also (e.g. tests). The organization has in its turn responded by telling the graduate that it wishes to continue the exchange. What is to happen next? Traditionally, the organization has interviewed the applicant at her university at this point, but this procedure seems to violate the fairness of the social exchange. We have seen in Chapter 6 how parties have different expectations of the interview, with the applicant wishing to use the opportunity to learn more about the organization while the interviewer wishes to learn more about the applicant. This confounding of objectives both distorts and ludicrously overloads the interview. Usually, the interviewer achieves more of his objective than does the applicant, given the unequal distribution of power in the social exchange.

At this point in the social exchange it seems far preferable to permit the applicant to find out more about the organization. One way of doing this is to hold a presentation at the applicant's university or at a regional centre. This presentation is not for the purpose of attracting applicants. It is further to inform those applicants who have passed the pre-selection stage. They have, after all, had no opportunity hitherto of asking questions, having been provided only with company literature. While a senior manager of the organization may answer certain questions about the organization as a whole, younger employees are more likely to be asked the more personal questions of interest to graduates. Women employees and cultural minority employees should be included in the team. Their responses may be more likely to be trusted if they themselves attended the same university or studied the same degree course. They are, of course, instructed to give replies they believe to be true and they are to be given the privacy to enable them to do so securely. At the end of this presentation, the sole purpose of which is to inform the graduate of what she wants to know, the graduate can self-select in or out without any reflection upon herself; for she will have obtained detailed knowledge of how graduates' careers develop within the organization. We might expect considerable further reduction in numbers before the next stage; the interview.

The purpose of the interview can now be very clearly specified. It is to obtain more information about the applicant than that provided on the application form. By this stage the interviewer should also have available a reference containing responses to carefully phrased, specific questions. Such responses are usually best obtained from the applicant's personal tutor. The purpose of the interview is best achieved by close reference to the applicant's completed application form. The interviewer will be requiring the applicant to expand upon those responses to questions which do not provide enough information, or which are unclear. Since the questions on the application form are chosen because they are hypothesized to predict the organizations's criteria, such additional information should be entirely relevant to a select/ reject decision. The interviewer will then avoid the dangers of drawing inferences from the actual form-filling behaviour and from the interview behaviour of the applicant. Compared to the biographical information and self-concept indices, such inferences are unreliable and invalid.

Given the importance of the biographical information for the whole exercise, the organization may have found it useful to check on the accuracy of some of the information before the interview, or at least during it. Moreover, interviewers will seek to discover information which has not been supplied on the application form despite opportunity provided to do so. Such information may have positive or negative weight. One UK applicant wrote in very small letters in the middle of a large open space, asking her to write anything more about herself that might be relevant, the statement 'I suffer from bad health'! On a more serious note, the interview has traditionally served the function of avoiding false positive choices as well as false negatives. In other words, interviewers have considered the face-to-face meeting the only way of spotting what some of them are pleased to call bad eggs. Some interviewers insist on forming negative judgements on the basis of interview behaviour—'she wouldn't look me in the eye', etc. However, a more appropriate method is to try and discover biographical information which the applicant has not, in her own interests, chosen to present. Such information might be obtained by questions relating to periods in the applicant's history left unaccounted for, or reasons for a sudden change (e.g. leaving a job or a course of study). As we saw in our review of the research, negative information may be more heavily weighted than positive information by the interviewer. It may well be the case that for some organizations the cost of false positives is far greater than that of false negatives; hence concentration upon discovering negative information unrevealed in the application form is understandable. It is important to note, however, that inferences from single specific behaviours in particular situations are highly dangerous, whether the behaviour is creditable or not. It is only when several different instances of, e.g., failure to complete a project once stated, or disregard for welfare of others, are available that inferences are worth drawing about probable future behaviour. Moreover, the interviewer will remember that such evidence is only relevant if it is reasonably hypothesized to predict the criteria.

This careful examination of her biographical history, however, is likely to be paralleled by an equally detailed examination of the applicant's self-concept as she reports it. Inconsistencies between different aspects of the self-concept may be pursued and elucidated and, in particular, the applicant's aspirations further elaborated. How far do they extend into the future? Upon what level of position does the applicant have her sights set? How far do her aspirations relate to her occupation or profession and how far to the organization? How consistent are they with her biographical history? How closely do they relate to the organization's career policy for graduates of this type?

This form of interview appears to be very much one-way traffic. It is, however, entirely consistent with the social exchange sequence, in which information is required of each party in turn by the other. Brochure and application form have each provided information from one of the parties to the other; presentation and interview have permitted each party to ask and obtain the information they desire. Such episodes can in principle be less ambiguous in their objectives and rules than they are at present. Graduates can be clearer what is going on, if their purpose is made explicit.

It was suggested earlier that the interview might be an opportunity for bargaining to occur. However, such a use of the interview implies that the interviewer has succeeded in matching the information obtained in the interview with the organization's expectations for the applicant during the course of the interview. This is an extraordinarily difficult task, and is likely to be far more effectively accomplished subsequently, after any immediate judgements based on interview behaviour have been consciously put aside. The decision whether to proceed further with the applicant on the basis of the matching procedure may be improved by a joint discussion with other selectors, rather than an individual process.

In the traditional procedure a final stage is still required, often in the form of an assessment centre. Our review of assessment centres suggested that some of the outcomes were serendipitous: managers improve their assessment skills, while successful applicants may reduce their cognitive dissonance by concluding that the organization must be worth joining, having suffered such a demanding entry ritual. We noted that the only features of the assessment centre not present in the selection procedure hitherto were the exercises and the final group assessment. With reference to the exercises, it was argued that, where they did predict criteria, it was not clear why they did so. If the reason was that the exercise was in effect a job-sample test, and therefore predicted similar subsequent performance, this seems irrelevant to graduate recruitment where specific task success is unlikely to be an adequate criterion. If the exercises are aimed at revealing personal qualities, then all the arguments against making inferences from single specific behaviours may be adduced. Otherwise, the assessment centre procedure seems to be reproducing events (interviews, psychological tests, consideration of application forms) which have occurred earlier in the recruitment process. The conclusion seems to be that a final stage is required because the previous stages have not succeeded in reducing the number of applicants down to slightly above the number to be taken on. It is worth noting at this point that certain UK organizations report quite a considerable rejection rate even of offers made after the final stage.

Perhaps we may attribute the apparent need for the third stage at present to ineffective social exchange at earlier stages. Graduates may not discover enough in the brochures to enable them to self-select out; organizations may not have designed their application forms so as to obtain the relevant information; presentations may not occur, or if they do, are aimed at attracting applicants to accept a job if offered one, or general public relations, rather than at telling the graduate what she wants to know; interviews may have confounded objectives, with the graduate by now very concerned to know more. Self-selection out, and rejection by the organization, may both be facilitated if the prochure, application form, presentation, and interview are designed and conducted appropriately. Hence a final assessment centre stage should not be needed in order finally to reduce the number of applicants to the number to whom offers of employment are to be made.

However, an alternative final stage may be suggested. It is a stage of negotiation and bargaining, explicitly designated as such. Hitherto, the social exchange has been one of the giving and receiving of information and the making of individual decisions by either party. These activities should have resulted in a modicum of trust, since both parties will have been open in supplying accurate information which the other requested. Further, the probable inequalities in power between the parties have not been exploited by the organization, since equal opportunity for obtaining information and matching self-concept and organizational expectations has been provided to both parties. Perhaps one remaining inequality relates to the organization's criteria; by what will it judge my success or failure, the graduate may wish to know, and what information will it use in selection to predict such criteria? On the other hand, the graduate may conclude from the application form and the questions at interview what are the predictors being used.

Given a certain degree of mutual trust and respect, the bargaining stage may now be entered into with some expectation of success. The bargain relates to the conditional commitments each party is prepared to make to the other. Within its general graduate policy the organization may be prepared to offer specific opportunities or make specific demands of individuals. These may be in response to a highly desirable potential employee's bargaining position, or they may be an indication to a less desirable graduate that the organization will expect her to undertake somewhat different work from that for which she hoped. Either way, the outcome of the bargaining procedure is that both parties will have made or have refused to make undertakings to each other that are mutually acceptable. This final, bargaining, stage recognises *par excellence* the social exchange character of the relationship between individual and organization. It allows the recruitment procedure to become part of this relationship, and it places it within the wider social context; for graduates' expectations and their bargaining behaviour will reflect currently held ideas of equity. Presentation and acceptance of a job offer after such negotiation cement the relationship and formalize in a general sense the 'contract' entered into by both parties, although the legal contract of employment will not, and cannot, contain the elements of the informal contract.

CONCLUSIONS

One of the reasons for suggesting the social exchange model for the recruitment process was that it appears to encapsulate more of what is going on than either the assessment or the counselling models. Another reason was the more political one of providing a common theoretical framework for both recruiters and counsellors. The social exchange model implies participation by an educated graduate; educated with respect to careers and organizations, and prepared for the social exchange process. This means a basic commitment to careers education at an institutional level, with careers counsellors being perceived as part of the academic community rather than as people to whom you send your students when they have a problem. Given the inertia of the higher education system and its total obsession with academic subjects and disciplines, one approach would be for large organizations to sponsor careers education within universities. They already sponsor teaching and research in technical subjects related to their own functions, and arguments could clearly be made that careers education would benefit organizations much more directly than some of the highly academic research and teaching which they currently support. Not only sponsorship of careers education but also participation in it would be beneficial. In particular, the provision of work experience would be of immense benefit.

The social exchange model has the benefit of directing attention away from the individual student, with recruiters assessing her qualities and counsellors helping her develop and self-actualize. Instead, attention is drawn towards social process, with inevitable consideration of the context of that process. From the perspective of social process, we have considered the relationship between recruiters and counsellors, between universities and organizations. We have discussed the nature of individuals at particular stages of their lives; the way in which organizations socialize their employees and adapt to them; the profound influence of socioeconomic class and sex stereotypes; the role played by her self-concept in the individual's social actions; the relationships of organizations with their environments. We have been forced to move out from the safe confines of the academic fields of individual differences and of self-actualization into the social world; for psychology is social. Like the student, we have to come down from the ivory tower.

Bibliography

Abe, C., and Holland, J. L. 1965. *A description of college freshmen: students with different vocational choices*. Iowa City: The American College Testing Program, Research reports no. 3 and 4.

Adams, J. S. 1976. The structure and dynamics of behavior in organisational boundary roles. In Dunnette, M. D. (ed.) *Handbook of Industrial and Organisational Psychology*. Chicago: Rand McNally.

Adams, J., Hayes, J., and Hopson, B. 1980. *Transition—understanding and managing personal change*. Bath: Martin Robertson.

Ajzen, I., and Holmes, W. H. 1976. Uniqueness of effects in causal attribution. *Journal of Personality*, **44**, 98–108.

Albrecht, P. A., Glaser, E. M., and Marks, J. 1964. Validation of a multiple assessment procedure for managerial personnel. *Journal of Applied Psychology*, **48**, 351–360.

Alderfer, C. P., and McCord, C. G. 1970. Personal and situational factors in the recruitment interview. *Journal of Applied Psychology*, **54**, 377–385.

Almquist, E. E. 1974. Sex stereotypes in occupational choice: the case for college women. *Journal of Vocational Behavior*, **5**, 13–21.

Alper, T. G. 1973. The relationship between role-orientation and achievement motivation in college women. *Journal of Personality*, **41**, 9–31.

Anastasi, A. 1982. *Psychological Testing*. 5th edition. New York: Macmillan.

Anstey, E. 1971. The civil service administrative class: a follow up of post-war entrants. *Occupational Psychology*, **45**, 27–43.

Anstey, E. 1977. A 30 year follow-up of the CSSB procedure, with lessons for the future. *Journal of Occupational Psychology*, **50**, 149–159.

Argyle, M., Furnham, A., and Graham, J. A. 1981. *Social Situations*. Cambridge: Cambridge University Press.

Aronson, E. 1981. The Social Animal. 3rd edition. San Francisco: W. H. Freeman & Co.

Aronson, E., and Mills, J. 1959. The effect of severity of initiation on liking for a group. *Journal of Abnormal and Social Psychology*, **59**, 177–181.

Arvey, R. D. 1979. Unfair discrimination in the employment interview: legal and psychological aspects. *Psychological Bulletin*, **86**, 736–765.

Arvey, R. D., and Campion, J. E. 1982. The employment interview: a summary and review of recent literature. *Personnel Psychology*, **35**, 281–322.

188

Ashby, J. D., Wall, H. W., and Osipow, S. H. 1966. Vocational certainty and indecision in college freshmen. *Personnel Guidance Journal*, **44**, 1037–1041.

Asher, J. J. 1972. The biographical item: can it be improved? *Personnel Psychology*, **25**, 251–269.

Asher, J. J., and Sciarrino, J. A. 1974. Realistic work sample tests: a review. *Personnel Psychology*, **27**, 519–533.

Astin, A. M. 1977. *Sex Discrimination in Career Counseling and Education*. New York: Harwood.

Astin, A. W. 1982. Paper presented to the National Commission on Excellence in Education, Washington, D.C.

Astin, A. W., and Panos, R. J. 1969. *The Educational and Vocational Development of College Students*. Washington, DC: American Council on Education.

Atkinson, R. C., and Shiffrin, R. M. 1968. Human memory: a proposed system and its control processes. In Spence, K. W., and Spence, J. T. (eds) *The Psychology of Learning and Motivation*, volume 2. New York: Academic Press.

Baird, L. L. 1979. The relation of vocational interests to life goals, self-ratings of ability and personality traits, and potential for achievement. *Journal of Counseling Psychology*, **17**, 233–239.

Bandura, A. 1977. Self-efficacy: toward a unifying theory of behavioral change. *Psychological Bulletin*, **84**, 191–215.

Bandura, A. 1978. The self system in reciprocal determination. *American Psychologist*, **33**, 344–358.

Barak, A., Carney, C. G., and Archibald, R. D. 1975. The relationship between vocational information seeking and educational and vocational decidedness. *Journal of Vocational Behavior*, **7**, 149–159.

Barrett, T. C., and Tinsley, H. E. A. 1977a. Measuring vocational self-concept crystallization. *Journal of Vocational Behavior*, **11**, 305–313.

Barrett, T. C., and Tinsley, H. E. A. 1977b. Vocational self-concept crystallization and vocational indecision. *Journal of Counseling Psychology*, **24**, 301–307.

Bartol, K. A., Anderson, C. R., and Schneier, C. E. 1981. Sex and ethnic effects on motivation to manage among college business students. *Journal of Applied Psychology*, **66**, 40–44.

Barton, K., Cattell, R. B., and Vaughan, G. M. 1973. Changes in personality as a function of college attendance or work experience. *Journal of Counseling Psychology*, **20**, 162–165.

Basow, S. A., and Howe, K. G. 1979. Model influence on career choices of college students. *Vocational Guidance Quarterly*, **27**, 239–243.

Bassis, M. S. 1977. The campus as a frog-pond. A theoretical and empirical reassessment. *American Journal of Sociology*, **82**, 1309–1326.

Baumgardner, S. R. 1976. The impact of college experience on conventional career logic. *Journal of Counseling Psychology*, **23**, 40–45.

Bayer, A. E., Roher, J. T., and Webb, R. M. 1973. Four years after college entry. *ACE Research Reports*, **1**, 1–45.

Bayne, R. 1977. Can selection interviewing be improved? *Journal of Occupational Psychology*, **50**, 161–167.

Beardslee, D. C., and O'Dowd, D. D. 1962. Students and the occupational world. In Standford, N. (ed.) *The American College*. New York: Wiley.

Bedeian, A. G. 1977. The roles of self-esteem and achievement in aspiring to prestigious occupations. *Journal of Vocational Behavior*, **11**, 109–119.

Behling, O., and Tolliver, J. 1972. Self-concept moderated by self-esteem as a predictor of choice among potential employers. *Academy of Management Proceedings*, **32**, 214–216.

Bem, S. L. 1974. The measurement of psychological androgyny. *Journal of Consulting and Clinical Psychology*, **42**, 155–162.

Bem, D. J., and Allen, A. 1974. On predicting some of the people some of the time: the search for cross-situational consistencies in behaviour. *Psychological Review*, **81**, 506–520.

Bentz, V. J. 1968. The Sears experience in the investigation, description, and prediction of executive behavior. In Myers, J. A. (ed.) *Predicting Managerial Success*. Ann Arbor: Foundation for Research on Human Behavior.

Berlew, D. E., and Hall, D. T. 1966. The socialization of managers: effects of expectations on performance. *Administrative Science Quarterly*, **11**, 207–223.

Bernardin, H. J., and Pence, E. C. 1980. Effects of rater training: Creating new response tests and decreasing accuracy. *Journal of Applied Psychology*, **65**, 60–66.

Betz, N. E., and Hackett, G. 1981. The relationship of career-related self-efficacy expectations to perceived career options in college women and men. *Journal of Counseling Psychology*, **28**, 399–340.

Biddle, B. J. 1979. *Role Theory. Expectations, Identities and Behaviors*. New York: Academic Press.

Bieri, J. 1966. Cognitive complexity and personality development. In Harvey, C. J. (ed.) *Experience, Structure and Adaptability*. New York: Springer.

Blackham, H. J. (ed.) 1978. *Education for Personal Autonomy*. London: British Association for Counselling.

Blakeney, R. N., and McNaughton, J. F. 1971. Effects of temporal placement of unfavourable information on decision-making during the selection interview. *Journal of Applied Psychology*, **55**, 138–142.

Blocher, D. H., and Schutz, R. A. 1961. Relationships among self-descriptions occupational stereotypes and vocational preference. *Journal of Counseling Psychology*, **8**, 314–317.

Bodden, J. L. 1970. Cognitive complexity as a factor in appropriate vocational choice. *Journal of Counseling Psychology*, **17**, 364–368.

Bodden, J. L., and Klein, A. J. 1973. Cognitive differentiation and effective stimulus value in vocational judgements. *Journal of Vocational Behavior*, **3**, 751–759.

Boehm, V. R. 1977. Differential prediction: a methodological artifact? *Journal of Applied Psychology*, **62**, 146–154.

Bolster, B. I., and Springbett, B. M. 1961. The reaction of interviewers to favorable and unfavorable information. *Journal of Applied Psychology*, **45**, 97–103.

Borgen, F. H., and Seling, M. J. 1978. Expressed and inventoried interests revisited: perspicacity in the person. *Journal of Counseling Psychology*, **25**, 536–543.

Borman, C. 1972. Effects of reinforcement style of counseling on information seeking behaviour. *Journal of Vocational Behavior*, **2**, 255–259.

Borman, W. C. 1973. *First Line Supervisor Validation Study*. Minneapolis: Personnel Decisions.

Borman, W. C. 1982. Validity of behavioral assessment for predicting military recruiter performance. *Journal of Applied Psychology*, **67**, 3–9.

Bowers, K. S. 1973. Situationism in psychology: an analysis and critique. *Psychological Review*, **80**, 307–336.

Bray, D. W. and Campbell, R. J. 1968. Selection of salesmen by means of an assessment centre. *Journal of Applied Psychology*, **52**, 36–41.

Bray, D. W., Campbell, R. J., and Grant, D. T. 1974. *Formative Years in Business. A Long-term A.T. & T. Study of Managerial Lives*. New York: Wiley.

Bray, D. W., and Grant, D. L. 1966. The assessment center in the measurement of potential for business management. *Psychological Monographs*, **80**, whole no. 625.

Brotherton, C. 1980. Paradigms of selection validation: Some comments in the light of British Equal Opportunities Legislation. *Journal of Occupational Psychology*, **53**, 73–79.

Broverman, I. K., Broverman, D. M., Clarkson, F. E., Rosenkrantz, P. S., and Vogel, S. R. 1972. Sex role stereotypes: a current appraisal. *Journal of Social Issues*, **28**, 59–78.

Brown, S. H. 1978. Long term validity of the personal history item scoring procedure. *Journal of Applied Psychology*, **63**, 673–680.

Bruch, M. A., and Krieshok, T. S. 1981. Investigative versus realistic Holland types and adjustment in theoretical engineering majors. *Journal of Vocational Behavior*, **18**, 162–173.

Bryant, P. E. 1974. *Perception and Understanding in Young Children*. London: Methuen.

Buchanan, B. 1974. Building organizational commitment: the socialization of managers in work organizations. *Administrative Science Quarterly*, **19**, 533–546.

Buel, W. D., Albright, L. E., and Glennon, J. R. 1966. A note on the generality and cross-validity of personal history data for identifying creative research scientists. *Journal of Applied Psychology*, **50**, 217–219.

Burns, T., and Stalker, G. M. 1961. *The Management of Innovation*, London: Tavistock.

Byrne, D. 1969. Attitudes and attraction. In Berkowitz, L. (ed.) *Advances in Experimental Social Psychology*, Volume 4. New York: Academic Press.

Campion, M. A. 1978. Identification of variables most influential in determining interviewers' evaluations of applicants in a college placement center. *Psychological Reports*, **42**, 947–952.

Cantor, J. H. 1976. Individual needs and salient constructs in interpersonal perception. *Journal of Personality and Social Psychology*, **34**, 519–525.

Cantor, N., and Mischel, W. 1977. Traits as prototypes: effects on recognition memory. *Journal of Personality and Social Psychology*, **35**, 38–48.

Cantor, N., and Mischel, W. 1979. Prototypicality and personality: effects on free recall and personality impressions. *Journal of Research in Personality*, **13**, 187–205.

Carlson, R. E. 1970. Effects of applicant sample on ratings of valid information in an employment setting. *Journal of Applied Psychology*, **54**, 217–222.

Carlson, R. E. 1976. Selection interview decisions: the effect of interviewer experience, relative quota situation, and applicant sample on interviewer decisions. *Personnel Psychology*, **20**, 259–280.

Carney, C. G., Savitz, C. J., and Weiskott, G. N. 1979. Students' evaluation of a university counseling center and their intentions to use its programs. *Journal of Counseling Psychology*, **26**, 242–249.

Carroll, S. J., and Nash, A. N. 1972. Effectiveness of a forced-choice reference check. *Personnel Administration*, **35**, 42–46.

Cascio, W. F., and Phillips, N. F. 1979. Performance testing: a rose among thorns? *Personnel Psychology*, **32**, 751–766.

Cascio, W. F., and Sibley, V. 1979. Utility of the assessment center as a selection device. *Journal of Applied Psychology*, **64**, 107–118.

Cash, T. F., Gillen, B., and Burns, D. S. 1977. Sexism and beautyism in personnel consultant decision-making. *Journal of Applied Psychology*, **62**, 301–311.

Cattell, R. B. 1973. *Personality and Mood by Questionnaire*. San Francisco: Jossey-Bass.

Cecil, E. A., Paul, R. J., and Olins, R. A. 1973. Perceived importance of selected variables used to evaluate male and female job applicants. *Personnel Psychology*, **26**, 397–404.

Chambers, J. A. 1964. Relating personality and biographical factors to scientific creativity. *Psychological Monographs; General and Applied*, **78** (7), whole no. 584.

Cherry, N. 1975. Occupational values and employment: a follow-up study of graduate men and women. *Higher Education*, **4**, 357–368.

Claiborn, C. D. 1982. Interpretation and change in counseling. *Journal of Counseling Psychology*, **29**, 439–453.

Cochran, D. J., Hoffman, S. D., Strand, K. H., and Warren, P. M. 1977. Effects of client–computer interaction on career decision-making processes. *Journal of Counseling Psychology*, **24**, 308–312.

Cohen, S. L., and Bunker, K. A. 1975. Subtle effects of sex role stereotypes on recruiters' hiring decisions. *Journal of Applied Psychology*, **60**, 566–572.

Cole, N. S., and Hanson, G. R. 1971. *An analysis of the structure of vocational interests*. Iowa City: American College Testing Program, research report no. 40.

Constantin, S. W. 1976. An investigation of information favorability in the employment interview. *Journal of Applied Psychology*, **61**, 743–749.

Constantinople, A. 1973. Masculinity–femininity: an exception to a famous dictum? *Psychological Bulletin*, **80**, 389–407.

Cook, M. 1979. *Interpersonal Perception*. London: Methuen.

Cooley, W. W., and Lohnes, P. R. 1968. *Predicting development of young adults*. Palo Alto, California: Project TALENT office, American Institute for Research and University Pittburgh, Contract No. OE-610-065.

Coombs, C. H., Dawes, R. M., and Tversky, A. 1970. *Mathematical Psychology*. Englewood Cliffs, New Jersey: Prentice-Hall.

Corey, G. 1977. *Theory and Practice of Counseling and Psychotherapy*. California: Brooks–Cole.

Cotgrove, S. 1972. Alienation and automation. *British Journal of Sociology*, **23**, 437–451.

Cotgrove, S., and Box, S. 1970. *Science, Industry and Society: Studies in the sociology of science*. London: George Allen & Unwin.

Cotgrove, S., and Fuller, M. 1972. Occupational socialisation and choice: the effects of sandwich courses. *Sociology*, **6**, 59–70.

Coxon, A. P. M. 1971. Occupational attributes: constructs and structure. *Sociology*, **5**, 335–354.

Crawford, J. D. 1978. Career development and career choice in pioneer and traditional women. *Journal of Vocational Behavior*, **12**, 129–139.

Crites, J. O. 1976a. A comprehensive model of career development in early adulthood. *Journal of Vocational Behavior*, **9**, 105–118.

Crites, J. O. 1976b. Career counselling: a comprehensive approach. *Journal of Counseling Psychology*, **6** (3), 2–12.

D'Andrade, R. G. 1965. Trait psychology and componential analysis. *American Anthropologist*, **67**, 215–228.

Dansereau, F., Graen, G., and Haga, W. J. 1975. A vertical dyad linkage approach to leadership within formal organisations: a longitudinal investigation of the role-making process. *Organizational Behavior and Human Performance*, **13**, 46–78.

Davis, J. A. 1966. The campus as a frog pond: an application of the theory of relative deprivation to career decisions of college men. *American Journal of Sociology*, **72**, 17–31.

Daws, P. P. 1970. Occupational information and the self-defining process. *Vocational Aspects of Education*, **22**, 52–56.

Deaux, K., and Emswiller, T. 1974. Explanations of successful performance on sex-linked tasks. *Journal of Personality and Social Psychology*, **29**, 80–85.

De Cotiis, T. A. 1977. An analysis of the external validity and applied relevance of three rating formats. *Organizational Behavior and Human Performance*, **19**, 357–366.

DeWinne, R. F., Overton, T. D., and Schneider, L. J. 1978. Types produce types—especially fathers. *Journal of Vocational Behavior*, **12**, 140–144.

Dipboye, R. L. 1977. A critical review of Korman's self-consistency theory of work motivation and occupational choice. *Organizational Behavior and Human Performance*, **18**, 108–126.

Dipboye, R. L., Arvey, R. D., and Terpstra, D. E. 1977. Sex and physical attractiveness of raters and applicants as determinants of resumé evaluations. *Journal of Applied Psychology*, **62**, 288–294.

Dipboye, R. L., Fromkin, H. L., and Wiback, K. 1975. Relative importance of applicant sex, attractiveness and scholastic standing in evaluation of job applicant resumés. *Journal of Applied Psychology*, **60**, 39–43.

Dipboye, R. L., and Wiley, J. W. 1977. Reactions of college recruiters to interviewee sex and self-presentation style. *Journal of Vocational Behavior*, **10**, 1–12.

Direnzo, G. J. 1974. Congruences in personality structure and academic curricula as determinants of occupational careers. *Psychological Reports*, **34**, 1295–1298.

Downs, S., Farr, R. M., and Colbeck, L. 1978. Self-appraisal: A convergence of selection and guidance. *Journal of Occupational Psychology*, **51**, 271–278.

Dreman, S. B., and Dolev, A. 1976. Expectations and preferences of nonclients for a university student counseling service. *Journal of Counseling Psychology*, **23**, 571–574.

Drew, D. E., and Astin, A. W. 1972. Undergraduate aspirations: a test of several theories. *American Journal of Sociology*, **72**, 17–31.

Duff, A., and Cotgrove, S. 1982. Social values and the choice of careers in industry. *Journal of Occupational Psychology*, **55**, 97–107.

Dulewicz, S.V., and Fletcher, C. 1982. The relationship between previous experience, intelligence, and background characteristics of participants and their performance in an assessment centre. *Journal of Occupational Psychology*, **55**, 197–208.

Dunnette, M. D. 1976. Aptitudes, abilities and skills. In Dunnette, M. D. (ed.) *Handbook of Industrial and Organizational Psychology*. Chicago: Rand McNally.

Dunnette, M. D., and Borman, W. C. 1979. Personnel selection and classification systems. *Annual Review of Psychology*, **30**, 477–525.

Dunnette, M. D., Kirchner, W. K., Erickson, J., and Banas, P. 1960. Predicting turnover among female office workers. *Personnel Administration*, **23**, 45–50.

Edwards, K. J., and Whitney, D. R. 1972. A structural analysis of Holland's personality types using factor and configural analysis. *Journal of Counseling Psychology*, **19**, 136–145.

Eiser, J. R. 1978. Interpersonal attributions. In Tajfel, H., and Fraser, C. (eds). *Introducing social psychology*. Harmondsworth: Penguin.

Elton, C. F. 1971. The interaction of environment and personality: a test of Holland's theory. *Journal of Applied Psychology*, **55**, 114–118. .

Elton, C. F., and Rose, H. A. 1970. Male occupational constancy and change: its prediction according to Holland's theory. *Journal of Counseling Psychology*, **17**, 2, 6.

Entwistle, N., and Wilson, J. 1977. *Degrees of Excellence*. London: Hodder & Stoughton.

Esposito, R. P. 1977. The relationship between the motive to avoid success and vocational choice. *Journal of Vocational Behavior*, **10**, 347–357.

Eysenck, H. J., and Eysenck, S. G. B. 1969. *Personality Structure and Measurement*. London: Routledge & Kegan Paul

Eysenck, M. W., and Eysenck, H. J. 1980. Mischel and the concept of personality. *British Journal of Psychology*, **71**, 191–204.

Farr, J. L. 1973. Response requirements and primacy–recency effects in a simulated selection interview. *Journal of Applied Psychology*, **57**, 228–233.

Farr, J. L., and York, C. M. 1975. Amount of information and primacy—recency effects in recruitment decisions. *Personnel Psychology*, **28**, 233–238.

Fear, R. 1978. *The Evaluation Interview*. 2nd edition. New York: McGraw-Hill.

Feather, N. T. 1975. Positive and negative reactions to male and female success and failure in relation to the perceived status and sex-typed appropriateness of occupations. *Journal of Personality and Social Psychology*, **31**, 536–548.

Feldman, D. C., and Arnold, H. J. 1978. Position choice: Comparing the importance of organisational and job factors. *Journal of Applied Psychology*, **63**, 706–710.

Feldman, K. A., and Newcomb, T. M. 1969. *The Impact of College on Students*. San Francisco: Jossey-Bass.

Feldman-Summers, S., and Kiesler, S. B. 1974. Those who are number two try harder. *Journal of Personality and Social Psychology*, **30**, 846–855.

Finkle, R. B. 1976. Managerial assessment centres. In Dunnette, M. D. (ed.) *Handbook of Industrial and Organizational Psychology*. Chicago: Rand McNally.

194

Fisher, C., Ilgen, D., and Hoyer, W. 1979. Source credibility, information favorability, and job offer acceptance. *Academy of Management Journal*, **22**, 94–103.

Fisher, T. J., Reardon, R. C., and Burck, H. D. 1976. Increasing information seeking behavior with a model reinforced videotape. *Journal of Vocational Behavior*, **8**, 234–238.

Fletcher, C. 1981. Candidates' beliefs and self-presentation strategies in selection interviews. *Personnel Review*, **10** (3), 14–17.

Forbes, R. J., and Jackson, P. R. 1980. Non-verbal behaviour and the outcome of selection intervies. *Journal of Occupational Psychology*, **53**, 65–72.

Forehand, G. A. 1968. On the interaction of persons and organizations. In Tagiuri, R. and Litwin, G. (ed.) *Organizational Climate: Explorations of a Concept*. Boston: Division of Research, Harvard Business School.

Forsyth, N. L., and Forsyth, D. R. 1982. Internality, controllability and the effectiveness of attributional interpretations in counseling. *Journal of Counseling Psychology*, **29**, 140–150.

Frese, M. 1982. Occupational socialization and psychological development: an underemphasized research perspective in industrial psychology. *Journal of Occupational Psychology*, **55**, 209–224.

Fretz, B. R. 1972. Occupational values as discriminants of pre-professional student groups. *Journal of Vocational Behavior*, **2**, 235–237.

Fullan, M. 1970. Industrial technology and worker integration in the organization. *American Sociological Review*, **35**, 1028–1039.

Gable, R. K., Thompson, D. L., and Glanstein, P. J. 1976. Perceptions of personal control and conformity of vocational choice as correlates of vocational development. *Journal of Vocational Behavior*, **8**, 259–267.

Gade, E. M., and Solia, D. 1975. Vocational preference inventory high point code versus expressed choices as predictors of college major and career entry. *Journal of Counseling Psychology*, **22**, 117–121.

Gardner, K. E., and Williams, A. P. O. 1973. A twenty-five year follow-up of an extended interview selection procedure in the Royal Navy. *Occupational Psychology*, **47**, 1–13, 149–161.

Gelatt, H. B. 1962. Decision-making: a conceptual frame of reference for counseling. *Journal of Counseling Psychology*, **9**, 204–245.

Gergen, K. J. 1971. *The Concept of Self*. New York: Holt, Rinehart, & Winston.

Ghiselli, E. E. 1966. *The Validity of Occupational Aptitude Tests*. New York: Wiley.

Ghiselli, E. E. 1973. The validity of aptitude tests in personnel selection. *Personnel Psychology*, **26**, 461–477.

Ginsberg, E. 1975. *The Manpower Connection: Education and Work*. Cambridge, Massachussetts: Harvard University Press.

Ginzberg, E. 1972. Toward a theory of occupational choice: a restatement. *Vocational Guidance Quarterly*, **20**, 169–176.

Glover, I., and Herriot, P. 1982. Engineering students and manufacturing industry—chalk and cheese? *Energy World*, **91**, 8–11.

Glueck, W. F. 1973. Recruiters and executives: how do they affect job choice? *Journal of College Placement*, **33**, 77–78.

Glueck, W. F. 1974. Decision making: organizational choice. *Personnel Psychology*, **27**, 77–93.

Goffman, E. 1959. *The Presentation of Self in Everyday Life*. New York: Anchor Books.

Goldman, R. D., and Hewitt, B. N. 1976. The scholastic aptitude test 'explains' why college men major in science more often than college women. *Journal of Counseling Psychology*, **23**, 50–54.

Goldstein, I. L. 1971. The application blank: how honest are the responses? *Journal of Applied Psychology*, **55**, 491–492.

Goldthorpe, J. H. 1980. *Social Mobility and Class Structure in Modern Britain.* Oxford: Clarendon Press.

Goldthorpe, J. H., Lockwood, D., Bechofer, F., and Platt, J. 1970. *The Affluent Worker: Industrial Attitudes and Behaviour.* Cambridge: Cambridge University Press.

Gottfredson, G. D., and Holland, J. L. 1974. *Vocational Choices of Men and Women: A Comparison of Predictions from S.D.S.* Centre of Social Organisation of Schools. John Hopkins University, No. 175.

Gottfredson, L. S., and Becker, H. J. 1981. A challenge to vocational psychology: How important are aspirations in determining male career development? *Journal of Vocational Behavior*, **18**, 121–137.

Gouldner, A. W. 1957. Cosmopolitans and locals: towards an analysis of latent social roles. *Administrative Science Quarterly*, **2**, 282–292.

Graen, G. 1976. Role-making processes in organizations. In Dunnette, M. D. (ed.) *Handbook of Industrial and Organizational Psychology.* Chicago: Rand McNally.

Graff, R. W., Danish, S., and Astin, B. 1972. Individual, group, and programmed counseling. *Journal of Counseling Psychology*, **19**, 224–228.

Grandy, T. G., and Stahman, R. F. 1974. Family influence on college students' vocational choice: predicting Holland's personality types. *Journal of College Student Personnel*, **15**, 404–409.

Greenhaus, J. H. 1971. Self-esteem as an influence on occupational choice and occupational satisfaction. *Journal of Vocational Behavior*, **1**, 75–83.

Greenhaus, J. H., and Simon, W. E. 1977. Career salience, work values, and vocational indecision. *Journal of Vocational Behavior*, **10**, 104–110.

Greenhaus, J. H., and Sklarew, N. D. 1981. Some sources and consequences of career exploration. *Journal of Vocational Behavior*, **18**, 1–12.

Greenhaus, J. H., Sugalski, T., and Crispin, G. 1978. Relationships between perceptions of organizational size and the organizational choice process. *Journal of Vocational Behavior*, **13**, 113–125.

Greenwood, J. M., and McNamara, W. J. 1967. Inter-rater reliability in situational tests. *Journal of Applied Psychology*, **51**, 101–106.

Gribbons, W. D., and Lohnes, P. R. 1968. *Emerging Careers.* New York: Teachers College Press.

Guion, R. M. 1976. Recruiting, selection and job replacement. In Dunnette, M. D. (ed.) *Handbook of Industrial and Organizational Psychology.* Chicago: Rand McNally, 1976.

Haase, R. F., Reed, C. F., Winer, J. L., and Bodden, J. L. 1979. Effect of positive, negative and mixed occupational information on cognitive and affective complexity. *Journal of Vocational Behavior*, **15**, 294–302.

Hackett, G., and Betz, N. E. 1981. A self-efficacy approach to the career development of women. *Journal of Vocational Behavior*, **18**, 326–339.

Hackman, J. R., and Oldham, G. R. 1976. Motivation through design of work: Test of a theory. *Organizational Behavior and Human Performance*, **16**, 250–279.

Hakel, M. D. 1971. Similarity of post-interview trait rating intercorrelations as a contributor in interrater agreement in a structured employment interview. *Journal of Applied Psychology*, **55**, 443–448.

Hakel, M. D., and Dunnette, M. D. 1970. *Checklists for Describing Job Applicants.* Minneapolis: University of Minnesota Press, 1970.

Hakel, M. D., and Schuh, A. J. 1971. Job applicant attributes judged important across seven divergent occupations. *Personnel Psychology*, **24**, 45–52.

Hakel, M. D., Dobmeyer, T. W., and Dunnette, M. D. 1970. Relative importance of three content dimensions in overall suitability rating of job applicants' resumés. *Journal of Applied Psychology*, **54**, 65–71.

Hakel, M. D., Hollman, T. D., and Dunnette, M. D. 1970. Accuracy of interviewers, certified public accountants, and students in identifying the interests of accountants. *Journal of Applied Psychology*, **54**, 115–119.

Hakel, M. D., Ohnesorge, J. P., and Dunnette, M. D. 1970. Interviewer evaluations of job applicants' resumés as a function of the qualifications of the immediately preceding applicants. *Journal of Applied Psychology*, **54**, 27–30.

Hall, D. T., and Schneider, B. 1972. Correlates of organizational identification as a function of career pattern and organizational type. *Administrative Science Quarterly*, **17**, 340–350.

Hall, D. T., Schneider, B., and Nygren, H. T. 1970. Personal factors in organizational identification. *Administrative Science Quarterly*, **15**, 176–190.

Halsey, A. H., Heath, A. F., and Ridge, J. M. 1980. *Origins and Destinations: Family Class and Education in Modern Britain*. Oxford: Clarendon Press.

Hampson, S. 1982. *The Construction of Personality*. London: Routledge & Kegan Paul.

Harkness, C. A. 1976. *Career Counseling*. Springfield, Illinois: Charles C. Thomas.

Harré, R., and Secord, P. F. 1972. *The Explanation of Social Behaviour*. Oxford: Basil Blackwell.

Harren, V. A. 1979. A model of career decision making for college students. *Journal of Vocational Behavior*, **14**, 119–133.

Harren, V. A., Kass, R. A., Tinsley, H. E. A., and Moreland, J. R. 1978. Influence of sex role attitudes and cognitive styles on career decision making. *Journal of Counseling Psychology*, **25** 390–398.

Harren, V. A., Kass, R. A., Tinsley, H. E. A., and Moreland, J. R. 1979. Influence of gender, sex-role attitudes and cognitive complexity on gender-dominant career choices. *Journal of Counseling Psychology*, **26**, 227–234.

Hartman, B. W., Utz, P. W., and Farnum, S. O. 1979. Examining the reliability and validity of an adapted scale of educational-vocational undecidedness in a sample of graduate students. *Journal of Vocational Behavior*, **15**, 224–230.

Hawkins, J. G., Bradley, R. W., and White, G. W. 1977. Anxiety and the process of deciding about a major and vocation. *Journal of Counseling Psychology*, **24**, 398–403.

Hayes, J. 1969. Occupational choice and the perception of occupational roles. *Occupational Psychology*, **43**, 15–22.

Hayes, J., and Hopson, B. 1971. *Careers Guidance*. London: Heinemann.

Hazel, E. 1976. Group counseling for occupational choice. *Personnel and Guidance Journal*, **54**, 437–438.

Healy, C. C. 1968. Relation of occupational choice to the similarity between self-ratings and occupational ratings. *Journal of Counseling Psychology*, **15**, 317–323.

Healy, C. C. 1973. The relation of esteem and social class to self-occupational congruence. *Journal of Vocational Behavior*, **3**, 43–51.

Healy, C. C. 1975. *Career Counseling for Teachers and Counselors*. Boston: Houghton-Mifflin.

Heilman, M. E. 1980. The impact of situational factors on personnel decisions concerning women: varying the sex composition of the applicant pool. *Organizational Behavior and Human Performance*, **26**, 386–396.

Heilman, M. E., and Guzzo, R. A. 1978. The perceived cause of work success as a mediator of sex discrimination in organizations. *Organizational Behavior and Human Performance*, **21**, 346–357.

Heilman, M. E., and Saruwatari, L. R. 1979. When beauty is beastly: the effects of appearance and sex on evaluations of job applicants for managerial and non-managerial jobs. *Organizational Behavior and Human Performance*, **23**, 360–372.

Heneman, H. G. 1980. Self-assessment: a critical analysis. *Personnel Psychology*, **33**, 297–300.

Heneman, H. G., Schwab, D. P., Huett, D. L., and Ford, J. J. 1975. Interviewer validity as a function of interview structure, biographical data, and interviewee order. *Journal of Applied Psychology*, **60**, 748–753.

Herriot, P. 1974. *Attributes of Memory*. London: Methuen.

Herriot, P. 1981. Towards an attributional theory of the selection interview. *Journal of Occupational Psychology*, **54**, 165–173.

Herriot, P., and Ecob, R. 1979. Expectancy-value theory and occupational choice: testing some modifications. *Journal of Occupational Psychology*, **52**, 311–324.

Herriot, P., Ecob, R., and Hutchison, M. 1980. Decision theory and occupational choice: some longitudinal data. *Journal of Occupational Psychology*, **53**, 223–236.

Herriot, P., and Rothwell, C. 1983. Expectations and impressions in the graduate selection interview. *Journal of Occupational Psychology*, **56**,

Himmelfarb, S., and Anderson, N. H. 1975. Integration theory applied to opinion attribution. *Journal of Personality and Social Psychology*, **31**, 1064–1071.

Hind, R. R., and Wirth, T. E. 1969. The effect of university experience on occupational choice among undergraduates. *Sociology of Education*, **42**, 50–70.

Hinkle, J. E., and Thomas, L. E. 1972, The life-planning workshop: A future oriented programme. *Journal of College Student Personnel*, **13**, 3–5.

Hinrichs, J. R. 1978. An eight year follow up of a management assessment center. *Journal of Applied Psychology*, **63**, 596–601.

Hinrichs, J. R., and Haanpera, S. 1976. Reliability of measurement in situational exercises: an assessment of the assessment center method. *Personnel Psychology*, **29**, 31–40.

Hinrichs, J. R., Haanpera, S., and Sonkin, L. 1976. Validity of a biographical information blank across national boundaries. *Personnel Psychology*, **29**, 417–422.

Hoffman, M. A., Spokane, A. R., and Magoon, T. M. 1981. Effects of feedback mode on counseling outcomes using the Strong-Campbell Interest Inventory: does the counselor really matter? *Journal of Counseling Psychology*, **28**, 119–125.

Holcomb, W. R., and Anderson, W. P. 1978. Expressed and inventoried vocational interests as predictors of college graduation and vocational choices, *Journal of Vocational Behavior*, **12**, 290–296.

Holland, J. L. 1968. Explorations of a theory of vocational choice. VI. A longitudinal study using a sample of typical college students. *Journal of Applied Psychology*, **52**, 1–37.

Holland, J. L. 1971. A theory-ridden computerless impersonal vocational guidance system. *Journal of Vocational Behavior*, **1**, 167–176.

Holland, J. L. 1972. *The Self-directed Search: A Guide to Educational and Vocational Planning*. Palo Alto, California: Consulting Psychologists Press.

Holland, J. L. 1973. *Making Vocational Choices: A Theory of Careers*. Englewood Cliffs, New Jersey: Prentice Hall.

Holland, J. L. 1976a. Vocational preferences. In Dunnette, M. D. (ed.) *Handbook of Industrial and Organizational Psychology*. Chicago: Rand McNally.

Holland, J. L. 1976b. A new synthesis for an old method and a new analysis of some old phenomena. *The Counseling Psychologist*, **6** (3), 12–13.

Holland, J. L., and Gottfredson, G. D. 1975. Predictive value and psychological meaning of vocational aspirations. *Journal of Vocational Behavior*, **6**, 349–363.

Holland, J. L., and Gottfredson, G. D. 1976. Using a typology of persons and environments to explain careers: some extensions and clarifications. *The Counseling Psychologist*, **6** (3), 20–29.

Holland, J. L., Gottfredson, G. D., and Nafziger, D. H. 1975. Testing the validity of some theoretical signs of vocational decision-making ability. *Journal of Counseling Psychology*, **22**, 411–422.

Holland, J. L., and Holland, J. E. 1977. Vocational indecision: more evidence and speculation. *Journal of Counseling Psychology*, **24**, 404–414.

Holland, J. L., and Nichols, R. C. 1964. Explorations of a theory of vocational choice. III. A longitudinal study of changes in major field of study. *Personnel and Guidance Journal*, **43**, 235–242.

198

Holland, J. L., and Whitney, D. R. 1969. Career development. *Review of Educational Research*, **39**, 227–237.

Holland, J. L., Sorensen, A. B., Clark, J. P., Nafziger, D. H., and Blum, Z. D. 1973 Applying an occupational classification to a representative sample of work histories. *Journal of Applied Psychology*, **58**, 34–41.

Hollander, M. A., and Parker, H. J. 1972. Occupational stereotypes and self-descriptions: their relationships to vocational choice. *Journal of Vocational Behavior*, **2**, 57–65.

Hollandsworth, J. G. Jr., Dressel, M. E., and Stevens, J. 1977. Use of behavioral versus traditional procedures for increasing job interview skills. *Journal of Counseling Psychology*, **24**, 503–510.

Hollandsworth, J. G. Jr., Kazelskis, R., Stevens, J., and Dressel, M. E. 1979. Relative contributions of verbal, articulative, and non-verbal communication to employment decisions in the job interview setting. *Personnel Psychology*, **32**, 359–367.

Hollman, T. D. 1972. Employment interviewers' errors in processing positive and negative information. *Journal of Applied Psychology*, **56**, 130–134.

Holmstrom, V. L., and Beach, L. R. 1973. Subjective expected utility and career preferences. *Organizational Behavior and Human Performance*, **10**, 201–207.

Hoppock, R. 1976. *Occupational Information*, 4th edition. New York: McGraw-Hill.

Hopson, B., and Scally, M. 1980. Change and development in adult life: some applications for helpers. *British Journal of Guidance and Counselling*, **8**, 175–187.

Huck, J. R. 1973. Assessment centers: a review of the external and internal validities. *Personnel Psychology*, **26**, 191–212.

Huck, J. R., and Bray, D. W. 1976. Management assessment center evaluations and subsequent job performance of white and black females. *Personnel Psychology*, **29**, 13–30.

Hudson, L. 1968. *Frames of Mind*. London: Methuen.

Hulin, C. L. 1982. Some reflections on general performance dimensions and halo rating error. *Journal of Applied Psychology*, **55**, 35–42.

Hunter, J. E., Schmidt, F. L., and Hunter, R. 1979. Differential validity of employment tests by race: a comprehensive review and analysis. *Psychological Bulletin*, **86**, 721–735.

Isaacson, L. E. 1971. *Career Information in Counseling and Teaching*. Boston: Allyn & Bacon.

Ivey, A. E. 1980. Counseling 2000: time to take charge! *The Counseling Psychologist*, **8**, 12–16.

Izraeli, D., Krausz, M., and Garber, R. 1979. Student self-selection for specialization in engineering. *Journal of Vocational Behavior*, **15**, 107–117.

Janis, I. L., and Mann, L. 1977. *Decision-making: A Psychological Analysis of Conflict, Choice and Commitment*. New York: Free Press.

Joesting, J., and Joesting, R. 1972. Sex differences in group belongingness as influenced by instructor's sex. *Psychological Reports*, **31**, 717–718.

Jones, A. 1981. Inter-rater reliability in the assessment of group exercises at a U.K. assessment centre. *Journal of Occupational Psychology*, **54**, 79–86.

Jones, A., and Harrison, E. 1982. Prediction of performance in officer training: using referees' reports. *Journal of Occupational Psychology*, **55**, 35–42.

Jones, C. L. 1973. 'A longitudinal study of students' attitudes towards teaching as a career'. PhD thesis, University of Edinburgh.

Jones, E. E. 1974. The rocky road from acts to dispositions. *American Psychologist*, **34**, 107–117.

Jones, E. E., and Davis, K. E., 1965. From acts to dispositions: the attribution process in person perception. In Berkowitz, L. (ed.) *Advances in Experimental Social Psychology*, Volume 2. New York: Academic Press.

Jones, E. E., and Goethals, G. R. 1971. Order effects in impression formation: Attribution context and the nature of the entity. In Jones, E. E., Kanouse, D. E., Kelley, H. H., Nisbett, R. E., Valins, S., and Weiner, B. (eds.) *Attribution: Perceiving the Causes of Behavior*. Morristown, New Jersey: General Learning Press.

Jones, E. E., and Harris, V. A. 1967. The attribution of attitudes. *Journal of Experimental Social Psychology*, **3**, 1–24.

Jones, E. E., and Nisbett, R. E. 1971. The actor and the observer: divergent perceptions of the causes of behavior. In Jones, E. E., Kanouse, D. E., Kelley, H. H., Nisbett, R. E., Valins, S., and Weiner, B. (eds) *Attribution: Perceiving the Causes of Behavior*. Morristown, New Jersey: General Learning Press.

Jones, E. E., Rock, L., Shaver, K. G., Goethals, G. R., and Ward, L. M. 1968. Pattern of performance and ability attribution: an unexpected primacy effect. *Journal of Personality and Social Psychology*, **10**, 317–340.

Jordaan, J.P. 1974. Life stages as organizing modes of career development. In Herr, E. L. (ed.) *Vocational Guidance and Human Development*, Boston: Houghton Mifflin.

Jordaan, J. P., and Super, D. E. 1974. The predictors of early adult behavior. In Ricks, D. F., Thomas, A., and Rott, M. (eds) *Life History Research in Psychopathology*. Minneapolis: University of Minnesota Press.

Kane, J. S., and Lawler, E. E. III. 1978. Methods of peer assessment. *Psychological Bulletin*, **85**, 555–586.

Katz, D., and Kahn, R. L. 1978. *The Social Psychology of Organizations*. 2nd edition. New York: Wiley.

Katz, J., Korn, H. A., Leland, C. A., and Levin, M. M. 1968. *Class, Character and Career: Determinants of Occupational Choice in College Students*. Stanford: Stanford University, Institute for the Study of Human Problems.

Katz, M. R. 1966. A model of guidance for career decision making. *Vocational Guidance Quarterly*, **15**, 2–10.

Kaufman, H. G. 1974. Relationships of early work challenge to job performance, professional contributions, and competence of engineers. *Journal of Applied Psychology*, **59**, 377–379.

Keenan, A. 1976. Interviewers' evaluations of applicant characteristics: Differences between personnel and non-personnel managers. *Journal of Occupational Psychology*, **49**, 223–230.

Keenan, A. 1977. Some relationships between interviewers' personal feelings about candidates and their general evaluation of them. *Journal of Occupational Psychology*, **50**, 275–283.

Keenan, A. 1978. Selection interview outcomes in relation to interviewer training and experience. *Journal of Social Psychology*, **106**, 249–260.

Keenan, A., and Wedderburn, A. A. I. 1980. Putting the boot on the other foot: candidates' descriptions of interviewers. *Journal of Occupational Psychology*, **53**, 81–89.

Kelley, H. H. 1972. Attribution in social interaction. In Jones, E. E., Kanouse, D. E., Kelley, H. H., Nisbett, R. E., Valins, S., and Weiner, B. (eds) *Attribution: Perceiving the Causes of Behavior*. Morristown, New Jersey: General Learning Press.

Kelley, H. H., and Michela, J. L. 1980. Attribution theory and research. *Annual Review of Psychology*, **31**, 457–501.

Kelman, H. 1961. Processes of opinion change. *Public Opinion Quarterly*, **25**, 57–78.

Kelsall, R. K. 1972. *Graduates: the Sociology of an Elite*. London: Methuen.

Kidd, J. M. 1981. Self and occupational awareness as influences in the career development of young people. In Watts, A. G., Super, D. E., and Kidd, J. M. (eds) *Career Development in Britain*. Cambridge: Hobsons Press.

200

Kingstrom, P. O., and Bass, A. R. 1981. A critical analysis of studies comparing behaviorally anchored rating scales (BARS) and other rating formats. *Personnel Psychology*, **34**, 263–289.

Kirton, M. 1976. *Career Knowledge of Sixth Form Boys*. London: Careers and Occupational Information Centre.

Kivlighan, D. M., Hageseth, J. A., Tipton, R. M., and McGovern, T. V. 1981. Effects of matching treatment approaches and personality types in group vocational counseling. *Journal of Counseling Psychology*, **28**, 315–320.

Klimoski, R. J., and Strickland, W. J. 1977. Assessment centers—valid or merely prescient? *Personnel Psychology*, **30**, 353–361.

Korman, A. K. 1966. Self esteem variable in vocational choice. *Journal of Applied Psychology*, **50**, 479–486.

Korman, A. K. 1967. Self-esteem as a moderator of the relationship between self-perceived abilities and vocational choice. *Journal of Applied Psychology*, **51**, 65–67.

Korman, A. K. 1968. The prediction of managerial performance—a review. *Personnel Psychology*, **21**, 295–322.

Korman, A. K. 1969. Self-esteem as a moderator in vocational choice: replications and extensions. *Journal of Applied Psychology*, **53**, 188–192.

Korman, A. K. 1977. An examination of Dipboye's 'A critical appraisal of Korman's self-consistency theory of work motivation and occupational choice.' *Organizational Behavior and Human Performance*, **18**, 127–128.

Kratzing, M. I., and Nystul, M. S. 1979. Effects of three methods of career counselling on vocational maturity and vocational preference. *British Journal of Guidance and Counselling*, **7**, 220–224.

Kraut, A. I., and Scott, G. J. 1972. Validity of an operational management assessment program. *Journal of Applied Psychology*, **56**, 124–129.

Krivatsy, S. E., and Magoon, T. M. 1976. Differential effects of three vocational counselling treatments. *Journal of Counseling Psychology*, **23**, 112–118.

Krumboltz, J. D., and Baker, R. D. 1973. Behavioral counseling for vocational decisions. In Borow, H. (ed.) *Career Guidance for a New Age*. Boston: Houghton-Mifflin.

Krumboltz, J. D., Mitchell, A. M., and Jones, G. B. 1976. A social learning theory of career selection. *The Counseling Psychologist*, **6**, 71–81.

Landy, F. J., and Bates, F. 1973. Another look at contrast effects in the employment interview. *Journal of Applied Psychology*, **58**, 141–144.

Landy, F. J., and Farr, J. L. 1980. Performance rating. *Psychological Bulletin*, **87**, 72–107.

Landy, F. J., and Trumbo, D. A. 1976. *Psychology of Work Behavior*. Illinois: The Dorsey Press.

Langdale, J. A., and Weitz, J. 1973. Estimating the influence of job information on interviewer agreement. *Journal of Applied Psychology*, **57**, 23–27.

Latham, G. P., Wexley, K. N., and Pursell, E. D. 1975. Training managers to minimize rating errors in the observation of behavior. *Journal of Applied Psychology*, **60**, 550–553.

Laurent, H. 1970. Cross-cultural cross-validation of empirically validated tests. *Journal of Applied Psychology*, **54**, 417–423.

Lawlis, G. F., and Crawford, J. D. 1975. Cognitive differentiation in women and pioneer—traditional vocational choices. *Journal of Vocational Behavior*, **6**, 263–267.

Lawrence, P. R., and Lorsch, J. W. 1967. Differentiation and integration in complex organizations. *Administrative Science Quarterly*, **12**, 1–47.

Leonard, R., Walsh, W., and Osipow, S. 1973. Self-esteem, self-consistency, and second vocational choice. *Journal of Counseling Psychology*, **20**, 91–93.

Levinson, D. J., Darrow, C. N., Klein, E. B., Levinson, M. H., and McKee, B. 1978. *The Seasons of a Man's Life*. New York: Knopf.

Lingle, J. H., Geva, N., Ostrom, T. M., Leippe, M. R., and Baumgardner, M. H. 1979. Thematic effects of person judgements on impression organization. *Journal of Personality and Social Psychology*, **37**, 674–687.

Little, D. M., and Roach, A. J. 1974. Videotape modeling of interest in nontraditional occupations for women. *Journal of Vocational Behavior*, **5**, 133–138.

Loeffler, D., and Fiedler, L. 1979. Woman—a sense of identity: a counseling intervention to facilitate personal growth in women. *Journal of Counseling Psychology*, **26**, 51–57.

Lofquist, L. H., and Dawis, R. V. 1978. Values as second order needs in the theory of work adjustment. *Journal of Vocational Behavior*, **12**, 12–19.

Looft, W. R. 1971. Sex differences in the expression of vocational aspirations by elementary school children. *Developmental Psychology*, **5**, 366.

Mabe, P. A. III and West, S. G. 1982. Validity of self-evaluation of ability: a review and meta-analysis. *Journal of Applied Psychology*, **67**, 280–296.

Macoby, E. E., and Jacklin, C. N. 1974. *The Psychology of Sex Differences*. Stanford, California: Stanford University Press.

Magnusson, D., and Endler, N. S. 1977. *Personality at the Crossroads*. New York: Wiley-Earlbaum.

Maier, D., and Herman, A. 1974. The relationship of vocational decidedness and satisfaction with dogmatism and self-esteem. *Journal of Vocational Behavior*, **5**, 95–102.

Mann, L. 1972. Use of a balance sheet procedure to improve the quality of personal decision making: a field experiment with college applicants. *Journal of Vocational Behavior*, **2**, 291–300.

Mansfield, R. 1973. Self-esteem, self-perceived abilities, and vocational choices. *Journal of Vocational Behavior*, **3**, 433–441.

Marks, E., and Webb, S. C. 1969. Vocational choice and professional experience as factors in occupational image. *Journal of Applied Psychology*, **53**, 292–300.

Markus, H. 1977. Self-schemata and processing information about the self. *Journal of Personality and Social Psychology*, **35**, 63–78.

Marshall, S. J., and Wijting, J. P. 1980. Relationships of achievement motivation and sex-role identity to college women's career orientation. *Journal of Vocational Behavior*, **16**, 299–311.

Mayfield, E. C. 1964. The selection interview: A re-evaluation of published research. *Personnel Psychology*, **17**, 239–260.

Mayfield, E. C., Brown, S. H., and Hamstra, B. W. 1980. Selection interviewing in the life insurance industry: an update of research and practice. *Personnel Psychology*, **33**, 725–740.

Mayfield, E. C., and Carlson, R. E. 1966. Selection interview decisions. First results of a long term research project. *Personnel Psychology*, **9**, 41–53.

McArthur, C., and Stevens, L. R. 1955. The validation of expressed interests as compared with inventoried interests: a fourteen-year follow-up. *Journal of Applied Psychology*, **39**, 184–189.

McCormick, E. J. 1976. Job and task analysis. In Dunnette, M. D. (ed.) *Handbook of Industrial and Organizational Psychology*. Chicago: Rand McNally, pp. 651–696.

McGovern, T. V., and Tinsley, H. E. 1978. Interviewer evaluations of interviewee non-verbal behavior. *Journal of Vocational Behavior*, **13**, 163–171.

McGowan, A. S. 1977. Vocational maturity and anxiety among vocationally undecided and indecisive students. *Journal of Vocational Behavior*, **10**, 196–204.

McGregor, D. 1960. *The Human Side of Enterprise*. New York: McGraw Hill.

McPherson, A. F., Swift, D., and Bernstein, B. 1972. *Eighteen-plus: the Final Selection*. Bletchley: Open University Press.

202

Meadows, S. E. 1983. *Developing Thinking*. London:Methuen.

Medvene, A. M. 1969. Occupational choice of graduate students in psychology as a function of early parent-child interactions. *Journal of Counseling Psychology*, **16**, 385–389.

Medvene, A. M., and Schueman, S. A. 1978. Perceived parental attitudes and choice of vocational speciality area among male engineering students. *Journal of Vocational Behavior*, **12**, 208–216.

Mencke, R. A., and Cochran, D. J. 1974. Impact of a counseling outreach workshop on vocational development. *Journal of Counseling Psychology*, **21**, 185–190.

Mendonca, J. D., and Siess, T. F. 1976. Counseling for indecisiveness: Problem solving and anxiety management training. *Journal of Counseling Psychology*, **23**, 339–347.

Meyer, H. H. 1980. Self-appraisal of job performance. *Personnel Psychology*, **33**, 291–296.

Miner, J. B. 1974. Motivation to manage among women: studies of college students. *Journal of Vocational Behavior*, **5**, 241–250.

Mischel, W. 1977. On the future of personality measurement. *American Psychologist*, **32**, 246–254.

Mitchel, J. O. 1975. Assessment center validity: a longitudinal study. *Journal of Applied Psychology*, **60**, 573–579.

Mitchell, T. R. 1982. Expectancy-value models in organizational psychology. In Feather, N. T. (ed.) *Expectation and Action: Expectancy-value Models in Psychology*. Hillsdale, New Jersey: Lawrence Erlbaum Associates.

Mitchell, T. R., and Beach, L. R. 1976. A review of occupational preference and choice research using expectancy theory and decision theory. *Journal of Occupational Psychology*, **49**, 231–248.

Mitchell, T. R., and Knudsen, B. W. 1973. Instrumentality theory predictions of students' attitudes towards business and their choice of business occupation. *Academy of Management Journal*, **16**, 410–415.

Moreland, J. R., Harren, V. A., Krimskey-Montague, E., and Tinsley, H. E. A. 1979. Sex-role concept and career decision-making. *Journal of Counseling Psychology*, **26**, 329–336.

Mortimer, J. T., and Lorence, J. 1979. Work experience and occupational value socialization: A longitudinal study. *American Journal of Sociology*, **84**, 1361–1385.

Mosel, J. N., and Goheen, H. W. 1958. The validity of the employment recommendation questionnaire in personnel selection. I. Skilled traders. *Personnel Psychology*, **11**, 481–490.

Moses, J. L. 1973. The development of an assessment center for the early identification of supervisory potential. *Personnel Psychology*, **26**, 569–580.

Muchinsky, P. M. 1979. The use of reference reports in personnel selection: a review and evaluation. *Journal of Occupational Psychology*, **52**, 287–297.

Muchinsky, P. M., and Harris, S. L. 1977. The effect of applicant sex and scholastic standing on the evaluation of job applicant resumés in sex-typed occupations. *Journal of Vocational Behavior*, **11**, 95–108.

Mulaik, S. 1964. Are personality factors raters' conceptual factors? *Journal of Consulting Psychology*, **28**, 506–511.

Munley, P. H. 1975. Erik Erikson's theory of psychological development and vocational behavior. *Journal of Counseling Psychology*, **22**, 314–319.

Neiner, A. G., and Owens, W. A. 1982. Relationships between two sets of biodata with seven years separation. *Journal of Applied Psychology*, **67**, 146–150.

Nelson-Jones, R. 1982. *The Theory and Practice of Counselling Psychology*. London: Holt, Rinehart, & Winston.

Nisbett, R. E., Caputo, C. G., Legant, P., and Maracek, J. 1973. Behavior as seen by the actor and as seen by the observer. *Journal of Personality and Social Psychology*, **27**, 154–164.

O'Connor, J. P., and Kinnane, J. F. 1961. A factor analysis of work values. *Journal of Counseling Psychology*, **8**, 263–267.

O'Donnell, J. A., and Andersen, D. G. 1978. Factors influencing choice of major and career of capable women. *Vocational Guidance Quarterly*, **26**, 214–222.

Ohlde, C. D., and Vinitsky, M. H. 1976. Effects of values-clarification workshop on value-awareness. *Journal of Counseling Psychology*, **23**, 489–491.

Okanes, M. M., and Tschirgi, H. 1978. Impact of the face-to-face interview on prior judgements of a candidate. *Perceptual and Motor Skills*, **46**, 322.

Oldham, G. R. 1976. Organizational choice and some correlates of individual expectancies. *Decision Science*, **3**, 873–884.

Oliver, L. W. 1974. Achievement and affiliation motivation in career-oriented and home-making oriented college women. *Journal of Vocational Behavior*, **4**, 275–281.

Oliver, L. W. 1974. The relationship of parental attitudes and parent identification to career and homemaking orientation in college women. *Journal of Vocational Behavior*, **7**, 1–12.

Olweus, D. 1977. Modern interactionism in personality psychology and the analysis of variance components approach: a critical examination. In Magnusson, D. and Endler, N. (eds) *Personality at the Crossroads*. New York: Wiley-Earlbaum.

O'Neil, J. M., and Magoon, T. M. 1977. The predictive power of Holland's investigative personality type and consistency levels using the self-directed search. *Journal of Vocational Behavior*, **10**, 39–46.

O'Neil, J. M., Magoon, T. M., and Tracey, T. O. 1978. Status of Holland's investigative personality types and their consistency levels seven years later. *Journal of Counseling Psychology*, **25**, 530–535.

Oppenheimer, E. A. 1966. The relationship between certain self constructs and occupational preferences. *Journal of Counseling Psychology*, **13**, 191–197.

Ory, J. C., and Helfrich, L. M. 1978. A study of individual characteristics and career aspirations. *Vocational Guidance Quarterly*, **27**, 43–49.

Osburn, H. G., Timmreck, C., and Bigby, D. 1981. Effect of dimensional relevance on accuracy of simulated hiring decisions by employment interviewers. *Journal of Applied Psychology*, **66**, 159–165.

Osgood, C. E. 1962. Studies on the generality of affective meaning systems. *American Psychologist*, **17**, 10–28.

Osipow, S. H., Carney, C. G., and Barak, A. 1976. A scale of educational-vocational undecidedness: A typological approach. *Journal of Vocational Behavior*, **9**, 233–243.

Owens, W. A. 1976. Background data. In Dunnette, M. D. (ed.) *Handbook of Industrial and Organizational Psychology*. Chicago: Rand McNally.

Owens, W. A. 1982. 'A Classification of Persons: Longitudinal Evidence and Potential Utility.' Paper presented at the International Congress on Applied Psychology, Edinburgh.

Owens, W. A., Glennon, J. R., and Allbright, L. E. 1966. *A Catalog of Life History Items*. Greensboro, N. C.: Richardson Foundation.

Parsons, D., and Hutt, R. 1981. *The Mobility of Young Graduates*. Brighton: Institute of Manpower Studies.

Passini, F. T., and Norman, W. T. 1966. A universal conception of personality structure? *Journal of Personality and Social Psychology*, **4**, 44–49.

Peres, S. H., and Garcia, J. R. 1962. Validity and dimensions of descriptive adjectives used in reference letters for engineering applicants. *Personnel Psychology*, **15**, 279–286.

Peters, L. H., and Terborg, J. R. 1975. The effects of temporal placement of unfavorable information and attitude similarity on personnel selection decisions. *Organizational Behavior and Human Performance*, **13**, 279–293.

204

Phares, E. J. 1978. Locus of control. In London, H. and Exner, J. E. (eds.) *Dimensions of Personality*. New York: Wiley.

Posner, B. Z. 1981. Comparing recruiter, student and faculty perceptions of important applicant and job characteristics. *Personnel Psychology*, **34**, 329–340.

Prior-Wandesforde, G. 1978. Helping unemployed graduates. *British Journal of Guidance and Counselling*, **6**, 251–219.

Pryor, R. G. L. 1980. Some types of stability in the study of students' work values. *Journal of Vocational Behavior*, **16**, 146–157.

Rammage, F. A. 1975. Career choice processes of graduates entering three manufacturing companies. *British Journal of Guidance and Counselling*, **3**, 66–81.

Rand, T. M., and Wexley, K. N. 1975. Demonstration of the effect 'similar to me' in simulated employment interviews. *Psychological Reports*, **36**, 535–544.

Reilly, R. R., and Chao, G. T. 1982. Validity and fairness of some alternative employee selection procedures. *Personnel Psychology*, **35**, 1–62.

Resnick, H., Fauble, M. L., and Osipow, S. H. 1970. Vocational crystallisation and self-esteem in college students. *Journal of Counseling Psychology*, **17**, 465–467.

Richards, J. M. Jr. 1971. The prediction of career plans. In Flanagan, J. C. (ed.) *Five Years after High School*. Palo Alto, California: American Institutes for Research.

Richards, J. M., Jr., Seligman, R., and Jones, R. K. 1970. Faculty and curriculum as measures of college environment. *Journal of Educational Psychology*, **61**, 324–332.

Ridgeway, C. 1978. Parental identification and patterns of career orientation in college women. *Journal of Vocational Behavior*, **12**, 1–11.

Roberts, K. 1981. The sociology of work entry and occupational choice. In Watts, A. G., Super, D. E., and Kidd, J. M. (eds) *Career Development in Britain*. Cambridge: Hobsons Press.

Robertson, I. T., and Downs, S. 1979. Learning and the prediction of performance: Development of trainability testing in the United Kingdom. *Journal of Applied Psychology*, **64**, 42–50.

Robertson, I. T., and Kandola, R. S. 1982. Work sample tests: validity, adverse impact, and applicant reaction. *Journal of Occupational Psychology*, **55**, 171–184.

Rodger, A., and Cavanagh, P. 1968. Personnel selection and vocational guidance. In Welford, A. T. (ed.) *Society: Psychological Problems and Methods of Study*. London: Routledge & Kegan Paul.

Roe, A. 1956. *The Psychology of Occupations*. New York: Wiley.

Roe, R. G. 1974. Effect of the college placement process on occupational stereotype. *Journal of Counseling Psychology*, **21**, 101–105.

Rogers, C. R. 1959. A theory of therapy, personality, and interpersonal relationships as developed in the client-centred framework. In Koch, S. (ed.) *Psychology: A Study of a Science*. New York: McGraw Hill.

Rokeach, M. 1973. *The Nature of Human Values*. New York: Free Press.

Rosen, B., and Jerdee, T. H. 1974. Effects of applicants' sex and difficulty of job on evaluations of candidates for managerial positions. *Journal of Applied Psychology*, **59**, 511–512.

Rosen, B. and Jerdee, T. H. 1975. The psychological basis for sex role stereotypes: A note on Terborg and Ilgen's conclusions. *Organizational Behavior and Human Performance*, **14**, 151–153.

Rosenberg, M. 1957. *Occupations and Values*. Glencoe, Illinois: Free Press.

Rosenberg, S., Nelson, C., and Vivekananthan, P. S. 1968. A multi-dimensional approach to the structure of personality impressions. *Journal of Personality and Social Psychology*, **9**, 283–294.

Ross, J. 1977. The intuitive psychologist and his shortcomings: Distortions in the attribution process. In Berkowitz, L. (ed.) *Advances in Experimental Social Psychology*, Volume 10. New York: Academic Press.

Ross, J., Greene, D., and House, P. 1977. The false consensus phenomenon: an attributional bias in self-perception and social perception processes. *Journal of Social Psychology*, **13** 279–301.

Rothstein, M., and Jackson, D. N. 1980. Decision making in the employment interview: an experimental approach. *Journal of Applied Psychology*, **65**, 271–283.

Rotter, J. B. 1966. Generalised expectancies for internal versus external control of reinforcement. *Psychological Monograph*, **80**, whole no. 609.

Rynes, S. L., Heneman, H. G., and Schwab, D. P. 1980. Individual reactions to organizational recruiting: A review. *Personnel Psychology*, **33**, 529–542.

Saal, F. E., Downey, R. G., and Lahey, M. A. 1980. Rating the ratings: Assessing the psychometric quality of rating data. *Psychological Bulletin*, **88**, 413–428.

Saal, F. E., and Landy, F. J. 1977. The mixed standard rating scales: an evaluation. *Organizational Behavior and Human Performance*, **18**, 19–35.

Sackett, P. R., and Wilson, M. A. 1982. Factors affecting the consensus judgement process in managerial assessment centers. *Journal of Applied Psychology*, **67**, 10–17.

Sampson, E. E. 1977. Psychology and the American ideal. *Journal of Personality and Social Psychology*, **35**, 767–782.

Sawyer, J. 1966. Measurement and prediction, clinical and statistical. *Psychological Bulletin*, **66**, 178–200.

Schaie, K. W. 1973. Methodological problems in descriptive developmental research on adulthood and old age. In Nesselroade, J. R., and Reese, H. W. (eds) *Life-span Developmental Psychology: Methodological Issues*. New York: Academic Press.

Schaie, K. W., and Parham, A. 1976. Stability of adult personality traits: Fact or fable? *Journal of Personality and Social Psychology*, **34**, 146–158.

Schein, V. E. 1973. The relationship between sex-role stereotypes and requisite management characteristics. *Journal of Applied Psychology*, **57**, 95–100.

Schein, V. E. 1978. Sex role stereotyping, ability and performance: Prior research and new directions. *Personnel Psychology*, **31**, 259–268.

Schlossberg, N. K., and Goodman, J. A. 1972. Woman's place: children's sex stereotyping of occupations. *Vocational Guidance Quarterly*, **20**, 266–270.

Schmitt, N. 1976. Social and situational determinants of interview decisions: Implications for the employment interview. *Personnel Psychology*, **29**, 79–101.

Schmitt, N. 1977. Interrater agreement in dimensionality and combination of assessment center judgements. *Journal of Applied Psychology*, **62**, 171–176.

Schmitt, N., and Coyle, B. N. 1976. Applicant decisions in the employment interview. *Journal of Applied Psychology*, **61**, 184–192.

Schneider, B. 1978. Person–situation selection: a review of some ability–situation interaction research. *Personnel Psychology*, **31**, 281–298.

Schneider, D. J., Hastorf, A. H., and Ellsworth, P. G. 1979. *Person Perception*. Reading, Mass.: Addison-Wesley.

Schuh, A. J. 1978. Contrast effect in the interview. *Bulletin of the Psychonomic Society*, **11**, 195–196.

Schwab, D. P., Heneman, H. G. III, and De Cotiis, T. 1975. Behaviorally anchored rating scales: a review of the literature. *Personnel Psychology*, **28**, 549–562.

Scott, N. A., and Sedlacek, W. E. 1975. Personality differentiation and prediction of persistence in physical science and engineering. *Journal of Vocational Behavior*, **6**, 205–216.

Semin, G. R. 1980. A gloss on attribution theory. *British Journal of Social and Clinical Psychology*, **19**, 291–300.

Sewell, W. H., and Hauser, R. M. 1975. *Education, Occupation and Earnings*. New York: Academic Press.

Shaw, E. A. 1972. Commonality of applicant stereotypes among recruiters. *Personnel Psychology*, **25**, 421–432.

Sheehy, G. 1976. *Passages: Predictable Crises of Adult Life*. New York: E. P. Dutton.

Shinar, E. H. 1975. Sexual stereotypes of occupations. *Journal of Vocational Behavior*, **1**, 99–111.

Shouksmith, G. 1978. *Assessment Through Interviewing*. 2nd edition. Oxford: Pergamon.

Shrauger, J. S., and Schoeneman, T. J. 1979. Symbolic interactionist view of self-concept: through the looking glass darkly. *Psychological Bulletin*, **86**, 549–573.

Simas, K., and McCarrey, M. 1979. Impact of recruiter authoritarianism and applicant sex on evaluation and selection decisions in a recruitment interview analogue study. *Journal of Applied Psychology*, **64**, 483–491.

Singer, J. N. 1974. Sex-differences-similarities in job preference factors. *Journal of Vocational Behavior*, **5**, 357–365.

Smith, P. C. 1976. Behaviors, results and organizational effectiveness: the problem of criteria. In Dunnette, M. D. (ed.) *Handbook of Industrial and Organizational Psychology*. Chicago: Rand McNally.

Sneath, F., Thakur, M., and Medjuck, B. 1976. *Testing People at Work*. London: Institute of Personnel Management.

Snyder, M. L., Tanke, E. D., and Berscheid, E. 1977. Social perception and interpersonal behavior: On the self-fulfilling nature of social stereotypes. *Journal of Personality and Social Psychology*, **35**, 656–666.

Snyder, M. L., and White, P. 1981. Testing hypotheses about other people. Strategies of verification and falsification. *Personality and Social Psychology Bulletin*, **7**, 39–43.

Spence, J. T., Helmreich, R., and Stapp, J. 1975. Ratings of self and peers on sex role attributes and their relation to self-esteem and conceptions of masculinity and femininity. *Journal of Personality and Social Psychology*, **32**, 29–39.

Spokane, A. R., and Derby, D. P. 1979. Congruence, personality pattern, and satisfaction in college women. *Journal of Vocational Behavior*, **15**, 36–42.

Spokane, A. R., Malett, S. D., and Vance, F. L. 1978. Consistent curriculum choice and congruence of subsequent changes. *Journal of Vocational Behavior*, **13**, 45–53.

Spool, M. D. 1978. Training programs for observers of behavior. *Personnel Psychology*, **31**, 853–888.

Springbett, B. M. 1958. Factors affecting the final decision in the employment interview. *Canadian Journal of Psychology*, **12**, 13–22.

Stake, J. E. 1979. Women's self-estimates of competence and the resolution of the career/home conflict. *Journal of Vocational Behavior*, **14**, 33–42.

Starishevsky, R., and Matlin, N. 1968. A model for the translation of self-concepts into vocational terms. In Hopson, B., and Hayes, J. (eds) *The Theory and Practice of Vocational Guidance*. Oxford: Pergamon.

Stephenson, G. 1978. Social behaviour in organisations. In Tajfel, H., and Fraser, C. (eds) *Introducing Social Psychology*. Harmondsworth: Penguin.

Sterrett, J. H. 1978. The job interview: body language and perceptions of potential effectiveness. *Journal of Applied Psychology*, **63**, 388–390.

Stockton, N., Berry, J., Shepson, J., and Utz, P. 1980. Sex role and innovative major choice among college students. *Journal of Vocational Behavior*, **16**, 360–367.

Storms, M. D. 1973. Videotape and the attribution process: reversing actors' and observers' points of view. *Journal of Personality and Social Psychology*, **27**, 165–175.

Super, D. E. 1953. A theory of vocational development. *American Psychologist*, **8**, 185–190.

Super, D. E. 1963. Self concepts in career development. In Super, D. E., Starishevsky, R., Matlin, N., and Jordaan, J. P. (eds) *Career Development: Self-concept Theory*. New York: College Entrance Examinations Board.

Super, D. E. 1973. The work values inventory. In Zytowski, D. G. (ed.) *Contemporary Approaches to Interest Measurement*. Minneapolis: University of Minnesota Press.

Super, D. E. 1977. The identity crisis of counseling psychologists. *The Counseling Psychologist*, **7** (2), 13–15.

Super, D. E. 1978. From information retrieval through matching to counselling and to career development: some lessons from the U.S.A. *Journal of Occupational Psychology*, **51**, 19–28.

Super, D. E. 1980. A life-span life-space approach to career development. *Journal of Vocational Behavior*, **16**, 282–298.

Super, D. E. 1981. Approaches to occupational choice and career development. In Watts, A. G., Super, D. E., and Kidd, J. M. (eds) *Career Development in Britain*. Cambridge: Hobson's Press.

Super, D. E., Kowalski, R., and Gotkin, E. 1967. *Floundering and trial after high school*. New York: Teachers College, Columbia University, Mimeo.

Super, D. E., Thompson, A. S., Lindeman, R. H., Jordaan, J. P., and Myers, R. A. 1981. *Career development inventory*. Palo Alto, California: Consulting Psychologists Press.

Tangri, S. S. 1972. Determinants of occupational role innovation among college women. *Journal of Social Issues*, **28**, 177–199.

Taylor, R. 1979. Career orientations and intra-occupational choice: a survey of engineering students. *Journal of Occupational Psychology*, **52**, 41–52.

Taylor, R. G., and Hanson, G. R. 1972. Interest changes as a function of persistence and transfer from an engineering major. *Journal of Counseling Psychology*, **19**, 130–135.

Terborg, J. R. 1977. Women in management: a research review. *Journal of Applied Psychology*, **62**, 647–664.

Tessler, R., and Sushelsky, L. 1978. Effects of eye contact and social status on the perception of a job applicant in an employment interviewing situation. *Journal of Vocational Behavior*, **13**, 338–347.

Thistlethwaite, D. L., and Wheeler, N. 1966. Effects of teacher and peer subcultures upon student aspirations. *Journal of Educational Psychology*, **57**, 35–47.

Thomson, H. A. 1970. Comparison of predictor and criterion and judgement of managerial performance using the multi-trait approach. *Journal of Applied Psychology*, **54**, 496–502.

Thoresen, C. E. and Ewart, C. K. 1976. Behavioral self-control and career development. *The Counseling Psychologist*, **3**, 29–43.

Thornton, G. C. 1980. Psychometric properties of self-appraisals of job performance. *Personnel Psychology*, **33**, 263–272.

Tilden, A. J. Jr. 1978. Is there a monotonic criterion for measures of vocational maturity in college students? *Journal of Vocational Behavior*, **13**, 327–337.

Titley, R. W., Titley, B., and Wolff, W. M. 1976. The major changers: Continuity or discontinuity in the career decision process? *Journal of Vocational Behavior*, **8**, 105–111.

Toffler, A. 1970. *Future Shock*. London: The Bodley Head.

Tolbert, V. 1980. *Counseling for Career Development*. Boston: Houghton Mifflin.

Tom, V. R. 1971. The role of personality and organizational images in the recruiting process. *Organizational Behavior and Human Performance*, **6**, 573–592.

Touchton, J. G., and Magoon, T. M. 1977. Occupational daydreams as predictors of vocational plans of college women. *Journal of Vocational Behavior*, **10**, 156–166.

Tucker, D. H., and Rowe, P. M. 1979. Relationship between expectancy, causal attributions and final hiring decisions in the employment interview. *Journal of Applied Psychology*, **64**, 27–34.

Tullar, W. L., and Barrett, G. V. 1976. The future autobiography as a predictor of sales success. *Journal of Applied Psychology*, **61**, 371–373.

Tullar, W. L., Mullins, T. W., and Caldwell, S. A. 1979. Effects of interview length and applicant quality on interview decision time. *Journal of Applied Psychology*, **64**, 669–674.

Tulving, E. 1972. Episodic and semantic memory. In Tulving, E., and Donaldson W. A. (eds) *Organization of Memory*. New York: Academic Press.

Tyler, F. 1978. Individual psychological competence: a personality configuration. *Educational and Psychological Measurement*, **38**, 309–323.

Ulrich, L., and Trumbo, D. 1965. The selection interview since 1949. *Psychological Bulletin*, **63**, 100–116.

Underhill, R. 1966. Values and post-college career change. *American Journal of Sociology*, **72**, 163–172.

Underwood, B. J. 1969. Attributes of memory. *Psychological Review*, **76**, 559–573.

Utz, P. W., and Hartman, B. 1978. An analysis of the discriminatory power of Holland's types for business majors in three concentration areas. *Measurement and Evaluation in Guidance*, **11**, 175–182.

Valenzi, E., and Andrews, L. R. 1973. Individual differences in the decision process of employment interviews. *Journal of Applied Psychology*, **58**, 49–53.

Van Maanen, J., and Schein, E. H. 1977. Career development. In Hackman, J. R., and Suttle, J. L. (eds.) *Improving Life at Work*. Santa Monica: Goodyear.

Vecchiotti, D. I., and Korn, J. H. 1980. Comparison of student and recruiter values. *Journal of Vocational Behavior*, **16**, 43–50.

Villwock, J. D., Schnitzen, J. P., and Carbonari, J. P. 1976. Holland's personality constructs as predictors of stability of choice. *Journal of Vocational Behavior*, **9**, 77–85.

Wagman, M. 1965. Sex and age differences in occupational values. *Personnel and Guidance Journal*, **44**, 258–262.

Wallace, S. R. 1974. How high the validity? *Personnel Psychology*, **27**, 399–407.

Wallace, W. L. 1965. Peer influences and undergraduates' aspirations for career study. *Sociology of Education*, **38**, 375–392.

Wallis, D. 1978. Some pressing problems for research in vocational guidance. *Journal of Occupational Psychology*, **51**, 7–18.

Walsh, W. B. 1974. Consistent occupational preferences and personality. *Journal of Vocational Behavior*, **4**, 145–153.

Walsh, W. B., and Hanle, N. A. 1975. Consistent occupational preferences, vocational maturity, and academic achievement. *Journal of Vocational Behavior*, **7**, 89–97.

Walsh, W. B., Horton, J. R., and Gaffey, R. L. 1977. Holland's theory and college degreed working men and women. *Journal of Vocational Behavior*, **10**, 180–186.

Walsh, W. B., and Lacey, D. W. 1969. Perceived change and Holland's theory. *Journal of Counseling Psychology*, **16**, 348–352.

Walsh, W. B., and Lacey, D. W. 1970. Further exploration of perceived change and Holland's theory. *Journal of Counseling Psychology*, **17**, 189–190.

Walsh, W. B., and Lewis, R. O. 1972. Consistent, inconsistent and undecided career preferences and personality. *Journal of Vocational Behavior*, **2**, 309–316.

Walsh, W. B., Vaudrin, D. M., and Hummel, R. A. 1972. The accentuation effect and Holland's theory. *Journal of Vocational Behavior*, **2**, 77–85.

Wanous, J. P. 1972. Occupational preferences: perceptions of valence and instrumentality and objective data. *Journal of Applied Psychology*, **56**, 152–155.

Wanous, J. P. 1976. Organisational entry: from naive expectations to realistic beliefs. *Journal of Applied Psychology*, **61**, 22–29.

Wanous, J. P. 1977. Organisational entry: newcomers moving from outside to inside. *Psychological Bulletin*, **84**, 601–618.

Wanous, J. P. 1978. Realistic job previews: can a procedure to reduce turnover also influence the relationship between abilities and performance? *Personnel Psychology*, **31**, 249–258.

Wanous, J. P. 1979. *Organisational Entry*. Reading, Mass: Addison-Wesley.

Ward, G. R., Cunningham, C. H., and Wakefield, J. A. 1976. Relationships between Holland's VPI and Cattell's 16PF. *Journal of Vocational Behavior*, **8**, 307–312.

Ware, M. E. 1980. Antecedents of educational/career preferences and choices. *Journal of Vocational Behavior*, **16**, 312–319.

Warnath, C. F. 1975. Vocational theories: direction to nowhere. *Personnel and Guidance Journal*, **53**, 422–428.

Warren, J. R. 1961. Self-concept, occupational role expectation and change in college major. *Journal of Counseling Psychology*, **8**, 164–169.

Warren-Piper, D. (ed.) 1981. *Is Higher Education Fair?* London: Society for Research into Higher Education.

Watts, A. G. 1977. Careers education in higher education: principles and practice. *British Journal of Guidance and Counselling*, **5**, 167–194.

Watts, A. G. 1981. Career patterns. In Watts, A. G., Super, D. E., and Kidd, J. M. (eds) *Career Development in Great Britain*. Cambridge: Hobson's Press.

Webster, E. C. 1964. *Decision Making in the Employment Interview*. Montreal: Eagle.

Weinrach, S. G. (ed.) 1979. *Career Counseling*. New York: McGraw Hill.

Weishaar, M. E., Green, B. J., and Craighead, L. W. 1981. Primary influencers of initial vocational choices for college women. *Journal of Vocational Behavior*, **18**, 67–78.

Weiss, D. J., and Dawis, R. V. 1960. Objective validation of factual interviewer data. *Journal of Applied Psychology*, **44**, 381–385.

Weller, L. 1979. Authoritarian personalities in the natural and social sciences. *Journal of Vocational Behavior*, **15**, 259–264.

Weller, L., and Nadler, A. 1975. Authoritarianism and job preference. *Journal of Vocational Behavior*, **6**, 9–14.

Wernimont, P. F. 1962. Re-evaluation of a weighted application blank for office personnel. *Journal of Applied Psychology*, **46**, 417–419.

Wernimont, P. F., and Campbell, J. P. 1968. Signs, samples, and criteria. *Journal of Applied Psychology*, **52**, 372–376.

Wertheim, E. G., Widom, C. S., and Wortzel, L. H. 1978. Multivariate analysis of male and female professional career choice correlates. *Journal of Applied Psychology*, **63**, 234–242.

Werts, C. E. 1966. Social class and initial career choice of college freshmen. *Sociology of Education*, **39**, 74–85.

Werts, C. E. 1967. Career changes in college. *Sociology of Education*, **40**, 90–95.

Werts, C. E., and Watley, D. J. 1969. A student's dilemma; big fish—little pond or little fish—big pond. *N.M.S.C. Research Reports*, **5**, 3.

Wexley, K. N., Yukl, G. A., Kovacs, S. Z., and Sanders, R. E. 1977. Importance of contrast effects in employment interviews. *Journal of Applied Psychology*, **56**, 43–48.

Wheeler, K. G. 1981. Sex differences in perceptions of desired rewards, availability of rewards and abilities in relation to occupational selection. *Journal of Occupational Psychology*, **54**, 141–148.

Wheeler, K. G. 1983. Comparisons of self-efficacy and expectancy models of occupational preference for college males and females. *Journal of Occupational Psychology*, **56**, 73–78.

Whiteley, J. M., Burkhart, M. Q., Harway-Herman, M., and Whiteley, R. M. 1975. Counseling and student development. *Annual Review of Psychology*, 337–366.

Wiener, Y., and Schneiderman, M. L. 1974. Use of job information as a criterion in employment decisions of interviewers. *Journal of Applied Psychology*, **59**, 699–704.

Wiggins, N., Hoffman, P. J. and Taber, T. 1969. Types of judges and cue utilization in judgments of intelligence. *Journal of Personality and Social Psychology*, **12**, 52–59.

Williamson, P., and Whitehead, L. 1980. Career attitudes of final year undergraduates. *Department of Employment Gazette*, January, pp. 13–20.

Wittmer, J., Jeffers, M. S., and Persons, W. E. 1974. Parental behavior and vocational choice: a comparison of counsellors and engineers. *Journal of Employment Counselling*, **11**, 16–21.

Wolfe, L. K., and Betz, N. E. 1981. Traditionality of choice and sex-role identification as moderators of the congruence of occupational choice in college women. *Journal of Vocational Behavior*, **18**, 43–55.

Wolfson, M. R., and Salancik, G. R. 1977. Observer orientation and actor-observer differences in attributions for failure. *Journal of Experimental Social Psychology*, **13**, 441–451.

Wolkon, K. A. 1972. Pioneer vs. traditional: two distinct vocational patterns of college alumnae. *Journal of Vocational Behavior*, **2**, 275–282.

Wollowick, H. B., and McNamara, W. J. 1969. Relationship of the components of an assessment center to management success. *Journal of Applied Psychology*, **53**, 348–352.

Woodward, J. 1965. *Industrial Organisation: Theory and Practice*. London: Oxford University Press.

Wooler, S., and Humphreys, P. 1979. *Modelling and Aiding of Career Transitions*. Decisions Analysis Unit, Brunel Institute of Organisation and Social Studies, working paper, 76–9.

Wylie, R. C. 1974. *The Self-concept*. Lincoln, Nebraska: University of Nebraska Press.

Yanico, B. J. 1978. Sex-bias in career information: effects of language on attitudes. *Journal of Vocational Behavior*, **13**, 26–34.

Yanico, B. J., Hardin, S. I., and McLaughlin, K. B. 1978. Androgyny and traditional versus nontraditional major choice among college freshmen. *Journal of Vocational Behavior*, **12**, 261–269.

Yen, F. B., and Healy, C. C. 1977. The effects of work experience on two scales of career development. *Measurement and Evaluation in Guidance*, **10**, 175–178.

Ziegler, D. J. 1970. Self-concept, occupational member concept, and occupational interest area relationships in male college students. *Journal of Counseling Psychology*, **17**, 133–136.

Ziegler, D. J. 1973. Distinctive self and occupational member concepts in different occupational preference groups. *Journal of Vocational Behavior*, **3**, 53–60.

Zikmund, W. G., Hitt, M. A., and Pickers, B. A. 1978. Influence of sex and scholastic performance on reactions to job applicant resumés. *Journal of Applied Psychology*, **63**, 252–254.

Zytowski, D. C. 1965. Avoidance behavior in vocational motivation. *Personnel Guidance Journal*, **43**, 746–750.

Author Index

216

218

WheelerWheeler, K. G., 135, 209
Wheeler, N., 123, 207
White, G. W., 196
White, P., 72, 206
Whitehead, L., 156, 209
Whiteley, J. M., 157, 209
Whiteley, R. M., 209
Whitney, D. R., 30, 117, 148, 193, 198
Wiback, K., 192
Widom, C. S., 209
Wiener, Y., 65, 209
Wiggins, N., 23, 209
Wijting, J. P., 143, 201
Wiley, J. W., 75, 192
Williams, A. P. O., 86, 194
Williamson, P., 156, 209
Wilson, J., 155, 159, 193
Wilson, M. A., 86, 205
Winer, J. L., 195
Wirth, T. E., 124, 197

Wittmer, J., 129, 209
Wolfe, L. K., 142, 209
Wolff, W. M., 207
Wolfson, M. R., 28, 210
Wolkon, K. A., 138, 210
Wollowick, H. B., 86, 210
Woodward, J., 45, 210
Wooler, S., 102, 177, 210
Wortzel, L. H., 209
Wylie, R. C., 28, 210

Yanico, B. J., 140, 142, 210
Yen, F. B., 125, 210
York, C. M., 64, 193
Yukl, G. A., 209

Ziegler, D. J., 115, 210
Zikmund, W. G., 136, 210
Zytowski, D. C., 109, 210

Subject Index